Stalinist Rule in the Ukraine

A Study of the Decade of Mass Terror
(1929 - 39)

by

HRYHORY KOSTIUK

Published for the
INSTITUTE FOR THE STUDY OF THE USSR

Frederick A. Praeger · *Publishers* · New York

The Institute for the Study of the USSR is a body of emigre scholars from the Soviet Union whose aim is to furnish reliable information regarding conditions and trends in the Soviet Union today. The head-quarters of the Institute, which was founded in 1950, are in Munich, Germany. Its studies embrace the general field of the social sciences, including various aspects of economics, law, government and Party, history, education, religion, literature, and social organization. The authors of all books published under the auspices of the Institute assume their own responsibility for statements of fact and expressions of opinion. It is the sole responsibility of the Institute to determine that these facts and opinions are worthy of presentation to the public.

BOOKS THAT MATTER

Published in the United States of America in 1960
by Frederick A. Praeger, Inc., Publishers,
64 University Place, New York 3, N. Y.

© 1960 by the
Institute for the Study of the USSR, Munich, Germany

Library of Congress catalog card number 60-9940

This book is Number 89 in the series
of *Praeger Publications in Russian History and World Communism*

TABLE OF CONTENTS

PART TWO

The Consolidation of Stalinism in the Ukraine

FOREWORD

The smiles, the blandishments and the more flexible though no less calculated policies of Stalin's heirs have led to an understandable, if dubious, tendency in some quarters to relegate Stalinism to the historical dust bin and to view it as having been a temporary aberration on the Russian political scene. While it is true that a final verdict must await the future development of the Communist Party of the Soviet Union, the policies and purpose of the latter cannot be evaluated fully and the answer to this question obtained except by means of a careful comparison with *all* aspects of Stalinism. Thus the study of the quarter century of Soviet rule from 1928 to 1953 which has become synonymous with the late dictator's name is not of purely historical interest for it provides an indispensable yardstick by which to determine the degree to which Stalin's successors actually have or have not broken with their late mentor, have retained certain of his policies and practices while abandoning or modifying others.

Superficial comparison of the Stalin and post-Stalin periods usually results in emphasis being placed upon the more obvious recent changes such as the diminished role of direct terror, the granting to collective farms of permission to purchase agricultural machinery, the policy of localizing certain operational economic decision-making as a result of the establishment of the regional economic councils and the like. However, preoccupation with the more spectacular recent Soviet policies which have led to certain changes may result in the neglect of more fundamental and persistent policies and techniques of rule developed by Stalin and retained by his heirs.

One such area in which the post-Stalin regime has retained the basic Stalinist program is that of nationality policy. Here the persistence of Russian great-power chauvinism and the apparently unceasing pressure to impose the Russian language and way of life upon the Soviet Union's non-Russian peoples have outweighed the relatively minor concessions accorded the non-Russians by N. S. Khrushchev as a result of his personal knowledge of nationality matters based upon his experience in the second largest republic in the twenties as well as from 1938 to 1949. Thus Stalinism, when viewed in its entirety, cannot be regarded as little more than a nightmare which the awakened victim casts off with a shudder and then quickly forgets. This period not only lasted too long but also left far too many marks upon the Soviet body politic and was an integral part of Soviet development.

The need for a continuing understanding of Stalinism makes Mr. Hryhory Kostiuk's study of Stalinist rule in the Ukrainian SSR a welcome contribution to the existing literature on this vital period. Mr. Kostiuk has painstakingly analyzed no fewer than thirteen alleged anti-Soviet Ukrainian conspiracies and purge trials—both public and secret—which took place between 1930 and 1937. While much has been published on the infamous Moscow purge trials of 1936–38, nothing has been written prior to this study on the no less significant Ukrainian trials which were fabricated in order to provide a pretext for the physical destruction of a substantial part of the Ukrainian nation's intellectual cadres. Mr. Kostiuk's study includes a painful recital of the names of Ukrainian artists, writers, professors, scientists, academicians, civil servants, journalists, poets, and even commissars who were caught in the toils of a cruel purge based primarily on national affiliation.

A second reason for the importance of Mr. Kostiuk's study is that it is based upon unimpeachable sources which he cites and utilizes fully. These include the *Visti* of the All-Ukrainian Central Executive Committee (VUTsVK) and the Moscow *Pravda* as well as other official publications. Ironically, Soviet scholars are not in a position to utilize certain published Soviet sources and archival materials. One reason for this is that certain earlier Soviet scholars and spokesmen have not been fully rehabilitated. Thus when the present writer visited the two leading libraries in the Ukrainian SSR during the summer of 1957 he was unable to find in the public catalogs any record of the published works of Mykola Skrypnyk and Volodymyr Zatonsky, who figure prominently in Mr. Kostiuk's study.* In a Communist society even the dead are dangerous. Thus when a purged figure from the past has not been posthumously rehabilitated Soviet scholars cannot well cite his published works and speeches nor can they give adequate treatment to the role which he played during the period under consideration. Nor can proper attention be given to the activities of fully rehabilitated figures since they represent a period which Soviet scholars cannot treat objectively because of the compromising nature of Stalin's regime. Therefore Soviet historians must treat this ineffaceable blemish upon the regime's record with great caution.

Mr. Kostiuk's work is of value for still another reason. It lays bare the tragedy of the Ukrainian "national Communists" who had accepted uncritically Lenin's devious promises only to pay with their lives for the folly of believing that the Soviet regime would respect the right of national self-determination. Even more tragic is the record, which Mr. Kostiuk unfolds, of Ukrainian Communists like Zatonsky or Khvylya who for a time played Moscow's game as the pressure increased and were perfectly willing to sacrifice certain of their comrades in combatting "bourgeois nationalism" either in the dubious hope of saving something or in order to further their own careers.

The account of the decade from 1929 to 1939 which Mr. Kostiuk has provided makes it clear why Ukrainians defected from the Soviet system in such large numbers during World War II. It also provides the background for an understand-

---

* In contrast, new cards had been introduced into the catalogs for Postyshev, Kosior, and Chubar, whose works had been removed from the shelves at the time they were purged but were restored following the Twentieth Congress of the Communist Party of the Soviet Union in 1956.

ing of the endless denunciations of "bourgeois nationalism" which occurred after the war during Khrushchev's tenure as Party chief in the Ukrainian SSR.

The present volume also throws light on the milieu in which Khrushchev emerged in 1939 as a full member of the CPSU Politburo and obtained Stalin's confidence. Mr. Kostiuk has made clear Khrushchev's complicity in the purging of Stanislaw Kosior, his predecessor as First Secretary of the Party organization in the Ukrainian SSR. For Khrushchev did not appear in Kiev in January of 1938 as a mere innocent ordered to a new post but had helped prepare the groundwork for his own promotion when he journeyed to the Ukrainian capital with Molotov and the hated Nikolai Yezhov in August of 1937 in order to engineer the liquidation of almost the entire Central Committee of the Communist Party of the Ukraine. It was this step that prompted the head of the Ukrainian Soviet government, Panas Lyubchenko, to commit suicide.

One of the virtues of the present volume is the author's use of an episodic approach which conveys the pathos and tragedy of these traumatic events. While fully utilizing all available documentary sources, he has also incorporated into this study a wealth of somber detail obtained from eyewitnesses and participants.

Mr. Kostiuk has had the unusual experience of personally witnessing many of the events which he has described and analyzed. As a native of the Ukraine he not only witnessed Stalin's depredations during the thirties but fell victim to them. Upon completing Kiev University, Mr. Kostiuk continued his higher education in the field of literature, obtaining the candidate's degree in 1932, and then pursued a teaching career in institutions of higher education in the eastern part of the Ukrainian SSR. During this period he wrote scholarly works which were published by the Ukrainian State Publishing House (DVU) and in Soviet journals. In the latter part of 1935 his career was abruptly interrupted when he was caught up in the wave of repression against Ukrainians and, without a trial, was confined in the infamous Soviet concentration camp at Vorkuta. Since World War II, Mr. Kostiuk has lived and worked in the West and has edited and written a number of studies.

All who are interested in the veracity of the Soviet historical record and in its completeness cannot but be grateful to Hryhory Kostiuk for his significant contribution to this end.

JOHN S. RESHETAR, JR.

University of Washington
Seattle

PREFACE

The present study was completed before the Twentieth Congress of the Communist Party in 1956, that is, before the sensational secret speech by Nikita Khrushchev delivered at that Congress. The object of the study was to survey only one decade of the Stalinist regime (1929–39) in the Ukraine. The documentary material published by the Twentieth Congress, Khrushchev's revelations on February 24 and 25 of 1956, and the ensuing internal tensions within the Soviet orbit have confirmed that the crimes of Stalin and the Stalinists are a festering and mortal wound of the Communist dictatorship.

It was hoped that the present work would, for the first time, bring together all the available evidence relating to Stalin's policy in the Ukraine and would help to clarify the general panorama of that era, the motives for and the results of the reign of terror. At no time during the writing of this text did the author hope that the next Party Congress and the First Secretary of the Communist Party would, under the pressure of circumstances, make revelations which bear out some of the conclusions of this study.

Any reader, however, will perceive at once the difference in treatment of the Stalinist regime as offered by the author and by Khrushchev. The latter, in his secret speech, only slightly lifted the veil which shrouds Stalin's era. Our study attempts to go further and present all available evidence, both documentary and historical.

Khrushchev attributes Stalin's crimes to his "evil" character. The present author, while giving Stalin his due, attempts to explore how far such characters as his were conditioned by the Soviet system. Hence the analysis embraces not only Stalin but also his lieutenants, above all Khrushchev, to whom two chapters of the work are devoted.

The reader will find on the ensuing pages the names of hundreds of persons who were the victims of Stalinism. They range from Ukrainian Hetmanites (Monarchists), to Communists. All were swept by the same hand into the same pit.

Today some of these persons have been "rehabilitated." So far, the "rehabilitation" has been timid and rather surreptitious. The present Soviet rulers, forced by historical factors to make such reinstatements, thereby admitted Stalin's crimes, since they were unable to conceal them any longer. They have tried desperately to remove from themselves all suspicion of complicity in these crimes. Only time will tell if they will succeed in this. In the opinion of this author they are accomplices, and no amount of "rehabilitation" will make them less guilty. It is for this reason that the recent "rehabilitations," although reported wherever possible in this study, are not regarded as significant. They do not, in any way, affect the historical analysis of the decade.

Most studies of Stalinism which have appeared up to now have dealt with the Moscow trials in the Russian Soviet Republic. But terror and oppression had been organized by Stalin and the Stalinists much earlier in other Union Republics, especially in the Ukraine where 1930 marked the beginning. It is hoped that the present study, devoted to the Ukraine with its own specific history and unique, unforgettable significance for the historian and the sociologist, will contribute to an understanding of the period in all its aspects. Without claiming to be definitive, it is hoped that a necessary corrective to the one-sided and biased work produced under Soviet circumstances has been supplied and that a modest beginning to further research in this field has been made.

HRYHORY KOSTIUK

New York, N. Y.

ACKNOWLEDGEMENTS

It is with great pleasure that the author expresses his deep gratitude to Dr. Merle Fainsod of Harvard University, Dr. John S. Reshetar, Jr., of the University of Washington, Prof. Iwan Majstrenko and Prof. Peter P. Kurinny in Munich, Germany, Prof. O. P. Ohloblin and Dr. Jurij Lawrynenko of the Ukrainian Free Academy in the United States, Dr. George S. N. Luckyj of the University of Toronto, Prof. Anthony Adamovich of the Belorussian Institute of Arts and Sciences in the United States, and Mr. V. S. Holubnychy of Columbia University, whose reading of the manuscript, valuable criticism, advice, and comments have been of inestimable help in the preparation and the publication of this book. The author is also grateful to the members of the Free Ukrainian Academy's Commission for the Study of the Post-Revolutionary Ukraine and the USSR for their valuable study and discussion of individual parts of the manuscript.

He extends his special thanks to Dr. Philip E. Mosely and to Dr. Alexander Dallin, former Director and Associate Director, respectively, of the Research Program on the USSR, who first made possible the collection and analysis of the materials on which this study is based.

TERMS AND ABBREVIATIONS

All-Union CP(b) .... All-Union Communist Party (Bolshevik)

Borotbists .... Members of the Ukrainian Communist Party (Borotbist)

Bundists .... Members of the Jewish Social Democratic Workers' Party

CC .... Central Committee

CCC .... Central Control Commission

CEC .... Central Executive Committee

Cheka .... Extraordinary Commission for the Suppression of Counterrevolution

CP(b)U .... Communist Party (Bolshevik) of the Ukraine

CPSU .... Communist Party of the Soviet Union

CPWU .... Communist Party of the Western Ukraine

DVU .... Ukrainian State Publishing House

GPU .... State Political Administration

Komnezamy .... Committees of Poor Peasants

MTS .... Machine-and-Tractor Station

NKVD .... People's Commissariat of Internal Affairs

NTS .... National Labor Alliance

OGPU .... Unified State Political Administration

POW .... Polish Military Organization

Rabfak .... Worker's Faculty

Russian CP(b) ...... Russian Communist Party (Bolshevik)

SD .... Social Democrat

SR .... Social Revolutionary

SSR .... Soviet Socialist Republic

SUM .... Union of Ukrainian Youth

SVU .... Union for the Liberation of the Ukraine

UCEC .... Ukrainian Central Executive Committee

UCP .... The Ukrainian Communist Party

UCP(b) .... The Ukrainian Communist Party (Borotbist)

Ukapists .... Members of the Ukrainian Communist Party

UkSSR .... Ukrainian Soviet Socialist Republic

UNTs .... Ukrainian National Center

USSR .... Union of Soviet Socialist Republics

UVO .... Ukrainian Military Organization

VUAMLIN .... All-Ukrainian Association of Marx and Lenin Institutes

VUSPP .... All-Ukrainian Society of Proletarian Writers

VUTsVK .... All-Ukrainian Central Executive Committee

PART ONE

Stalinist Centralism and the Ukraine

Chapter I

Stalin's Plans

During the late twenties the Communist Party of the Soviet Union was shaken by a series of major internal conflicts. It had experienced the so-called "Left Opposition" (led by Trotsky), the "Workers' Opposition" (Shlyapnikov, Medvedev, Kollontay), the "Democratic Centralists" (Saprovnov, Drobnis, Boguslavsky, Smirnov), the Leningrad "New Opposition" (1925), the Trotsky-Zinoviev Bloc (1926), and the "Right Opposition" (led by Bukharin, 1928–29). As a result of this internal strife the Party became the battleground of mighty forces fighting for control both of theory and of actual power. A no less violent struggle was being waged inside the Party over the national problem. The struggle arose from the relationship between the national republics within the Union, and the existence of much national deviation and opposition in the Communist parties of these republics.

The *Short History of the Communist Party of the Soviet Union,* published in 1950,[1] contains this laconic comment on the events in the national republics arising out of the struggle of the local Communist parties against centralist Moscow:

> In several republics (the Ukraine, Belorussia and others) Party organizations relaxed their struggle against local nationalism, allowing it to spread to such an extent that it made contact with hostile forces, with interventionists, and became a threat to the state.[2]

True or not, the quotation from the *Short History,* which Trotsky called a "codified collection of falsifications,"[3] reveals that the state of affairs it describes was so obvious that it could not be passed over in silence. It is sufficient to recall that in seven years the question of Ukrainian national opposition was discussed five times by the leaders of the Comintern at, among other places, the Fifth Con-

---

[1] *Istoriya Vsesoyuznoi Kommunisticheskoi Partii (bolshevikov), Kratky Kurs* (History of the Communist Party of the Soviet Union (Bolshevik)—a Short Course), Moscow, Gospolitizdat, 1950. Hereafter cited as the *Short History.*

[2] *Ibid.,* p. 307.

[3] *Byulleten oppozitsii* (Bulletin of the Opposition), Paris, No. 81, January 1940, p. 15.

gress of that organization.[4] National deviations and oppositions within the Communist Party in the Ukraine (Shumskism, Khvylovism, Volobuevism, Skrypnykism), the expulsion, in 1928, of the Communist Party of the Western Ukraine (KPZU) from the Comintern and, finally, the great purge and campaign of terror (1933–38) are the main stages in the struggle of the Ukraine against the Kremlin.

There were two reasons for the origin of oppositionist movements within national Communist parties. First, the national republics, following the Revolution of 1917, enjoyed a certain measure of political and economic independence which the Bolshevik Party found it impossible to stifle. The Russian Communist Party, although centralist in nature, was forced to compromise with the national revolutionary forces in the non-Russian republics and to make concessions to them in the cultural, political and economic spheres. The creation, in 1923, of the Union of Soviet Socialist Republics was the result of the circumstances which made such compromise inevitable. After persistent demands,[5] the non-Russian republics were granted a constitution which guaranteed them equal partnership and limited independence within the Union, including the theoretical right of secession.

Second, the Russian Communist Party, having been compelled to compromise with the national republics, did not renounce its centralist principle. On the contrary, in order to retain control over the entire Soviet Union, it did everything in its power to uproot the centrifugal tendencies within the local Communist parties of the various republics. Implementing the Party statutes which, in the

---

[4] For source material on the "nationalist deviation" in the CP(b)U in the twenties see:

Budivnytstvo radyanskoi Ukrainy, Zbirnyk (Construction of the Soviet Ukraine—A Compendium)—Part I, Chapter V: "Zayava TsK KP(b)U do Vykonkomu Kominterna" (The Declaration of the CC of the CP(b)U to the Executive Committee of the Comintern), pp. 215-28: "Rezolyutsiya plenumu VKKI pro rozlam u kompartii Zakhidnoi Ukrainy" (The Resolution of the Plenum of the Executive Committee of the Comintern about the Split in the Communist Party of the Western Ukraine), pp. 255-56; "Vidozva Kominternu" (The Proclamation of the Comintern), pp. 256-58.

Kommunistische Partei der West-Ukraine (KPZU) — Die Ukrainische Nationale Frage (Materialen zur Frage der sogenannten ukrainischen Abweichungen "Schumskismus" in der Kommunistischen Partei der Ukraine und der Kommunistischen Partei der West-Ukraine), Lemberg, im Selbstverlag des ZK der KPZU, 1928.

Ye. F. Hirchak, *Shumskizm i rozlam v KPZU* (Shumskism and the Split in the CPWU), Kharkov, Ukrainian State Publishing House, 1928.

Mykola Kovalevsky, *Ukraina pid chervonym yarmom: Dokumenty, fakty* (The Ukraine under the Red Yoke: Documents and Facts), Warsaw, Lvov, 1936 (Chapter: "Shumsky, Maksymovych pered sudom III Internatsionalu" (Shumsky and Maksymovych on Trial before the III International)), pp. 59-62; 63-67.

Mykhailo Volobuyev, "Do problemy ukrainskoi ekonomiky" (Concerning the Problem of Ukrainian Economy), *Bilshovyk Ukrainy* (The Bolshevik of the Ukraine), 1928, No. 2, pp. 46-72; No. 3, pp. 42-63.

A. Richytsky, *Do problemy likvidatsii perezhytkiv koloniyalnost ta natsionaliszmu* (Concerning the Problem of the Liquidation of Vestiges of Coloniality and Nationalism), Kharkov, 1928.

[5] *XII sezd Rossiiskoi Kommunisticheskoi Partii (bolshevikov), Stenografischesky otchet 17-23 aprelya 1923 g.* (The Twelfth Congress of the Russian Communist Party (Bolshevik), Stenographic Report, 17-23 April 1923.) Moscow, Krasnaya nov, 1923, p. 705.

2

same form, were binding on all national Party organizations, it conducted periodic purges designed to favor the centralist elements and to paralyze the national movements. This policy led to complex and tense relations between the center and the periphery. This conflict in the Ukraine was trenchantly described by an American observer, William Henry Chamberlin. "The Communist Party in the Ukraine," he wrote, "was subjected to more frequent and violent purges than the same organization in Russia, because the impulse to assert national independence frequently cropped up even among Ukrainian Communists."[6] Similarly, Trotsky in an article "On the Ukrainian Question" wrote:

> Nowhere do repression, purges, subjection and all types of bureaucratic hooliganism in general assume such deadly proportions as in the Ukraine in the struggle against powerful subterranean strivings among the Ukrainian masses toward greater freedom and independence.[7]

The consolidation of absolute power in the Kremlin resulted in the gradual transformation of the non-Russian republics into administrative and economic provinces of Russia. Therefore the destruction of all national opposition in local Party organizations was conducted simultaneously with the liquidation of the inner opposition within the CPSU(b).

Having defeated Trotsky's "Left Opposition" at the Thirteenth Party Congress in May 1924, Zinoviev's "new Leningrad opposition" at the Fourteenth Party Congress in December 1925, the "Trotsky-Zinoviev Bloc" in November 1927, and Bukharin's "Right Opposition" at the Sixteenth Party Conference in April 1929, and having crushed a series of national opposition movements within Party organizations in the Ukraine, Georgia, Belorussia, Uzbekistan, the Tatar Republic, and Armenia, Stalin emerged in 1930 as the sole master of the Party in which all power in the Soviet state is vested. In subduing the various opposition movements by terror and by use of the Party apparatus, Stalin must have realized that in order to maintain his position and to carry out his further plans, he must transform the Party into his tool. This was difficult as long as the old cadres, familiar with Stalin's insignificant role in the early history of the Party, were still alive. The relations between the Soviet republics and Moscow also had to be altered and the entire structure of the Soviet state drastically changed. In order to fulfill Stalin's objectives three conditions had to be met:

1) Centralization of the Party apparatus and elimination from it of the Bolshevik "Old Guard."

2) Complete subordination of the State administration to the Party.

3) Economic unification of all the national republics and their subordination to the Kremlin.

The Soviet history of the thirties bears witness to the execution of these plans. The resistance which arose was ruthlessly crushed. The Bolshevik "Old Guard"

---

[6] W. H. Chamberlin, *The Ukraine—A Submerged Nation*, New York, 1944, p. 55.

[7] *Byulleten oppozitsii*, Paris, No. 77-78, May, June, July, 1939, p. 5.

was exterminated in Russia and the national republics,[8] all traces of national autonomy were wiped out and all those who could not or would not comply with Stalin's policies were branded as "enemies of the people," "spies," "saboteurs" or "foreign agents" and were subsequently dispatched to oblivion by the GPU-NKVD.

While still further concentrating all power in his hands, Stalin embarked on the industrialization of the country in order to bolster its economic strength and defensive capacity. To achieve this, it was necessary to "find the means."[9] The means, indeed, were crucial. They had to be sought "only within the country itself."[10] Workers and peasants alike were asked to sacrifice all their efforts, and often their lives, to enable Stalin to fulfill his dream.

---

[8] The history of the destruction of the Old Bolshevik Guard of the Party has been brilliantly analyzed by A. Avtorkhanov in his study *Pokorenie partii* (Subjugation of the Party), published in *Posev* (Sowing), No. 40-52, 1950, and No. 1-16, 1951. It first appeared in book form in French translation: Alexander Ouralov, *Staline au Pouvoir*, Paris, 1951. An English translation from the French by L. J. Smith followed: Alexander Uralov, *The Reign of Stalin*, London, 1953. Avtorkhanov's study is based primarily on his recollections, not on documentary sources.

[9] Cf. *Short History of the CPSU*, p. 268.

[10] *Ibid.*

Chapter II

The Plans in Action

One of the most important resolutions adopted by the Sixteenth Party Conference which met in April 1929 paved the way for the initiation of the First Five-Year Plan, according to the so-called "optimum variant."[1] It committed the entire Soviet Union to the utmost exertion and sacrifice in order to meet the demands of the required industrial construction. Agriculture came to play a crucial part in this plan. Thirdly, oppositionist tendencies in the Party were eliminated and the so-called "Right" (Bukharin) deviation was crushed.[2]

The issue of collectivization of agriculture soon appeared on the Party agenda. In order to obtain complete control of agricultural production and marketing, the Party began to introduce collectivization on a mass scale and at a rapid pace. In practise this meant that the peasants were denied all those property rights which had been guaranteed them by the decree on land, issued on November 8, 1917.[3] A prerogative, which they had regarded as the great reward of the Revolution, was swept away. It was obvious that such a measure would increase the hostility of the peasantry towards the regime, yet without it the full control which the Party sought over the peasants, would be impossible.

In declaring war on the peasants, Stalin simultaneously initiated his first major move against the Ukraine, where the tradition of individual farming was especially strong. That country, the second largest in the Soviet Union, and famous for its agricultural and mineral resources, was destined to play a leading role in the conflict which was obviously impending. The plans worked out in the Kremlin for the "grain-collection campaign" and for the "collectivization of agriculture" were aimed against the basic economic and social order of the Ukrainian peasantry. The peasants soon understood their meaning and reacted against them with the force and determination of a people fighting for life itself. The resistance of the Ukrainian peasantry to collectivization, glibly described by Soviet historians as the

---

[1] According to the *Short History*, the conference rejected the so-called "minimum variant" proposed by the "Rightists" and accepted the "optimum variant" of the Five-Year Plan proposed by Stalin (p. 283).

[2] For details see: *VKP(b) v rezolyutsiyakh i resheniyakh sezdov, konferentsii i plenumov* (The CPSU in Resolutions and Decisions of Congresses, Conferences and Plenums), Part II, 1925-35. 5th ed., Moscow, Partizdat TsK VKP(b), 1936, pp. 318-330 (United Plenum of the CC and CCC CPSU, April 15-23, 1929), pp. 331-32, 340-42 (the Sixteenth Conference).

[3] "Deklaratsiya prav trudyashchegosya i ekspluatiruemogo naroda" (The Declaration of the Rights of the Working and Exploited People), *Sistematicheskoe sobranie zakonov RSFSR* (Systematic Collection of the Laws of the RSFSR), Moscow, 1929, I, pp. 3-4.

"recalcitrance of the kulaks," spread to such an extent that, at the end of 1930, it became a serious threat to the regime. Stalin and his lieutenants realized that if they were to overcome this resistance they must use stark terror and brute force. To justify these Stalin issued the battle-cry "For the Liquidation of the Kulaks as a Class," which initiated one of the bloodiest eras of his reign.

This campaign received the following interpretation in the *Short History of the CPSU:*

> During 1930–34 the Bolshevik Party accomplished a historic task, the most difficult (after the establishment of the Soviet government) of the whole proletarian Revolution—the transference of millions of small-propertied peasants' farms to the collective farms and onto the path of socialism.[4]

How was this difficult task successfully completed? The official version reads as follows:

> The transition to total collectivization did not take place with a peaceful and orderly entry of the large masses of the peasants into the kolkhozes, but with a mass struggle of the peasants against the kulaks. Total collectivization meant the transfer of all land in the villages to the kolkhozes. However, since a sizeable part of the land was in the hands of the kulaks, the peasants drove the kulaks away, "dekulakized" them, took away their cattle, and demanded that the Soviet authorities arrest and evict the kulaks.[5]

The impression created by this quotation suggests that the Soviet authorities were performing a service to the peasants, that they confined themselves to aiding the peasants who rose against the kulaks, and that the "liquidation of the kulaks as a class" was ordered only after "persistent demands" for such action on the part of the peasants.[6] Do the facts recorded in the Soviet press and literature of the period support this contention?

A leading article, "Against Opportunism in the Work of the Soviet Apparatus," in the organ of the All-Ukrainian Central Executive Committee, *Radyanska Ukraina* (The Soviet Ukraine),[7] presents a survey of the situation in agriculture which offers a different picture from that presented in the *Short History*. The article confesses that the campaign for collectivization was far from satisfactory. It charges that the Party leaders in many areas were highly opportunistic and were sabotaging the effort. Frequently, the mainstay of the Party in the villages— the *Komnezamy* (Committees of Poor Peasants)—were directing the sabotage, having turned themselves into organizations hostile to the Soviet government. According to this article, the chairman of the Petrovsky village soviet, Shevchenko,

---

[4] *Short History of the CPSU*, p. 314.

[5] *Ibid.*, p. 290.

[6] *Ibid.*, p. 291.

[7] "Proty oportunizmu v roboti radyanskoho aparatu" (Against Opportunism in the Work of the Soviet Apparatus), *Radyanska Ukraina*, No. 10, November 1930.

had declared that there were no kulaks in his village and that he did not know, therefore, how he should conduct the class struggle. The village soviet, he complained, had received no "firm assignments."[8]

The chairman of the Oleksandrivsk village soviet also declared that there were no kulaks in his village, and that therefore collectivization was proceeding there without "firm assignments," that is, without terror and extortion. The chairman of the Novo-Petrovsk village soviet in Bilopolsky district advised the peasants who had been threatened with "firm assignments" to deliver 50 poods of grain to appease the authorities. Similarly, the chairman of the Bolshe-Fontansky village soviet confessed that since there were no kulaks in his village, he saw no reason why any stern measures should be used in collectivization. Moreover, he refused the aid of the government in the form of a "towing brigade,"[9] protesting that it was "a children's game, unnecessary to anyone." Nor could the chairman of the Sofievsky village soviet of the Andree-Ivanovsky district find any kulaks in his village, and he thought, therefore, that "firm assignments" were unneccessary. In the village of Stepok, in the district of Andrushkovo, the entire village soviet, the presidium of the *Komnezam*, the executive committee of the village kolkhoz and of the co-operative were disbanded for sabotaging the collection of grain.

The article in *Radyanska Ukraina* ends with the following conclusion: "One could cite scores and hundreds of other examples of 'Right' opportunism in the practical work of the soviets. Those cited above are, however, sufficient." In our opinion, they serve to expose the Soviet perversion of the history of collectivization. They clearly show how wide and spontaneous was the resistance to forced collectivization among the peasants not excluding chairmen of the soviets and other officials.

Another aspect of life during collectivization, amplifying this picture, is revealed in an article by M. Marchenko, also published in *Radyanska Ukraina*.[10] The author gives a grim account of the economic decay in the Khorol district, of

---

[8] The "firm assignments" *(tvyordye zadaniya)* were, like the terms "grain delivery" *(khlebozagotovka)* and "collectivization," Communist euphemisms disguising the policy of lawless terror against the peasantry. For a peasant to receive a "firm assignment" meant that he was declared a kulak and therefore had to be destroyed together with his family. Before his liquidation, however, he was given a special "grain delivery quota," which was made extremely difficult to fulfill. If a peasant was able to fulfill it, he was usually given another, even more difficult. Failure to fulfill an assignment was a criminal offense, for which he was then liquidated. This could mean death before a firing squad, or deportation to a concentration camp, from which he rarely returned. His family was also deported, and his home and farm became the property of the kolkhoz.

[9] The so-called "towing brigades" *(buksirnye brigady)* were yet another aid to collectivization. They were chiefly formed in towns, and consisted of Communist enthusiasts and Komsomol members. They were sent to the villages to help with the "grain delivery." These brigades of youths, armed, well-fed, and using all the methods of punitive police detachments, were hated by the peasants as much as the police. In 1930-33, during several peasant uprisings, some members of these brigades were the victims of peasant retribution.

[10] M. Marchenko, "Khorolsky rayon, ohlyad" (The Khorol Raion: A Survey), *Radyanska Ukraina*, No. 11, December 1930, pp. 75-76.

the flight of the peasants, and the protests of the small Party officials against the inhuman methods of collectivization. "Khorol district, in the province of Poltava," he writes, "fulfilled the plan of grain collection only as far as 40 to 41 per cent of the total target. The kulaks are fleeing to the Donbas and other places, leaving behind bare walls in their houses ... In the village of Melyushky two members of the village soviet have refused to participate in grain collection ... The District Executive Committee has ordered all the village soviets to organize the work in the village 'by sections.'"[11]

Similar accounts of peasant resistance to collectivization can be gleaned from the pages of another organ of the CP(b)U, the daily *Komunist*. Thus, in the issue of November 24, 1932, we read that in the village of Katerynovtsi (the paper was published in Kharkov), the secretary of the local Party cell, "after receiving the plan for grain collection, refused to fulfill it and asked to be relieved of his duties." The secretary of the Party cell in the village of Ushakivtsi refused to accept the written order of his superiors, specifying the tasks of the forthcoming drive for grain deliveries. The chairman of the Lenin kolkhoz in the Slavyansk district of Donets province, Zagorelsky, declared that first of all the peasants themselves must be given bread, and only then could they be asked to fulfill the grain deliveries. Many similar reports from *Komunist* could be cited.[12]

On the basis of material contained in the Soviet press as well as in accounts by escapees from the Soviet Union[13] it is possible to conclude that it was not the peasants who, with the aid of the government, drove out the kulaks, as the *Short History* contends, but that the government, with the armed forces and police, was responsible for the mass destruction of all peasants, both poor and rich, during collectivization. It is even possible to conjecture that the well-to-do peasants, who were also the most enlightened and educated, suffered less than the middle and poor peasants. Most of them, having realized that the Party was determined to uproot them, left their farms at the very beginning of collectivization (1929) and moved to industrial cities. The full brunt of the terror, which started in 1930 and culminated in the famine of 1932–33, was borne by those peasants who stayed

---

[11] This characteristic Ukrainian expression *(po kutkakh)* refers to another practice common during collectivization. Often unable to crush the opposition of the villagers, the authorities conducted grain collections in several sections of the village, which was split up for that purpose. Each section comprised from 100 to 150 peasants whose work was supervised by a brigade. The peasants of each section were exposed to constant abuse, threats and beatings. They were often arrested, or expelled from the village.

[12] The source for the material contained in *Komunist,* which is unobtainable in libraries in the United States or Canada, is M. Kovalevsky, *Polityka narodowościowa na Ukrainie* (Nationality Policy in the Ukraine), Instytut Badań Spraw Narodowościowych (Institute for the Study of Nationality Problems), Warsaw, 1938.

[13] D. Solovey, *Stezhkamy na Holhotu* (Along the Paths to Calvary), New York, Detroit, Scranton, 1952; also *Holhota Ukrainy* (The Calvary of the Ukraine), Winnipeg, 1952. A. Vysochenko, *SSSR bez masky* (The USSR Without a Mask), Buenos Aires, 1951. L. Drazhevska, "Ukrainska selyanka v Paryzhi. Vystup Olhy Marchenko na protsesi V. Kravchenka" (A Ukrainian Peasant Woman in Paris; the Appearance of Olha Marchenko at the Trial of V. Kravchenko), *Hromadyanka*, Munich, No. 1-2, 1949.

behind on their farms. Hundreds of thousands of them who lost their lives at that time were probably not kulaks but poor peasants who, in 1917, were active partisans in the Civil War.[14]

A partial admission of the truth of this statement is made by the anonymous author of the *Short History* who concedes that this "revolution" was "carried out from above."[15] The responsibility for the outrages of collectivization rests entirely with Stalin and the Communist Party.

---

[14] This view is supported by many accounts of victims of the Soviet terror. Cf. Solovey, *op. cit.;* Vysochenko, *op. cit.;* V. Skuybida, "Pamyati nevidomykh; Ryabchenko i bunt 21 polku" (To the Memory of the Unknown: Ryabchenko and the Mutiny of the 21 Regiment), *Nedilya,* No. 13, 1951. Also: "O tempe kollektivizatsii i merakh pomoshchi gosudarstva kolkhoznomu stroitelstvu, postanovleniye TsK VKP(b)" (Concerning the Rate of Collectivization and Government Measures to Aid the Establishment of the Kolkhozes, Resolution of the CC of the CPSU), *Pravda,* January 6, 1930.

[15] *Short History of the CPSU,* p. 291.

Chapter III

The Collapse of Agriculture

The implementation of Stalin's grandiose plans led to open conflict between the peasantry and the regime. The Ukrainian peasants' resistance to collectivization was expressed not only in passive protest against the grain collections, in sabotaging the five-year plan effort, in wrecking machinery, slaughtering cattle, and in flight from the villages to the cities. It often took the form of open revolt against the Soviet state. Many such spontaneous rebellions occurred in various parts of the country during the first stage of collectivization. Evidence of this may be found in Soviet and emigre sources.

One such rebellion took place in the Proskuriv district and in other areas in the Moldavian Autonomous Republic. According to an eye-witness account,

> at first the militia was sent to pacify the enraged peasants. Mounted militia moved into the villages of Zoslava and Slavuta. However, in a day or two, only a few of the entire detachment of militia men had escaped alive. The others had been killed by the peasants. The movement spread to Pohonny, Antonin, and other regions of the Shepetivka district. The peasants killed the government representatives, they seized the property which had been taken away from them and in some villages, especially in the region of Antonin, they even proclaimed a new "soviet government without Communists." A small GPU detachment, sent to relieve the militia, was also decimated. The chief of the GPU in the Shepetivka district reported to the Party that in this area there was a spontaneous anti-kolkhoz uprising, headed by inexperienced leaders, and that the regular army units could easily localize and suppress it.[1]

Similar peasant rebellions broke out in the Drabove[2] and Holo-Prystan districts in Kherson province,[3] and in the provinces of Kamenets-Podolsk and Vinnitsa.[4] In the province of Chernigov (Horodno, Tupychiv and Snov districts) the peasant risings had the support of the 21st Chernigov regiment, and were crushed only after major concentrations of the GPU and regular army troops were dispatched against them.[5] Other revolts occurred in the district of Tarashcha[6] in

---

[1] Vysochenko, *op. cit.*, p. 8.

[2] Solovey, "Holhota Ukrainy" (The Calvary of the Ukraine), *Ukrainsky holos* (Ukrainian Voice), Winnipeg, January 23, 1952.

[3] Yuriy Horlis-Horsky, *Ave Dictator*, Lvov, 1941, p. 31.

[4] S. Pidhayny, *Ukrainska intelligentsiya na Solovkakh* (Ukrainian Intellectuals on the Solovky), Prometey, 1947.

[5] Skuybida, *op. cit.*; Solovey, "Holhota Ukrainy," *Ukrainsky holos*, January 30, 1952.

[6] B. K. "1930-33 na Tarashchanshchyni" (The Years 1930-33 in the Tarashcha Area), *Novy shlyakh* (The New Path), Winnipeg, August 18, 1948.

Volhynia and in the Mykhailivka, Pereshchepyna,[7] and Pavlograd districts of Dnepropetrovsk province.[8]

Resistance to collectivization was widespread in other republics and areas of the USSR, especially in Kuban, the North Caucasus, Georgia, Uzbekistan, and Kazakhstan. Some evidence on peasant rebellions in the North Caucasus is contained in Avtorkhanov's *The Reign of Stalin.*

The official records of the Party also mention the peasant revolts in the Ukraine. Speaking at the March plenum of the Central Committee of the All-Union CP(b) in 1937,[9] Stalin, recalling the year 1930, said: "It was one of the most dangerous periods in the life of our Party." An even more open admission of peasant resistance is contained in the *Short History:*

> As a result of errors committed by the Party organizations . . . there appeared in the second half of February 1930 dangerous symptoms of serious peasant discontent. In some places the kulaks and their agents succeeded in provoking the peasants to direct anti-Soviet demonstrations.[10]

The *Short History* does not describe just how these anti-Soviet demonstrations were crushed. However, thousands of former Soviet citizens who are now in the West can confirm from their experience the brutal methods of mass terror used against the peasants during collectivization. And the fact that this quotation with the phrases "dangerous symptoms of serious peasant discontent" and "direct anti-Soviet demonstrations" appears at all in the *Short History,* the anonymous author of which usually attempts to pass over such things in silence, clearly indicates how widespread and how violent resistance was. Often it was only the NKVD troops and the regular Red Army who saved the Soviet regime from being overthrown by mass rebellions of the hungry, tortured, and ferocious peasants, determined to drive the government officials from the countryside. The effect of this reign of

---

[7] D. Solovey, *op. cit.*

[8] The author of this study met one of the participants in this revolt, Ivan Mykhailovych Prykhodko, in the Vorkuta concentration camp in 1936-40. He was eighteen years old when the rebellion broke out. He was sentenced to ten years forced labor for his participation in the revolt. The rebellion took place in the spring of 1930, during the worst of the terror in the villages. Headed by a Red Army lieutenant who happened to be on leave from the army and whose parents were placed on the list of those to be liquidated, the revolt spread like lightning to other villages. Many government officials, members of "towing brigades," contact men, informers and others were killed by the enraged peasants. The revolt was finally crushed by the army, which was supported by tanks and armor as well as by planes. The rebels, armed with axes, pitchforks, revolvers and other homemade weapons, surrendered after a fierce battle which lasted for five days. Their leader, the Red Army lieutenant, was killed in battle. Many other peasants were executed following their surrender. All those who had any connection with the uprising, together with their families, were deported for ten years.

[9] "O nedostatkakh partiinoi raboty i merakh likvidatsii trotskistkikh i inykh dvurushnikov; doklad tov. Stalina na plenume TsK VKP(b) 3 marta 1937 goda" (Concerning the Shortcomings of Party Activity and Measures for Liquidating the Trotskyite and Other Double-Dealers. Report by Comrade Stalin at the Plenum of the CC of the All-Union CP(b) on March 3, 1937), *Pravda,* March 27, 1937. Stalin's concluding speech at the plenum was printed in *Pravda,* April 1, 1937.

[10] *Short History of the CPSU,* p. 294.

terror[11] on the Ukrainian peasants was terrifying. The most usual reprisal against the more active participants in the resistance was execution on the spot; less active participants were given long sentences in concentration camps, while of the rest of the population, women and children, the aged and the sick, hundreds of thousands were deported to distant, unpopulated regions in the North of the USSR,[12] and there the majority of them perished. Not until these draconic measures had been applied would the Ukrainian villages submit to collectivization.

---

[11] The forced nature of collectivization is best attested in the secret directive to all organs of the GPU, the Court and the Procurator, signed by Stalin and Molotov on May 8, 1933. This document, seized by the German army in Smolensk, was published in *Sotsialistichesky vestnik,* New York and Paris, February-March, 1955, pp. 50-52.

[12] Fedir Rogiles, "Z nahody 17 richya znyshchennya stanytsi Poltavskoi" (On the Seventeenth Anniversary of the Destruction of the Poltavska Settlement), *Vilna Kuban* (The Free Kuban), Toronto, No. 2, December 1949.

Chapter IV

The Drabove Incident

In spite of the "successes" of the Party and the GPU-NKVD in dealing with the peasants, the Soviet dictator was alarmed by the resistance and by the means used to crush it.

In order to pour oil on troubled waters and to appease the enraged peasants, Stalin published his "Dizziness from Success" article in *Pravda* on March 2, 1930. Soviet historians attempt to interpret this statement as a radical change in the policy of collectivization. Subsequent events show, however, that no such change occurred. The policy remained just as ruthless and uncompromising as it had been before Stalin's speech. All that happened as a result of this speech was the removal of several thousand minor Communist executives who were thus made public scapegoats. This tactic was employed by Stalin on other occasions with the same purpose: minor officials were removed to create the illusion that justice had been done and that from then on there would be no further abuse of law and order. In reality, however, the men who replaced those who had grown "dizzy from success" pursued the old policy, and it became even more brutal as time went on.

The pronouncements by Lenin[1] and Stalin[2] that the enrollment of peasants in the kolkhozes should be voluntary remained in the realm of theory. The practice of collectivization differed sharply from the principles originally enunciated by Lenin. For it must not be assumed that the peasants were ready to capitulate before the first wave of terror which spread over the Ukraine in 1929–30. The struggle against collectivization went on, and the reprisals which followed were aimed at annihilating the remnants of the resistance.

The Soviet press of 1932 is full of accounts which testify to the violence of the struggle in the villages.[3] As an example of the indiscriminate terror used by the government against the peasants at that time we may recall the so-called Drabove Incident *(Drabovshchyna)*. It concerned a trial of Party and government

[1] V. Lenin, *Sochineniya* (Works), Vol. XXIV, pp. 167-168 and 579.

[2] J. Stalin, "Politichesky otchet tsentralnogo komiteta" (Political Report of the Central Committee) and "Otvet tovarishcham kolkhoznikam" (Answer to the Comrade Kolkhozniks) in *Sochineniya* (Collected Works), Moscow, 1949, Vol. 10, pp. 305-306, and Vol. 12, pp. 203-206.

[3] In addition to the reports in *Pravda*, *Visti (Visti VUTsVK*—News of the All-Ukrainian Central Executive Committee, hereafter referred to as *Visti), Komunist, Radyanska Ukraina*, and *Chervony shlyakh* (The Red Pathway), see The Resolutions of the Third Party Conference of the CP(b)U in *Pravda*, July 15, 1932, and *Visti*, July 11, 1932. The records of this conference also contain speeches by Skrypnyk, Chubar, Zatonsky, and Shlikhter. From June 2 to July 2, 1932, *Visti* printed regular reports on the "Drabove affair."

officials of the Drabove district, in the province of Poltava, which took place in July 1932.

At the beginning of 1932 the government policy of expropriation and exploitation of the peasants in the Drabove district reached catastrophic proportions. The Central Committee of the CP(b)U and the Council of People's Commissars of the Ukraine were deluged with complaints from collective farmers about the outbreak of famine and the flight of the peasants from the district. In response to these mass complaints a special government commission was sent to the area to investigate the state of affairs and to conduct an enquiry. The commission found that the economic life of the district was completely dislocated and laid the blame on several Party and government officials of the district, whom it charged with criminal neglect of duty and other malpractices. Following the recommendations laid down in the commission's report, the Soviet of People's Commissars requested the State Procurator to place all those accused of breaking the law under arrest, and to try them in the public courts. As a result, 30 men were arrested; among them were the secretary of the District Party Committee, Bodok, the chairman of the District Executive Commitee, Shirokov, the chairman of the Central Commission of Workers' and Peasants' Inspection, Shopenko, the chairman of the District Trade Union Council, Nevvazhai, and other officials taking part in the campaign for grain deliveries.

The public trial was held in Drabove. The accused were found guilty of "conspiring with the kulaks" in antigovernment activities and drew two- or three-year sentences. There is ample evidence to suggest that the conditions prevailing in the Drabove district were characteristic of many parts of the country.[4]

Although the Drabove trial had an obvious propaganda value, since it helped to brand the "criminals" responsible for the catastrophic state of Ukrainian agriculture, it revealed indirectly the processes of collectivization as well as the attempt on the part of the Soviet Ukrainian government to expose the worst abuses. An article by Ya. Tumarkin, "Letters from a Trial," published in the Party organ *Visti*,[5] gives the following list of offenses committed by the accused:

1) They had concealed and ignored the complaints of the peasants about the lawlessness practised during the grain deliveries.

2) They had suppressed all complaints and self-criticism with threats and violence.

3) They had tolerated the rule of force, lawlessness, and terror.

4) They had made kulaks out of middle and poor peasants, and even Party members.

5) Ignoring the actual situation, they had been guided by the slogan "Take grain wherever it is easiest to take." They did this without regard to the means used, or to the one from whom the grain was taken.

[4] Cf. The Resolutions of the Third Party Conference of the CP(b)U, *Visti*, July 11, 1932, in which similar practices are mentioned in several regions of Moldavia.

[5] Ya. Tumarkin, "Lysty z protsesu" (Letters from a Trial), *Visti*, July 2, 1932.

6) According to the testimony of district officials (Bodok, Shirokov, and Shopenko) the kolkhozes had been deprived of seed.

7) Criminals had been used for terrorization and plundering in the villages.

It is little wonder that under such conditions agricultural production in the Ukraine showed a rapid decline. Some figures for the years 1930–32 may be found in the report which Postyshev delivered before the Twelfth Congress of the CP(b)U, in 1934. According to Postyshev, grain deliveries in 1930 were satisfactory. Up to December 400 million poods of grain were delivered to the state. The annual plan was 95 per cent fulfilled. In 1931 the degree of collectivization of agriculture progressed from 38 per cent to 65 per cent. The number of machine-and-tractor stations rose from 47 in 1930 to 300, and the number of tractors from 15,000 to 25,000. But in spite of these technological and administrative advances the plan for grain deliveries was only 74 per cent fulfilled. In 1932 collectivization embraced 70 per cent of the farms in the country. The number of MTS rose to 445, and the number of tractors to 35,000. However, grain deliveries sharply decreased. In comparison with the 400 million poods obtained in 1930, and the 300 million poods in 1931, only 195 million poods of grain were delivered to the state in 1932.[6] The above figures speak for themselves. The country was on the brink of economic disaster. The first signs of famine became evident in the Ukraine early in 1932. The peasants were leaving their homes en masse and moving to industrial cities in search of employment. Those who remained died by the thousand.[7] Hungry

[6] "Sovetskaya Ukraina na novom podeme; Politichesky otchet TsK KP(b)U na XII sezde KP(b)U; doklad t. P. P. Postysheva" (The Soviet Ukraine in a New Advance: Political Report of the CC of the CP(b)U at the Twelfth Congress of the CP(b)U: Report of Comrade P. P. Postyshev), *Pravda*, January 24, 1934; also: *Visti*, January 24, 1934.

[7] Reports of famine in the Ukraine were systematically carried by *Sotsialistichesky vestnik*. Its leading articles (e. g. No. 13, June 25, 1932), special reports (e. g. A. Yugov, "Golod na Ukraine," No. 12, 1932) and regular colums (e. g. "Po Rossii") contained a great deal of factual information. The column "Across Russia" (No. 11, 1932, p. 23) reports:

> The railroad stations of the Ukraine, the Don region, the North Caucasus and other formerly rich agricultural areas are over-crowded with hungry peasants from the neighboring villages, who beg travellers for a "crumb of bread." One sees the horrible figures of women with famine-stricken children in their arms ... At present great crowds of peasants surge into the towns, drawn by rumors of free markets, hoping to buy something or to beg. Even in Kharkov there is a multitude of peasants, begging for bread. However, they are caught and sent away by the militia.

In the same column in No. 14, July 23, 1932, we read:

> I have just returned from Odessa. Conditions there, as well as the general food situation in the Ukraine, are beyond description. There the famine is real with all its attributes—the bark of trees and pig-weeds eaten as a substitute for bread. A veritable migration of people is taking place, carried by the railroads. I cannot vouch for figures, but eyewitnesses maintain that almost three million people are on the move. They are travelling with their families and small children; thousands of them crowd all the stations. In carriages and on the stations—all around there are so many hungry eyes that although one feels hungry, one does not take out a piece of black bread from one's bag.

A few years later, A. Ciliga reported after his escape from Soviet prisons (*Sotsialistichesky vestnik*, No. 11, 1936):

> In 1932-33 the country was literally starving ... In the villages of the Ukraine, the North Caucasus and Central Asia cannibalism was, if not an extensive, at least a widely spread phenomenon.

children left their homes in search of food. Everyone who lived in the Soviet Union at that time saw hundreds of thousands of these unfortunate five to ten year old children flooding the cities and railway stations of the country. One was particularly struck by the five or six year old children who resembled skeletons, were pale as death, emaciated, and, as Arthur Koestler noted with horror, "looked like embryos out of alcohol bottles."[8] These children begged for bread at all the crossroads and in all the railway stations of the USSR. An eyewitness account of the "waifs" (bezprizornye) appeared in Trotsky's *Bulletin of the Opposition*.[9]

> The peasants are leaving their children in the cities; the young people leave their villages and travel as stowaways to the North and East. Many *bezprizornye* have appeared in Moscow. The majority of them are Ukrainians.

The American journalist, Mark Khinoy, visiting the USSR in 1934, saw the last stages of the tragedy suffered by the children in the Ukraine. He wrote:

> The situation was better in the Volga regions and in Siberia. However, the Ukraine presents a picture of utter desolation. There is no plenty, no cheerfulness, everywhere there are the *bezprizornye* children. One cannot see them in Moscow, but in Kharkov, and especially in Dnepropetrovsk, there are whole bands of them. They are the remnants of the 1932 famine.[10]

At the time of the worst plight of the Ukrainian peasantry Stalin made the following statement on the achievements of collectivization:

> What, in fact, has changed during this time? First of all, we have liquidated unemployment, consequently we have destroyed the force which oppressed the "labor market." Secondly, we have uprooted the stratification of the village and as a result of this we have overcome the mass poverty which drove the peasants from the villages to the cities. Lastly, we have provided the villages with tens of thousands of tractors and machines, we have crushed the kulaks, organized kolkhozes, and given the peasants an opportunity to live and work like human beings. Now the village can no longer be called the peasant's stepmother, and because of this the peasant has begun to settle down in the village; there is no longer any "flight of the peasants from the village to the city," no waste of manpower.[11]

Terrible as it was, the year 1932 was only a prelude to the mass starvation of the peasants in the following year.

The Soviet Ukrainian press carried limited reports of the economic disaster in the Ukraine. The spring of 1932 exposed the inability of the government to cope with the seeding of grain.[12] This became especially obvious in the cultivation

---

[8] Cf. Koestler's article in *The God that Failed*, New York, Harper, 1949.
[9] *Byulleten oppozitsii*, No. 29-30, September 1932.
[10] "Po Rossii," *Sotsialistichesky vestnik*, No. 19, October 1934.
[11] Stalin, *Sochineniya*, XIII, GIPL, Moscow, 1951, pp. 51-80.
[12] Cf. Chubar's speech at the Third Party Conference of the CP(b)U, *Visti*, July 11, 1932.

of the large areas of sugar beet. The correspondent of *Visti*, having surveyed the problem in the Izyum district, reported that: "Only 25 per cent of the peasants reported for work ... More than one hundred hectares of sugar-beet were ruined because they were not weeded a single time ... 20 hectares of beetroot, 15 hectares of tomatoes, carrots, and watermelon were lost." Another correspondent reported that in the district of Znamenka, Kiev province, "by July 1, out of 7,086 only 812 hectares (36 per cent) have been weeded."[13]

Alarmed by this state of affairs, the Central Committee of the CP(b)U issued instructions to supply the regions which were suffering most from the famine with some bread and fish.[14] These foodstuffs were to be given exclusively to those who were actually working in the fields. However, the district and kolkhoz officials often handed the food out to all peasants and village teachers suffering from the famine.[15] This, admitted a correspondent, was considered a crime and a "waste of bread and fish."[16]

It would be possible to cite many such reports, revealing the hunger and distress of the Ukrainian peasants. But even then, it would be difficult to comprehend the magnitude of the suffering caused by collectivization.

[13] *Visti*, July 5, 1932.
[14] *Visti*, July 28, 1932.
[15] Report from Vinnitsa, *Visti*, July 5, 1932.
[16] *Ibid.*

Chapter V

The Failure of a Mission: V. Molotov and L. Kaganovich
at the Third All-Ukrainian Party Conference

If the Party was worried about the impending catastrophe in the Ukraine, this was not because of forced collectivization and brutal centralization, but because of the inability of the Ukrainian Party organization either to apply the correct policy in that republic or to fulfill the plans for collectivization and grain delivery. It was decided, therefore, to find the members of the organization guilty of misapplication of Party policy in the Communist Party of the Ukraine. They, as well as the recalcitrant peasants who would not obey them, were to be blamed for the catastrophic decline in food production.

The leaders of the CP(b)U were by no means inclined to accept the harshness of collectivization and they felt uneasy in acting as the main executors of this policy. They saw that the failure of collectivization was not due to sabotage by the kulaks and nationalists. It may be said that in this matter they had their own point of view, which differed from the official view of the All-Union CP(b). This difference led to a major conflict between the CP(b)U and the All-Union CP(b). Documentary evidence of this conflict is scanty, yet on the basis of analysis of records of the Third Party Conference of the CP(b)U in 1932, it is possible to gain an insight into this internal strife.

The Third All-Ukrainian Party Conference was convened on July 6, 1932. The first report was delivered by S. Kosior, the Secretary of the CP(b)U. All the delegates were anxious to hear two guests from Moscow, Chairman of the Council of People's Commissars V. Molotov and L. Kaganovich, member of the Politburo and Second (after Stalin) Secretary of the Central Committee of the All-Union CP(b). They, however, reserved to themselves the privilege of being the last two speakers, after the general discussion. This meant, of course, that while the views of all the other speakers were open to discussion, the pronouncements of Molotov and Kaganovich had to be accepted as final verdicts, against which there was no appeal. Such an agenda, obviously dictated by the visitors, was a slap in the face for the Ukrainian Communists.

In his introductory speech, Kosior clearly said that

> some comrades are inclined to explain the difficulties in the spring sowing campaign by the magnitude of the plans for grain deliveries, which they consider unrealistic... Many say that our pace and our plans are too strenuous ... Everything is blamed on the plans... This criticism comes from the Central Committee of the CP(b)U and from the districts.[1]

---

[1] "Iz doklada S. Kosiora na III vseukrainskoi partiinoi konferentsii" (From the Report of S. Kosior at the Third All-Ukrainian Party Conference), *Pravda*, July 9, 1932.

The effect of the pre-arranged agenda, and of Kosior's speech, was contrary to what Molotov and Kaganovich might have expected. Instead of browbeating the Ukrainian Communists, they infuriated them by their tactics, which were insulting to the CP(b)U.

Skrypnyk was the next to speak after Kosior. He told the conference that he had just returned from a trip during which he had visited three districts and scores of villages. Stressing that "our situation is difficult," that "we have breaches in grain collection," that "we have failed to collect 70 million poods of grain from the peasants," he admitted that "we are now experiencing great difficulties in providing food." This latter phrase was the Soviet euphemism for "famine." "I was in a district," Skrypnyk declared, "where there were great provisioning difficulties. It was in the village of Novo-Krasne, in the Oknyansk district, in Moldavia." Then, citing several other examples, Skrypnyk told the conference that the peasants blamed the government for the present state of affairs. They had told him that their farms had been "swept clean."

Probing into the real causes of the disaster, Skrypnyk, cautiously suggested that perhaps the fault lay not so much with the people as with the system itself:

> Instead of the question *what* is the cause of our failures [in production], a different question is being posed here, namely: *who* is the cause of our breakdown? This is not the correct way to formulate the question. We must explain the reason for our failures, and not substitute for it the philistine and petty bourgeois question— who is to blame? We are people. We live and we struggle; our faults must have their reasons.[2]

With these words Skrypnyk decisively refuted the insinuation that the men who were in charge of collectivization in the Ukraine were to blame for its failure. The reason, in his opinion, could not be attributed to human failure; it lay deeper, in the political and economic plan of the entire scheme. Skrypnyk left it to Molotov and Kaganovich to draw their own conclusions.

The next speaker was V. Zatonsky, People's Commissar of Workers' and Peasants' Inspection. While making a general admission that "since there are serious breakdowns . . . our work must have been bad," he claimed that "no one could accuse us of an incorrect political line . . . We stood and still stand on the ground of the general Party line."[3]

O. Shlikhter, Ukrainian Commissar of Agriculture, and Director of the Marx and Lenin Scientific Research Institutes, spoke about the class struggle, about the opposition of the kulaks, and about the loss of Party vigilance. "However," he concluded his speech, "that is not the question. Reasons for the loss of the harvest must be sought . . . elsewhere. The basic reason is poor economics, absence of correct organization of labor."[4] Consequently he devoted more time in his speech to the economic problems involved in collectivization.

[2] *Visti,* July 11, 1932.
[3] *Visti,* July 17, 1932.
[4] *Ibid.*

The highlight of the conference was the speech by the head of the Soviet Ukrainian government, Vlas Chubar.[5] He pointed to three chief reasons which, in his opinion, had led to the catastrophe in Ukrainian agriculture. The first he called "kolkhoz gigantism," an obsession of many high and low officials engaged in the supervision of collectivization. The plans for giant collective farms, he claimed, were the dreams of phantasists, and did not correspond to the economic realities of the country. From the point of view of the peasant, such large kolkhozes were, at the present time, he said, wasteful and unprofitable.[6] The second reason was the acceptance by kolkhoz managers of unrealistic plans, and their attempts to realize them later by illegal and ruinous methods. "It is wrong," said Chubar, "to accept an order [from above] regardless of its practicability, and then to try to distort Party policy, to destroy revolutionary law and order, to ruin the economy of the kolkhozes, justifying all this by orders from above. This is what has happened."[7] The third reason was connected with the exodus of young and industrious peasants from the villages. Here Chubar mentioned several incidents to prove his point. He said that in the district of Holoprystansk, the collective planners had found that they were 3,503 men short and, as a result, could not fulfill their plans.

The head of the Soviet Ukrainian government, himself the son of a peasant from the district of Dnepropetrovsk, a former leader of the Bolshevik revolution in the Putilov Works in Leningrad and in 1923 Lenin's choice as the head of the Soviet Ukrainian government, was not afraid to make this disclosure before the emmissaries from the Kremlin. Instead of accepting their veiled charges that he and the Ukrainian Comunists were to blame, he challenged Molotov and Kaganovich to see conditions as they really were. His answer to them was clear. Neither the peasants nor the Ukrainian government but the unrealistic plans of Moscow were to blame for the failure of collectivization.

Just how serious this failure, as reviewed by the Third Party Conference, was for the entire Soviet industrial development may be seen from an alarm sounded by a *Pravda* editorial on the occasion of the Conference, about the effects of the "agricultural shortages" in the Donbas.[8] However, the plea of all the Ukrainian Communists for an understanding of the real economic situation in the Ukraine was firmly rejected by Stalin's two envoys. Speaking after the discussion, they

---

[5] *Ibid.*

[6] Twenty years later, in 1950, the idea of "super-kolhozes" was revived by Nikita Khrushchev, who was then the dictator of the Ukraine. (See *Pravda,* February 19, 1950, also *Bolshevik,* No. 10, 1948 and No. 3, 1949.)

[7] There is reason to believe that Chubar's opinion remained unchanged. When he visited the Uman district in Kiev province in 1932 he was approached by an old peasant whose body was swollen with hunger, with a request to send him some grain. "And where is your grain?" Chubar was reported to have said. "They took it from me," answered the old man. "And why did you let them?" inquired Chubar in the presence of all the officials. This incident was reported by the secretary of the Uman district Party Committee, Herashchenko, to a person who later became an emigre.

[8] *Pravda,* July 7, 1932.

20

ignored the explanations given by the Ukrainians. Molotov declared that the recent difficulties were the result of errors committed by the Ukrainian Party organization. "We must admit," he said emphatically, "that the Ukrainian Bolsheviks have failed to cope with the task [put before them]." He branded the attempts to blame "external" circumstances and "unrealistic" plans for the failure of collectivization as "anti-Bolshevik."[9] Both Molotov and Kaganovich gave the Ukrainian Communists clearly to understand that Party policy concerning collectivization could not change and that Moscow expected them to submit to it without hope of any concessions: "There will be no concessions or vacillations in the problem of fulfillment of the tasks set by the Party and the Soviet government."[10] These were Molotov's last words. The resolution adopted at the Third Party Conference was obviously dictated by Molotov and Kaganovich.[11] It dealt with strictly economic, not political, matters. Yet the disagreement, which the resolution tried to resolve, was not confined to agriculture.

Listening to the speeches and discussions at the Third Conference, Stalin's envoys must have been struck by a certain degree of unity and stubbornness evinced by the Ukrainian Communist leaders. This must have appeared very ominous to them. As yet, Molotov and Kaganovich had not expressed their views on the united Ukrainian front. All they had been told to do was to convince the Ukrainians that there would be no relaxation of collectivization by Moscow. But the insight they gained into the minds of the Ukrainian Communists must have alarmed them considerably. Returning to Moscow they were no doubt ready to report to their chief that a new, strongly deviationist trend was starting within the CP(b)U. The future held many imponderables, but the feeling of tension between Kharkov and Moscow remained acute. Having realized that there would be no concessions from Moscow, the Ukrainian delegates to the Third Party Conference were faced with a terrifying alternative: either to become the instruments of Moscow's tyranny over their people, or to perish.

[9] *Pravda*, July 14, 1932.
[10] *Ibid.*
[11] *Pravda*, July 15, 1932.

The Deepening Crisis: From the Third Party Conference to the Resolution of the Central Committee of the All-Union CP(b) on January 24, 1933

The Third All-Ukrainian Party Conference brought no improvement in the economic situation of Ukrainian agriculture. It reiterated the existing Party line and left the same targets to be met by the country in grain deliveries. Instead of easing the tension, the conference led to further contraction. On August 7, 1932, a decree was issued which imposed the possible penalty of death by execution on all peasants misappropriating farm property or stealing food.[1]

Because of the widespread famine, peasants were often tempted to cut down handfuls of unripened crops, and, having dried and ground them, to prepare a mixture of grain, tree-bark and other vegetation, to satisfy their hunger. This desperate action by the starving peasants was interpreted as criminal, since it damaged the harvest. It was to remedy this, that the Soviet government issued the decree of August 7, which may have helped in saving the crops for deliveries to the state, but scarcely relieved the famine. The crisis in agriculture was not averted; on the contrary, production fell and the hungry peasants remained unfed. The Soviet Ukrainian press—*Visti, Komunist, Selyanyn Kharkivshchyny, Proletarka pravda, Bilshovyk Ukrainy, Radyanska Ukraina*—published several accounts of the distress and hardship from which the country suffered.

According to the *Visti* correspondent:

> The weeding of sugar beet stopped in many districts. In the district of Khrystynovka only 36.1 per cent of the sugar-beet acreage was weeded; and in the district of Bratslav, 54.8 per cent; Makhnovka, 58 per cent.

> On the Chubar kolkhoz in Ivanov in the district of Novo-Ukrainsky 92 of 200 hectares of sugar-beet acreage were lost due to the negligence of the kolkhoz management, which failed to ensure the necessary care of the land. The remaining hectares of the plantation became so overgrown with weeds that it was difficult to see how they could produce any harvest.[2]

---

[1] "Ob okhrane imushchestva gosudarstvennykh predpriyatii, kolkhozov i kooperatsii i ukrepleniya obshchestvennoi sotsialisticheskoi sobstvennosti. Postanovleniye TsIK i SNK SSSR ot 7 avgusta 1932 g." (Concerning the Protection of Property of the State Establishments, the Kolkhozes and Cooperatives and the Strengthening of Public Socialist Property: Resolution of the Central Executive Committee and the Council of People's Commissars of the USSR, August 7, 1932), *Pravda*, August 8, 1932; reprinted in *Osnovnye direktivy partii i pravitelstva po khoz. stroitelstvu* (Basic Directives of the Party and Government on Economic Construction), Moscow, 1934, pp. 39-40.

[2] *Visti*, September 9, 1932.

A month later the same newspaper carried reports of the yield of the sugar-beet harvest. It fell well below expectations. Instead of the planned production of 100 centners per hectare, the yield was often less than half that amount. "In most cases," reported *Visti*, "20 to 25 centners per hectare are obtained."[3]

On October 18 *Visti* reported that deliveries of sugar beet to the refineries were lagging behind, especially in the Vinnitsa district. Most peasants were too weak to dig or to work in the field. In some cases the beets could not be brought to the factories because of lack of transportation. As a result, on October 20, which was the deadline for sugar-beet deliveries to the state, "only 55.9 per cent of the sugar-beet acreage was harvested."[4]

Press reports on the figures for grain deliveries are scantier. There are the usual directives and tirades about the urgency of the grain collection campaign, interspersed with threats of punitive action against sabotage and theft. Most revealing in regard to the famine are government orders allowing the peasants to take no more than 10 to 15 per cent of the newly harvested crops for their own use.[5] Often the amount the starving peasants claimed was much larger, and it seems that the local authorities were powerless to stop them, or rather condoned this action in order to relieve the famine.

Thus *Visti*, for September 1, 1932, contains the following account:

> In Holovchyntsi artel in the district of Zhmerinka 11 hectares of wheat and 8 hectares of rye were harvested and all the grain was immediately distributed among the peasants.

According to this report, similar violations occurred in the district of Derazhnya. There,

> in the Zorya kolkhoz 60 per cent of the threshed grain was given to the peasants, and in the Sivach artel the entire harvest was turned over to them ... In the Lenin's Memory artel the grain was earmarked for distribution among the peasants before it was ripe.

Visti's correspondent also notes that the chairmen of the kolkhozes ignored government orders to advance grain to the peasants only in proportion to their quotas of "work-days"; food was apparently distributed to all who needed it. The government, alarmed at these "misappropriations of state property," took measures to subdue the starving, declaring that their actions were "directed against the state."[6]

Local Party officials were probably conspiring in this scheme, since this was the only way to get the famished peasants to return to work. Otherwise the local

---

[3] *Visti*, October 14, 1932.
[4] *Visti*, October 24, 1932.
[5] *Visti*, September 1, 1932.
[6] Khataevich's speech before the Stalin artel in the Novo-Ukrainka village soviet, *Visti*, December 9, 1932.

Party bosses would themselves suffer because of non-fulfillment of set targets of production.

It is small wonder that, under such conditions, in spite of the presence in the villages of hundreds of overseers,[7] the yield of crops for 1932 was well below what was expected. Up to October 20, only 82.9 per cent of the total acreage was seeded for winter crops.[8] The figures for grain collection, as given by the press, were as follows:[9]

Up to October 5 .... 39.0 per cent
Up to November 1 .... 40.7 per cent
Up to November 26 .... 60.8 per cent
Up to December 1 .... 63.0 per cent
Up to December 6 .... 65.0 per cent
Up to December 18 .... 68.8 per cent
Up to December 26 .... 71.8 per cent

This was all that the Ukrainian peasantry could deliver. Frequently, it was also deprived of the minimum food supplies for the winter and of seed for the next year.[10]

There is evidence to suggest that, as a result of the Third Party Conference, the CP(b)U found itself in a state of internal confusion. It was suffering from the most serious consequence in Soviet reality—loss of confidence in the Kremlin. Two forces which were manifest in the CP(b)U from the day of its creation, headed toward a new conflict at the end of 1932. One of the forces was that of the native Ukrainian Communists who were convinced of the value of their own contribution to the growth of their country; the other was that of the Russian, "centralist and bureaucratic" elements which were often resented by the first group as aliens. In the contest between these tendencies, historical circumstances dictated which of them held the upper hand. In 1932, the tension expressed itself in the following series of events which, for the sake of convenience may be classified in two columns. The first shows the gains of the native, Ukrainian Communists:

1) The triumphant celebration of the 60th birthday of Skrypnyk, "the undying Bolshevik, one of the best representatives of the old Lenin guard, one of the best fighters and builders of the Soviet Socialist Ukraine."[11] All this—with no mention of Stalin.

2) The clearly demonstrative decision of the Ukrainian Economic Council on July 14, 1932 (six days after the Third Party Conference), modifying the decree of the Soviet of People's Commissars of the USSR dated June 29, 1932, concern-

---

[7] According to *Short History of the CPSU*, 17,000 Party workers were sent to the villages (p. 303).

[8] *Visti*, October 24, 1932.

[9] The above data are collected from reports published in *Visti* between October 28 and December 30, 1932.

[10] Cf. Postyshev's speech in *Pravda*, June 22, 1933.

[11] *Visti*, January 26, 1932.

24

ing the deliveries of butter in the Ukraine. According to this modification, the original target of 16,400 tons of butter was reduced to 11,214 tons.[12]

3) Chubar's speech at the Komsomol conference in Kharkov, pleading for more freedom and decentralization.[13]

4) The surge of local pride in the construction in the Ukraine of Dniprelstan—the first giant power station in the USSR.[14]

5) A series of decrees, issued by the Soviet Ukrainian government and the Central Committee of the CP(b)U, some of them granting greater cultural facilities to the villages,[15] others expressing concern with local party organizations[16] and with the deliveries of foodstuffs by the peasants.[17]

On the other hand, several measures taken by the CP(b)U showed that it was still fulfilling drastic orders from above:

1) The directive "to organize immediately the return of grain distributed [to the peasants], and to direct it toward the fulfillment of grain deliveries."[18]

2) The sanctioning of the complete surrender of the seed supplies of the kolkhozes.[19]

3) Threats to arrest and liquidate lower officials of the kolkhozes.[20]

This divergence in decisions and actions of the Ukrainian Communists is the primary indication of the struggle between Moscow and Kharkov which was raging at that time. There was no doubt that, like all similar conflicts in the past, this divergence of views would lead to open conflict. There is reason to believe that Stalin, through his private informers, was gathering "evidence" against the top Ukrainian Communists, who were desperately trying to cope with the chaotic situation and yet were powerless to act.

---

[12] *Visti*, July 17, 1932.

[13] *Visti*, September 10, 1932.

[14] The Ukrainian name *Dniprelstan* was later changed to *Dniprobud* (synonymous with the Russian *Dneprostroi*) and still later to *Dneproges*, which was used in Russian and Ukrainian newspapers.

[15] *Visti*, June 28, 1932; *Visti*, July 11, 1932.

[16] "Do vsikh oblkomiv i raykomiv KP(b)U vid TsK KP(b)U" (To all Provincial and District Committees of the CP(b)U from the CC of the CP(b)U), *Visti*, October 26, 1932.

[17] *Visti*, December 17, 1932; *Visti*, December 20, 1932.

[18] *Visti*, November 23, 1932.

[19] Terekhov, secretary of the Central Committee and the Kharkov Provincial Committee of the CP(b)U, made the following remark at the meeting of the rank-and-file Party members in Kharkov on November 23, 1932: "The seed supplies may be taken in the course of grain deliveries. This must be done prudently. We must not forget about the sowing campaign and its difficulties. Our approach to seed supplies must be flexible. At the moment we cannot put down in writing that the seed supplies must not be touched, but we also cannot say that they must be taken." (Postyshev's speech at the plenum of the CC CP(b)U, *Pravda*, June 22, 1932.)

[20] *Visti*, December 23, 1932. According to the resolution of the CC CP(b)U, the following Party workers were removed from their posts for negligence of duty: Shklyar and Kasiyan (province of Dnepropetrovsk); A. A. Bolyukevych, I. I. Lavtsov, M. P. Leshchenko, K. Novikov, L. Ya. Mykhailyk; see also resolution of the Council of People's Commissars of the UkSSR, *Visti*, January 5, 1932.

The first intimation of impending battle was given in the decision on the purge of the Party, adopted by the Central Committee of the All-Union CP(b) on December 10, 1932. On January 7, 1933, *Pravda* printed an article entitled "The Ukraine—the Deciding Factor in Grain Collection." It complained that up to December 25, the grain collection in the Ukraine decreased every five days. The republic was then one of the laggards in the fulfillment of the annual plan. Further, the article laid the blame on the Party organization in the Ukraine, which enabled the "class enemy to get organized." This was a clear sign that heads were going to roll.

The decision to precipitate the existing crisis was taken by Moscow. In January 1933, the curtain went up on a new act of the tragedy being directed by the Communist rulers in the Ukraine.

Chapter VII

The "Historic Resolution"

On January 24, 1933, the Central Committee of the All-Union CP(b) adopted a special resolution on the Ukrainian Party organization,[1] described later as "the turning point in the history of the CP(b)U, opening a new chapter in the victorious battle of the Bolsheviks in the Ukraine."[2]

Wherein lay its "historic" significance? The resolution stated bluntly that the CP(b)U had failed to carry out the tasks entrusted to it in connection with collectivization. In spite of the fact that the original target-figures for food deliveries were reduced three times, they were not reached, and hence the "major breakdown" ensued in grain collection. The resolution also pointed out that the three provinces most important in the agricultural production of the Ukraine—Odessa, Dnepropetrovsk and Kharkov— had been neglected. Therefore, the resolution went on, the Central Committee of the All-Union CP(b) decreed:

1) The appointment of Comrade P. Postyshev, secretary of the CC, All-Union CP(b), as second secretary of the CP(b)U and first secretary of the Kharkov Provincial Committee.

2) The appointment of Comrade Khataevich to the post of first secretary of the Dnepropetrovsk Provincial Committee, and permission for him to remain as one of the secretaries of the Central Committee of the CP(b)U.

3) The appointment of Comrade Veger as first secretary of the Odessa Provincial Committee.

4) The release of Comrades Maiorov, Stroganov, and Terekhov from their current duties, and their placement at the disposal of the Central Committee.

---

[1] It has been impossible to find the full text of this resolution. Parts of it were quoted in Kosior's speech "Itogi khlebozagotovok i zadachi KP(b)U v borbe za podnyatie selskogo khozyaistva Ukrainy" (Results of the Grain Deliveries and the Tasks of the CP(b)U in the Struggle for the Improvement of Agriculture in the Ukraine), printed in *Pravda*, February 15, 1933, in "O zadachakh vesennego seva i reshenii TsK VKP(b) ot 24 yanvarya 1933 goda. Doklad na ob'edinennom plenume kharkovskogo obkoma i gorkoma KP(b)U 4 fevralya 1933 g." (Concerning the Tasks of the Spring Seeding and the Resolution of the CC All-Union CP(b) of January 24, 1933. Report at the Joint Plenum of the Kharkov District Committee and City Committee of the CP(b)U of February 4, 1933), in the resolution of the same plenum under the same name, *Pravda*, February 6, 1933, in Postyshev's speech, printed in *Pravda*, February 8, 1933, and in Khvylya's address "Na movnomu fronti" (On the Linguistic Front), *Visti*, June 30, 1933.

[2] "Itogi 1933 selsko-khozyaistvennogo goda i ocherednye zadachi KP(b)U" (Results of 1933 in Agriculture and the Next Tasks of the CP(b)U), Rech P. P. Postysheva na plenume TsK KP(b)U 19 noyabrya, 1933, *Pravda*, November 24, 1933.

5) The assumption of their new duties by Comrades Postyshev, Khataevich and Veger no later than January 30.[3]

Now that the entire execution of Party policy by the CP(b)U had been condemned by the Kremlin, the discredited leaders of the CP(b)U were placed under the direct supervision of Moscow's emissary Postyshev. He was accompanied to the Ukraine not only by the assistants mentioned in the resolution, but also by thousands of agents whose task it was to keep an eye on Party activities in the Ukraine. V. A. Balitsky arrived from Moscow to take over the all-important post of Commissar of State Security in the Ukraine.

These facts were revealed by Postyshev a few months after he had assumed control of the Party organization in the Ukraine. Speaking at the November Plenum of the CP(b)U, Postyshev disclosed that

> 1,340 comrades were dispatched to the district managerial jobs. In the same period of time, 237 secretaries of District Party Committees, 279 chairmen of District Executive Committees, and 158 chairmen of District Control Commissions were replaced by more tenacious workers. With the aid of the All-Union CP(b), 643 MTS Political Detachments and 203 Sovkhoz Political Detachments were created in the Ukraine, where, in all, 3,000 worker leaders were sent in order to inculate new forms and methods of management.[4]

"Simultaneously," Postyshev continued, "no fewer than 10,000 men were sent for permanent employment to the kolkhozes, including 3,000 chairmen and secretaries of kolkhozes. *A large detachment of strong, experienced Bolsheviks was sent to the villages as organizers of collectivization.*"[5]

What was the significance of these measures which were intended to assist Postyshev? Bearing in mind that the Ukraine, according to the official data of the Board of Economic Statistics,[6] was divided into 525 districts, this meant that almost half of the district secretaries of the Party, half of the chairmen of the District Executive Committees, and a third of the chairmen of the District Control Commissions were replaced by "more tenacious workers," that is, those who enjoyed Postyshev's confidence and were brought with him from the center. If one adds to this 846 newly created Political Detachments, staffed with 3,000 of Postyshev's men (roughly 6 men per district), and 10,000 "experienced Bolsheviks" planted in the kolkhozes, the total picture is that of a wholesale occupation of key posts in the country by the staff of Stalin's satrap. To every district he sent 29 men to control Party activities and to watch over the most vital spheres of public life. There is little doubt that they were joined by thousands of local

---

[3] For the full text of this section of the resolution see Kosior's speech, *Pravda*, February 15, 1933.

[4] Postyshev's speech at the November plenum, *Pravda*, November 24, 1933.

[5] *Ibid.*, (italics are Postyshev's).

[6] *Sotsiyalistychna Ukraina. Statystychny zbirnyk upravlinnya narodnohospodarskoho obliku USSR* (The Socialist Ukraine: A Statistical Compendium of the Office of National Economic Statistics of the UkSSR), Kiev, January 1937, p. 103.

officials, eager to save their skins and to please their new master. With the help of this vast network of trusted employees, Postyshev could easily subdue any country, let alone the famine-ridden, terrorized Ukraine.

The January resolution of the All-Union CP(b) came like a bolt from the blue. Its effect was stunning, especially for such leading Ukrainian Communists and old Bolsheviks as Skrypnyk, Kosior, Chubar, Petrovsky, Shlikhter, Zatonsky, Lyubchenko, Dubovy, Sukhomlin, and Dudnyk, all of whom realized that they were being placed under Postyshev's supervision. The unprecedented appointment of Postyshev showed how little Moscow was prepared to respect the nominal rights of the Ukrainian Communists.

It is small wonder, therefore, that Postyshev's official reception in the Ukraine was far from enthusiastic. One document, in particular, revealed the open hostility of the Ukrainian Communists toward the new governor-general of the Ukraine. It is the report in *Pravda* of the joint plenum of the Kharkov Provincial and City Committees of the CP(b)U on February 6.[7]

> After listening to the report by Postyshev the plenum devoted itself to broad debate. The participants in the plenum sharply criticized management in the villages. They scored the attempts of this management to blur the most important decision of the Central Committee of the All-Union CP(b), dated January 24, and thus to nullify it.[8]

Moreover, we find even more striking evidence of the opposition to the January resolution in the words of Postyshev himself. Speaking at the joint plenum referred to above, Postyshev complained that

> the leadership of the Kharkov Party organization has attempted to interpret this exceptional . . . decision of the CC of the All-Union CP(b) simply as an ordinary change of personnel—as the recall of one person, Terekhov, and his replacement by another person, Postyshev. It is a fact that the plenum of the Provincial Committee, held on January 29, lasted only 20 minutes and that nobody even mentioned the most important resolution of the CC of the All-Union CP(b), thus testifying to its complete aloofness and revealing, to put it mildly, its political myopia. The plenary meeting was held, as it were, secretly, with only a few men present.[9]

These incidents are extremely significant. It seems that in spite of the resolution of January 24, the Kharkov committee had decided to ignore it at the meeting held on January 29. This move could only have been made with the knowledge of the Central Committee of the CP(b)U (the secretary of the Provincial Committee was at the same time the fourth secretary of the Central Committee and a member of the Politburo). The demonstration staged by the Ukrainian Communists, who, at the Kharkov meeting, refused even to discuss the January resolu-

---

[7] *Pravda*, February 6, 1933.
[8] *Ibid.*
[9] *Ibid.*

tion, could have been dictated by one consideration only. The top Ukrainian Communists must have felt that the whole affair was an incredible mistake on the part of the All-Union CP(b), which they would be able to rectify. It is also extremely likely that some of the top Ukrainian Communists hoped to discuss the matter with Stalin himself and to persuade him to revoke his decision.[10]

Very soon, however, these hopes completely vanished. Stalin stood firm, and Postyshev, together with his entourage, arrived in the Ukraine to take over from those who doubted his right. There was nothing else left for the Ukrainian Central Committee to do; they had to accept the orders from above. The February 6 resolution of the joint plenum expressed confidence that "the decision of the CC of the All-Union CP(b) of January 24, in which the CC of the Party condemned the Party organization in the Ukraine ... would be the turning point in the life and work of the Kharkov Party organization."[11] One day later, on February 7, this attitude was reaffirmed at the joint plenum of the CC and CCC of the CP(b)U. "The plenum considers the resolution of the CC, All-Union CP(b), as unquestionably correct; it welcomes the strengthening of management in the most vital provinces of the Ukraine and the arrival of the second secretary of the CC, CP(b)U, Comrade Postyshev."[12] Moreover, the plenum declared that the new resolution was in direct relation to the Third Party Conference and the advice of Molotov and Kaganovich. The humiliation of the native Communists was thus complete, and Postyshev could proceed to the execution of his many tasks. Having donned an embroidered Ukrainian shirt, he embarked on what turned out to be a most cruel subjugation of the Ukrainian people.

---

[10] In 1938 the present author met two old Ukrainian Bolsheviks in the Vorkuta concentration camp. They were A. Butsenko, former secretary of the Ukrainian Central Executive Committee and later chairman of the Executive Committee of the Far Eastern Kray, and Ivan Kasyanenko, former director of Ukrainian Civil Aviation. Both had received sentences of 25 years for "Ukrainian nationalism." Both maintained that negotiations between top Ukrainian Communists and Moscow had been held in January 1933, and that the result was unfavorable for the Ukrainians.

[11] "O zadachakh vesennego seva i o reshenii TsK VKP(b) ot yanvarya 1933 g." (Concerning the Tasks of the Spring Seeding and the Resolution of the CC All-Union CP(b) of January 1933), *Pravda*, February 6, 1933.

[12] "O itogakh khlebozagotovki na Ukraine i postanovlenie TsK VKP(b) ot 24 yanvarya 1933. Rezolyutsiya plenuma TsK KP(b)U, prinyataya na zasedanii 7 fevralya 1933 g." (Concerning the Results of Grain Deliveries in the Ukraine and the Resolution of the CC, All-Union CP(b), January 24, 1933, Resolution of the Plenum of the CC of the CP(b)U adopted at the meeting held on February 7, 1933), *Pravda*, February 10, 1933.

Chapter VIII

The Official Mission of Pavel Postyshev

Pavel Petrovich Postyshev was born in 1888 in the Russian city of Ivanovo-Voznesensk, into the family of a weaver.[1] A member of the Party since 1904, he was one of the Bolshevik Old Guard. Having received only a partial secondary education, Postyshev did not belong to the Party's theoreticians, intellectual leaders, or journalists. He was a typical professional revolutionary, an executive of Party organs. It is this quality which brought him to the top of the Party hierarchy during Stalin's dictatorship. During the Revolution he was one of the most active Party organizers in the Far East. In 1923, because of ill health, he was transferred to the Ukraine where the climate was more congenial to him. Beginning his duties as a member of the Control Commission of the CP(b)U in Kiev, he was quickly promoted to a post on the Central Committee and finally to the Politburo of the CC of the CP(b)U. In spite of reaching such a responsible position, Postyshev did not play a major part in the CP(b)U at that time. His colorless personality did not make him popular with the top Ukrainian Communists. Tall and gaunt, with a cropped moustache, sickly yellow complexion, and a hoarse voice, Postyshev possessed two qualities which earned him a high post in the Ukraine. First, he was an avowed enemy of the policy of Ukrainization pursued at that time by the CP(b)U. He never mastered the Ukrainian language and never entered into Ukrainian cultural life. Second, he was a reliable servant of the Kremlin and a trusted administrator of its policies.

These qualities stood Postyshev in good stead in 1930. On Stalin's orders he was transferred to Moscow, where, as secretary of the City Committee and Provincial Committee of the All-Union CP(b) and a member of the Orgburo of the Central Committee of the Party, he helped his master consolidate power in the Kremlin. Postyshev's role as "Stalin's associate and friend" lasted until January 1933. When, at that time, Stalin decided to crack down on the CP(b)U, he could find no better candidate for the difficult task than Postyshev. Even such a stalwart of the Party and former peacemaker in the Ukraine as Kaganovich would not fulfill all the requirements. Kaganovich, who in 1926–28 helped to cleanse the CP(b)U of "Shumskism," had, during his stay in the Ukraine, acclimatized himself entirely to Ukrainian life and had mastered the Ukrainian language. The situation in 1933 called for someone who would know the internal situation in the Ukraine, yet at the same time would be entirely incorruptible and unsusceptible to local elements. Postyshev, who was clearly hostile to the policy of Ukrainization,

---

[1] All biographical data on Postyshev are taken from *Kalendar kommunista*, Moscow, 1931, pp. 725-26.

fostered chiefly by Skrypnyk, was an ideal choice for the post of Stalin's viceroy in the Ukraine. Above all, he was, like his master, a "man of steel," ready to carry out any order, regardless of the consequences.

Postyshev's mission in the Ukraine was primarily concerned with the correction of errors made by the CP(b)U in agricultural policy, and with the salvation of the country from economic chaos. It was reasonable to believe that he would be guided in his task in the Ukraine by the resolution of January 24, as well as by two of Stalin's recent speeches which were concerned with agriculture: "The Results of the First Five-Year Plan," delivered before the plenum of the Central Committee of the All-Union CP(b) on January 7, 1933, and "On the Work in the Villages," an address made to the same assembly on January 11 of that year. What were the focal points of these speeches?

The first of these speeches, summing up the results of the First Five-Year Plan, made no mention of the economic difficulties in Ukrainian agriculture. On the contrary, it painted a glowing picture of progress. "The Party," said Stalin, "has succeeded in making it possible to purvey from 1,200 to 1,400 million poods of grain annually instead of the 500 to 600 million poods produced when individual farming predominated."[2] The position of the peasants, in Stalin's words, had been vastly improved.

> At the present time it no longer happens in our country that millions of peasants run away from their homes to distant parts in search of employment. Now, in order to draw the peasant to any work outside the kolkhoz, it is necessary [for the outside employer] to sign an agreement with the kolkhoz, and to pay for the travelling expenses of the collective farmer. Now there are no more cases of hundreds of thousands and millions of peasants lining up for work outside factories ... Now, the peasant is a master in his own right.[3]

Stalin, therefore, had no doubt "that the material condition of the workers and peasants is improving with every year. This can be doubted only by mortal enemies of the Soviet government."

This was said by Stalin at a time when both workers and peasants throughout the USSR, and especially in the Ukraine, were living on the verge of starvation. Even skilled workers were then earning no more than 250 to 300 rubles a month; they lived in extreme penury, their diet consisted chiefly of potatoes, black bread, salted fish and *kvas*, and they lacked the basic necessities of clothing and footwear.[4] The peasants, driven from the countryside to the towns by famine and

---

[2] *Pravda*, January 10, 1933.

[3] "Itogi pervoi pyatiletki" (Results of the First Five-Year Plan), *Pravda*, January 10, 1933; "O rabote v derevne" (On the Work in the Villages); Rech I. Stalina na obedinennom plenume TsK i TsKK VKP(b) (Speech by J. Stalin at the Joint Plenum of the CC and CCC of the All-Union CP(b)), *Pravda*, January 17, 1933.

[4] In 1935, the present author worked in a cement factory in Sukhoi Log in the Urals. The workers ate bread and *kvas* (a beer made from barley, malt, and rye) for lunch, because they could not afford to pay for hot soup.

terror, were begging for bread at all railroad stations and city squares, often perishing from hunger and exhaustion. However, to see the facts as they were, was, according to the words of the "Great Leader," tantamount to being a "mortal enemy of the Soviet government."

In his second speech, delivered on January 11, 1933, Stalin made some references to the fact that in spite of a good harvest and all the progress made in the mechanization and collectivization of agriculture, "the grain collection in 1932 was carried out under greater difficulties than the one in the previous year." "What happened? What are the reasons for our shortcomings?"[5] he asked rhetorically.

In his answer Stalin gave five reasons for past shortcomings.

First, the peasants were reluctant to deliver the grain to the state because they hoped to sell it at a higher price on the market, in accordance with the decree concerned with "collective trade in grain." The local Party authorities were not determined enough in breaking this practice of the peasants.

Second, the Party organizations, having introduced total collectivization, had ceased to be interested in the work of the kolkhozes. The Party should take "the management of the kolkhozes into its own hands."

Third, having created the kolkhozes, the Party had failed to infuse into them socialist content. It was not enough to give them socialist form. The kolkhozes must be filled with Communist content. Otherwise, counter-revolutionary elements, and in the Ukraine the "nationalists and Petlyurovites," could seize control. The slogan "kolkhozes without the Communists" was counter-revolutionary.

Fourth, the Party organizations had failed to realize that, of late years, the tactics of the class enemy had changed. Therefore it was necessary to change Communist tactics. The kulaks were no longer openly opposing the kolkhozes; they were insidiously accomplishing destructive work. "Today's anti-Soviet elements," said Stalin, "are mostly people who are 'quiet,' 'sweet,' and almost 'holy.'" Those who thought that there were no kulaks left were seriously mistaken. "The kulaks," said Stalin, "have been defeated, but they are not completely exterminated."

Fifth, the Party, not the peasants, was to blame for the failure in grain collection. "There has not been and there is not, anywhere in the world," said Stalin, "such a mighty and authoritative government as our Soviet government. In the whole world there has not been and there is not a party as mighty and authoritative as our Party. Nobody can stop us from managing the kolkhozes in the way demanded by their own interests, and the interests of the state."[6]

---

[5] "O rabote v derevne" (On the Work in the Villages), *Pravda*, January 17, 1933.
[6] *Ibid.*

Stalin's five-point program[7] may be reduced to one clear conclusion: The struggle against the "class enemy and the kulak" must be intensified. The Party was free to use all the means at its disposal to deal a final blow to those who still resisted the collective system in agriculture; it must exterminate the "hidden enemies."

This program gave Postyshev carte blanche to conduct an even more intensive campaign of terror against the Ukrainian peasantry.

---

[7] This is how Stalin's speech was described in *Pravda's* leading article, January 18, 1933.

Chapter IX

New Methods of Leadership

Stalin's analysis of the situation in the villages could hardly provide Postyshev with a guide to action. What Stalin said had little relation to existing conditions. In order to justify further tightening of controls over the peasant, he painted a sinister but unreal picture of the village seething with hidden enemies. The aim was to make the kolkhozes even more submissive to the Party, to permeate the village with active Communists, and thus to raise the food production level. Rapt in his dreams of turning the countryside into a large food and grain factory, Stalin cared little about the fate of the peasants themselves.

In keeping with Stalin's interpretation, Postyshev delivered his speech "On the Tasks of Spring Sowing and the Decision of the CC, All-Union CP(b), dated January 24, 1933," before the united plenum of the Kharkov Provincial and City Committees of the CP(b)U.[1] In it Postyshev painted in the most somber colors the remnants of the kulaks, the Petlyurovites, and the nationalists, who, having infiltrated the Party and the kolkhozes, were sabotaging collectivization. He quoted figures which were the new targets to be reached in agricultural production. Like Stalin, he was inflexible in his attitude toward the crying need of the peasants for food. "It is imperative," he said, "to make it clear to the broad masses of Party members and collective farmers who are not Party members, that there can be no talk about assistance from the state in the matter of seeding supplies, that the seed must be obtained and sown by the kolkhozes and the collective and individual farmers themselves."[2]

In the resolutions of the same plenum we read that "a necessary preliminary to the successful realization of spring sowing is the combination of persuasive methods with the methods of administrative influence."[3] This left no doubt that the Party policy remained inflexible.

In reality, however, there were no "class enemies" or "saboteurs" in the villages. Famine, exhaustion and utter privation were facts which could no longer be ignored. Therefore, life proved stronger than Stalin's fiction. And if life was to be sustained at all in the greater part of the Ukraine, people had to be fed. Realizing the desperate situation of the peasants who, during the height of the famine, often resorted to cannibalism, Postyshev had to face facts. What the Party actually did, therefore, was in clear contrast to the official harangues of Stalin and Postyshev.

---

[1] "O zadachakh vesennego seva i resheniye TsK VKP(b) ot 24 yanvarya 1933 g.," *Pravda,* February 8, 1933.

[2] *Pravda,* February 6, 1933.

[3] *Ibid.*

Quietly, without the usual fanfare accompanying the proclamation of Party resolutions, on February 23, 1933, the government issued the decree of the Council of People's Commissars "On Aid in Seeding to Kolkhozes of the Ukraine and the North Caucasus."[4] "In view of the fact," the decree ran, "that unfavorable climatic conditions during the summer of 1932 have resulted in the loss of the harvest[5] in several districts of the Ukraine and the North Caucasus, as a consequence of which the sovkhozes and kolkhozes of the steppe area of the Ukraine and certain districts in the North Caucasus [Kuban] were not able to stock enough seed for the spring sowing, the Council of People's Commissars and the Central Committee of the All-Union CP(b) decree:

"The release from government stocks of grain for the kolkhozes and sovkhozes of the Ukraine and the North Caucasus to be loaned for seeding supplies. The quantities are as follows: the Ukraine—20,300 poods; the North Caucasus—15,300 poods."

This was an obvious admission that the whip alone was no longer effective in the collectivization drive; the carrot had to be used too. Yet perhaps the most significant thing about this move is the way it was made. Demands for the release of seed from government stocks in order to relieve the food situation in the Ukraine had been made several times before.[6] The pleas of Skrypnyk, Chubar, and other Ukrainian Communists for lower targets for grain deliveries to the state had also been made with the aim of enabling the peasants to stock more grain for spring sowing. These pleas fell on deaf ears. There was to be no relaxation of the grain collections, no pampering of the peasants.

When, finally, the release of the seed was announced, it was only after Postyshev's arrival, and it was not an action of the Soviet Ukrainian government. The

---

[4] *Pravda*, February 26, 1933.

Similar measures were adopted later, in 1934. In one of the Resolutions of the Council of People's Commissars of the USSR and the Central Committee of the All-Union CP(b), published in December 1934, we read that state financial aid was to be given to all the kolkhozes which were in arrears in paying off the agricultural loan issued to them on January 1, 1933 (*Sobraniezakonov i rasporyazhenii Raboche-Krestyanskogo Pravitelstva SSSR izdavaemoe Upravleniem Delami SNK SSSR, 7 yanvarya 1935* goda (The Collection of Laws and Regulations of the Workers' and Peasants' Government of the USSR published by the Administration of the Affairs of the Council of People's Commissars, January 7, 1935) *No. 1, otdel pervy.*

On December 26, 1934, it was decreed that another 69,197,000 poods of grain should be released to the kolkhozes. This loan, however, covered the needs of "seed, food, and forage," not merely of seed, as it did in 1933. This shows that, to avoid a repetition of the famine, the government had decided to feed the peasants.

[5] This admission is in sheer contradiction to Stalin's speech of January 11, 1933, to Postyshev's speech of February 4, 1933, as well as to the pronouncements of Molotov and Kaganovich during the Third Ukrainian Party Conference. Stalin, in his speech, made a point of emphasizing that the failure in grain collection "cannot be explained by a poor harvest, since this year's harvest was no worse than that of last year. Nobody can deny that the total yield of grain in 1932 was larger than in 1931."

[6] Kosior's speech at the Third Party Conference, *Pravda*, July 9, 1932; Kosior's speech "Itogi khlebozagotovki, ..." *Pravda*, February 13, 1933; Postyshev's speech, *Pravda*, February 8, 1933.

obvious implication was that relief could only come from Moscow, not from Kharkov.

The impotence of the Soviet Ukrainian government, exposed by this move, was in reality far greater than might be believed. At no time during the terrible food crisis in the Ukraine was the government of this republic, or its Communist Party, able to dispose freely of a single pood of grain.

All stocks of grain were under the exclusive control of the "Committee of the Council of People's Commissars of the USSR for the Provision of Agricultural Products."[7] According to the decree of the Council of People's Commissars of the USSR, dated February 10, 1933, the Committee carried on its work only through "its representatives in the republics, regions, and provinces. The republican, regional, and provincial representatives are subordinate only to the Committee of the Council of People's Commissars of the USSR for the Provision of Agricultural Products. The orders issued by the Committee of the Council of People's Commissars of the USSR for the Provision of Agricultural Products are binding on all organs of the local governments; they can be revoked only by the Council of People's Commissars of the USSR." Only by keeping control of food supplies in his hands could Stalin dictate his terms to the union republics.

Another infringement of the authority of the CP(b)U was contained in the resolution of the Kharkov plenum which called for the dispatch of "active Communists" from the cities to the villages, to supervise and to assist with the spring sowing campaign.[8] These, surely, were some of the men whom Postyshev had brought with him.

The question which remains unanswered is this: Was Postyshev sent to the Ukraine solely to improve the situation in the kolkhozes by the simultaneous use of terror and soothing seed loans? There are strong reasons to believe that this was only part of his mission; its main purpose lay elsewhere.

---

[7] "O reorganizatsii komiteta po zagotovkam selsko-khozyaistvennykh produktov; postanovleniye SNK SSSR ot 10 fevralya 1933 g." (Concerning the Reorganization of the Committee on Deliveries of Agricultural Products; Resolution of the Council of People's Commissars of February 10, 1933), *Pravda*, February 14, 1933.

[8] Postyshev's speech, *Pravda*, February 8, 1933.

Chapter X

The Campaign for "Ukrainization"

The purpose of Stalin's offensive against the Ukraine was not only to force collectivization upon the recalcitrant and stubborn peasants. His plan was grand and far-reaching in scope. It was to destroy the spiritual and cultural backbone of the entire nation, as well as to terrorize the peasantry. Without this complete annihilation of spiritual resources and cultural achievements, Stalin's victory in the Ukraine could never be complete. Realizing this, he decided to unleash all the forces of devastation at his disposal against those who stood for an independent Ukrainian culture, tradition and consciousness, even though they were devoted Communists.

In the early thirties the Ukrainian SSR was one of the most thriving Soviet republics. Economically (in the production of steel, coal, agriculture) it was the most powerful unit of the USSR; numerically, it was second only to Russia; culturally, it represented a considerable achievement.[1]

The Ukraine's nominal ruler was the CP(b)U, which was not a monolithic party, but a conglomerate. It had been formed in the process of the revolution in the Ukraine and consisted of two contending elements: the national element, born in the Ukrainian Revolution of 1917, and the Russian element, traditionally centralist in its tendencies. As a result of these "twin roots" of the CP(b)U, the Party, as was always admitted by early Soviet Ukrainian historians,[2] was polarized between two divergent trends.

The leading representative of the Ukrainian trend within the CP(b)U was Mykola Skrypnyk, a prominent theorist and historian of Ukrainian Communism, the co-founder of the Soviet Ukrainian government (first chairman of the Soviet Ukrainian People's Secretariat), member of the Bolshevik Old Guard, close associate of Lenin, member of the Central Committee of the CP(b)U and the All-Union CP(b), head of the Ukrainian delegation to the Comintern and permanent member of the Executive Committee of the Comintern.

The centralist Russian trend in the CP(b)U was always headed by its general secretary who was appointed by Moscow and was never a Ukrainian.[3] During the twenties the Ukrainian tendency in the CP(b)U had the upper hand, although its victory was never complete. Under the influence of this dominant tendency,

---

[1] Cf. Kosior's speech at the November Plenum, *Pravda*, December 2, 1933.

[2] Cf. Ravich-Cherkassky, *Istoriya kommunisticheskoi partii (bolshevikov) Ukrainy* (A History of the Communist Party [Bolshevik] of the Ukraine), Kharkov, 1923; M. M. Popov, *Ocherk istorii kommunisticheskoi partii (bolshevikov) Ukrainy* (An Outline of the History of the Communist Party [Bolshevik] of the Ukraine), Kharkov, 1929; M. Skrypnyk, *Statti i promovy* (Articles and Speeches), I, Kharkov, 1930.

[3] Not until after Stalin's death, did the CP(b)U receive, in June 1953, a secretary with a Ukrainian name, A. I. Kirichenko.

the Ukrainian SSR developed into a clearly defined national, economic, and cultural organism. The centralist tendency was discredited during the Civil War when it held sway during the periods of Red Army occupation in the Ukraine. This trend was losing ground because of the pressures exerted by the non-Russian nationalities and also because of the international aspect of Communism. In 1923, during the Twelfth Congress of the All-Union CP(b), Great Russian nationalism was declared the major danger in the USSR. This decision strengthened the growth of national elements in the non-Russian Communist Parties.

Although the stimulation of a national culture in the Ukraine during the twenties could, in the absence of complete independence, lead to no permanent achievement, it nevertheless produced a vigorous flowering of literature, science and scholarship. It may be said that the forces released during the national revolution in the Ukraine in 1917,[4] which led to the establishment in the same year of the Ukrainian People's Republic, did not disintegrate with the fall of this state. They re-emerged in the Soviet Ukraine, and the Communists could not entirely suppress the urge of the Ukrainians to achieve full independence. After 1920 the CP(b)U came to be regarded by some as the continuator of the Ukrainian struggle for national independence, and of the country's cultural and political self-expression.[5]

The attempts to extinguish Ukrainian national Communism made by the Russian Bolsheviks during the periods of the Civil War and of so-called War Communism were unsuccessful. Among them were the unsuccessful attempt to block the formation of a separate Communist Party in the Ukraine,[6] the refusal on the part of the Russian CP(b) to recognize the CP(b)U as the nominal master of the Ukraine,[7] the anti-Ukrainian terror of Colonel Muravev and the chief of the Cheka, Lacis, when many people in Kiev were even executed for speaking Ukrainian in the streets,[8] and the decision of the All-Russian Central Council of Trade Unions, in March 1919, to ask for the immediate merger of the Ukrainian trade union movement with the Russian movement, as a prerequisite for the merger of the Ukraine with the Russian Soviet Republic.[9] All of these ended in failure.

In 1920, the Ukrainian Communist Party (Borotbist)[10] merged with the CP(b)U, adding to it thousands of former Ukrainian Left SR's. Five years later,

---

[4] Cf. John S. Reshetar, Jr., *The Ukrainian Revolution*, Princeton, Princeton University Press, 1952.

[5] "Postanovlenie TsK RKP(b) 18 maya 1918 g. *XI sezd RKP(b)*, Kiev, 1922, pp. 45-46 (Skrypnyk's speech).

[6] Cf. Ravich-Cherkassky, *op. cit., passim;* M. Skrypnyk, *Statti i promovy*, I, 1930; also: "Memorandum UKP (Borotbystiv) do Vykonavchoho Komitetu III-ho Kominternatsionalu" (The Memorandum of the UCP (Borotbist) to the Executive Committee of the Third Communist International), *Borotba* (The Struggle), Kiev, 1920.

[7] "K razresheniyu natsionalnogo voprosa" (Towards a Solution of the National Question), *Borotba*, Kiev, 1920.

[8] V. Zatonsky, one of the leading Ukrainian Communists, relates how he himself was nearly shot for this offence (V. Zatonsky, *Natsionalna problema na Ukraini*, (The National Problem in the Ukraine), Kharkov, 1926, pp. 33-40.

[9] *Visti*, March 16, 1919.

in 1925, after many prominent Ukrainian scholars and politicians returned to the Soviet Ukraine from abroad where they had gone in 1919,[11] the Ukrainian Communist Party (the so-called Ukapists) also joined forces with the CP(b)U. At that time, too, many Ukrainian Communists from Galicia and Bukovina came to the Soviet Ukraine and were active in the government and in cultural life. In this way the kernel of Ukrainian Communism, created in the CP(b)U by Skrypnyk in 1918, was reinforced to such an extent that the dominance of the Ukrainian tendency in the CP(b)U was undisputed.

It was because of the strength of the native Communist forces in the Ukraine that the Russian CP(b) decided to initiate in 1923 a policy of "Ukrainization."[12] This was a concession, made through necessity, not principle, to the overwhelming demand of the Ukrainians for active participation in every aspect of the culture and government of their country. "Ukrainization" was started in 1925, after the April Plenum of the CP(b)U. A year later, in 1926, the June Plenum of the CP(b)U gave specific instructions on the de-Russification of the trade unions and the Komsomol in the Ukraine.[13] Yet at the same plenum concern was expressed lest the Ukrainian national elements divorce themselves from Communism.[14]

The flowering of Ukrainian culture and intellectual life during the twenties manifested itself above all in literature,[15] the fine arts,[16] theater and music,[17] and

[10] Cf. I. Majstrenko, *Borot'bism: A Chapter in the History of Ukrainian Communism*, New York, Research Program on the USSR, 1954.

[11] Among them were: Professor Mykhailo Hrushevsky, former chairman of the Central Rada, a well-known historian and politician; M. F. Chechel, Professor of the Kharkov Technological Institute; General Yu. Tyutyunnyk, the leader of the Ukrainian democratic army against the Bolsheviks; A. Nikovsky, former Minister for Foreign Affairs in the Ukrainian People's Republic; P. Khrystyuk, member of the Central Rada, writer and politician, the author of *Zamitky i materiyaly do istorii ukrainskoi revolyutsii* (Notes and Materials Concerning the History of the Ukrainian Revolution), Vienna, 1921-22, the poet M. Vorony, and many others.

[12] Cf. *XII sezd Rossiiskoi Kommunisticheskoi Partii (bolshevikov)* (The Twelfth Congress of the Russian Communist Party [Bolshevik]); *Stenografichesky otchet 17-25 aprelya 1923 goda.*, Moscow, Krasnaya nov, 1923, V, 705.

[13] "Tezy TsK KP(b)U pro pidsumky ukrainizatsii" (Theses of the CC of the CP(b)U on of the Russian Communist Party [Bolshevik]); *Stenografichesky otchet 17-25 aprelya 1923 goda.*, Kharkov, 1928, II, 293-303.

[14] *Ibid.*, p. 297.

[15] Cf. George S. N. Luckyj, *Literary Politics in the Soviet Ukraine: 1917-1934*, New York, Columbia University Press, 1956.

Also Leytes and Yashek, *op. cit.*; Yuriy Skerekh, "Styli suchasnoi ukrainskoi literatury" (The Styles of Modern Ukrainian Literature), *MUR*, I, Munich, 1946; B. Podolyak, "Poet yunosty i syly" (The Poet of Youth and Strength), *MUR*, Almanakh, I, Germany, 1946.

[16] I. Vrona, "Na shlyakhakh revolyutsiinoho mystetstva" (On the Paths of Revolutionary Art), *Vaplite*, No. 3, Kharkov, 1927, p. 166.

[17] L. Kurbas, "Shlyakhy 'Berezolya'" (The Paths of "Berezil"), *Vaplite*, No. 3, 1927, pp. 141-65; M. Skrypnyk, *Pereznaky tvorchoho terenu—rekonstruktyvni linii v literaturi, muzytsi, obrazotvorchomu mystetstvi* (Changing Marks in the Creative Field: Trends of Reconstruction in Literature, Music and Painting), Kharkov, 1930; Ye. Olensky, "Do tvorchykh zavyazkiv suchasnoi ukrainskoi muzyky" (The Creative Origins of Contemporary Ukrainian Music), *Literaturno-naukovy zbirnyk* (Literary and Scientific Symposium), New York, I, 1952, pp. 287-89.

scholarship.[18] The works of such writers as Khvylovy, Kulish, Yanovsky, Anton-enko-Davydovych, Tychyna, Ivchenko, Lyubchenko, Vlyzko and Kosynka, the theatrical productions of Les Kurbas, the films of Dovzhenko, the paintings of Boychuk, the literary criticism of Zerov, and the scholarly studies by members of the Ukrainian Academy of Sciences were evidence of the beginning of a cultural renaissance in which an attempt at national self-expression was blended with a quest for universal aesthetic and intellectual values. In that decade, for the first time in Ukrainian history, complete editions of Ukrainian classics were published as well as many translations from Western literature. In schools, Ukrainian re-placed Russian as the language of instruction. On the initiative of the Commissar of Education, Skrypnyk, research institutes were established for the purpose of studying the national and colonial problem. Inquiries into the Ukrainian economy and history carried out by such men as Yavorsky, Hrynko, Shumsky, and Skryp-nyk tended to regard the Ukraine as an independent republic, tied to the USSR by the bonds of the Soviet Constitution.

This idea of Ukrainian Communist independence was expressed by the writer Mykola Khvylovy in his pamphlets which stirred wide public discussion. In the third part of his essay "The Apologists of Scribbling" Khvylovy wrote:

> The Ukrainian economy is not Russian and cannot be so, if only because the Ukrainian culture, which emanates from the economic structure [of the country] and in turn influences it, bears characteristic forms and features. So does our economy. In a word—the [Soviet] Union remains a Union and the Ukraine is an independent state.[19]

Other Ukrainian Communists accused Russia of pursuing the old tsarist policy of colonial exploitation of the Ukraine.[20]

The conflict within the CP(b)U, which the growth of Ukrainian national Communism made inevitable, was brought to a head in 1926, when the Commissar for Education and a member of the Politburo of the Central Committee of the CP(b)U, Shumsky, was branded by the All-Union CP(b) as a national deviationist when he demanded fuller cultural, economic, and political autonomy for the Soviet

---

[18] M. Vetukhiv, "Osnovni etapy rozvytku Ukrainskoi Akademii Nauk u Kyyevi" (Main Stages in the Development of the Ukrainian Academy of Sciences in Kiev), *Literaturno-naukovy zbirnyk*, New York, I, 1952; A. Ya. Artemsky, *Shcho take Vseukrainska Akademiya Nauk* (What is the All-Ukrainian Academy of Sciences), Kiev, 1931; N. Polonska-Vasylenko, *Ukrainska Akademiya Nauk (narys istorii)*, I, (1918-1930), Munich, Instytut dlya vyvchannya istorii i kultury SSSR, 1955.

[19] M. Khvylovy, "Apolohety pysaryzmu" (The Apologists of Scribbling), *Kultura i pobut* (Culture and Life), *(Visti)* No. 13, 1926, pp. 1-8.

[20] M. Volobuyev, "Do problemy ukrainskoi ekonomiky" (Concerning the Problem of Ukrain-ian Economics), *Bilshovyk Ukrainy* (Bolshevik of the Ukraine), Nos. 2, 3, 1928; A. Richytsky, *Do problemy likvidatsii perezhytkiv koloniyalnosty to natsionalizmu* (Concerning the Problem of the Liquidation of the Vestiges of Colonialism and Nationalism), Kharkov, 1928; H. Hrynko, "Narys ukrainskoi ekonomiky" (An Outline of the Ukrainian Economy), *Chervony shlyakh* (The Red Pathway), No. 5-6, 1926.

Ukraine. The crisis in the CP(b)U was all the more serious, because the Communist Party of the Western Ukraine sided with Shumsky. The first outbreak of this "Ukrainian Titoism" ended in the removal of Shumsky from his post, and in the liquidation of the Communist Party of the Western Ukraine.[21] The danger of Shumsky's deviation was best described by Stalin in his letter to Kaganovich, written on April 26, 1926.[22] In it he admitted that this movement "attracted the non-Communist intelligensia" because of the "weakness of the local Communist cadres in the Ukraine" and could "assume the character of a struggle for the alienation of Ukrainian cultural and social life from the common Soviet cultural and social life, of a struggle against Moscow and the Russians in general, against Russian culture."[23]

The fall of Shumsky, however, did not put an end to the Ukrainian resurgence within the CP(b)U. The fight of the Ukrainian Communists was carried on chiefly by Skrypnyk who replaced Shumsky as Commissar for Education.[24] It is against the background of Soviet Ukrainian history of the twenties that we must see Stalin's plans for the subjugation of that country, entrusted to Postyshev in 1933.

---

[21] Ye. Hirchak, *Shumskizm i rozlam v KPZU*, Kharkov, 1928; M. Skrypnyk, *Dzherela ta prychny rozlamu v KPZU* (Origins and Causes of the Split in the CPWU), Kharkov, 1928. It is interesting to record that after the dissolution of the Communist Party of the Western Ukraine (KPZU), its members were either deported to concentration camps (Vasylkiv-Turyansky, Bukshovany), or killed on Stalin's orders during the first Soviet occupation of the Western Ukraine (1939-40).

[22] Stalin's letter to Kaganovich, Stalin, *Sochineniya*, VIII, pp. 149-54.

[23] *Ibid.*

[24] The forthrightness with which Skrypnyk defended the interests of the Ukrainians and other non-Russian nationalities may be seen from his speeches, collected in *Druha konferentsiya komunistychnoi partii (bilshovykiv) Ukrainy, 9-14 Kvitnya 1929 roku* (The Second Conference of the Communist Party [Bolshevik] of the Ukraine, 9-14 April 1929). *Stenohrafichny zvit*, Kharkiv, DVU, 1929, and in *XVI sezd VKP(b), iyul, 1930, stenograficheskyi otchet*, 2nd ed., Moscow, 1931, pp. 242-44.

Chapter XI

First Signs of a New Course

Having overcome the opposition within the CP(b)U to his appointment and realizing that he would not be able to raise agricultural production in the Ukraine by terror alone, Postyshev arranged for a seed loan from the state and dispatched his trusted men to the villages to help with the sowing and harvesting. Now he could devote himself to his chief task, the destruction of Ukrainian "bourgeois nationalism."

First of all a suitable atmosphere had to be created to enable Postyshev to carry out his policy. The Ukrainian people had to look upon him as their friend and savior, the inhabitants of Kharkov as their patron and benefactor, schoolchildren as their beloved teacher, the local Party members as their trusted leader. Therefore, on Postyshev's orders, when famine and privation were at their height, both in the Ukraine and in Kharkov, the capital was slated to receive a "new look." With feverish speed the streets, the parks, the public squares, and all the buildings in the Ukrainian capital were cleaned and made to look their best. Several churches were demolished (e. g. the Cathedral of St. Nicholas, and the Church of the Holy Anointing) in order to make room for new public buildings, which, by the way, were never erected. The parks, in particular, were beautified with great care and received new lawns and flowerbeds. In the center of the University Park a large monument to Shevchenko by the well-known Leningrad artist, Manizer, was prepared for unveiling. In connection with this, Trotsky made the following trenchant remark:

> The Soviet Ukraine has become an administrative part of the economic complex and the military base of the USSR for the totalitarian bureaucracy. Stalin's bureaucracy, it is true, erects statues to Shevchenko, but only in order to press with this monument on the Ukrainian people, to force them to eulogize the Kremlin violators in the language of the *Kobzar*.[1]

At the same time, the so-called "commercial" or "Postyshev" bread appeared on sale in some of the stores. Although supplies were scanty, the propaganda value was considerable. In Kharkov legends were circulated by Soviet propagandists

---

[1] L. Trotsky, "Ob ukrainskom voprose" (About the Ukrainian Problem), *Byulleten oppozitsii*, 77-78, May, June, July, 1939, p. 6. When Taras Shevchenko, the great Ukrainian poet of the mid-nineteenth century, published his first collection of poems in 1840 it bore the title *Kobzar*. The kobzars, whose instrument was the kobza or bandura, were bards of the sixteenth and seventeenth centuries who represented to the Ukrainians a living link with their past (see Morris John Diakowsky, "The Bandura," *The Ukrainian Trend*, New York, Vol. IX, No. 1, 1958).

about Postyshev's concern for the welfare of the ordinary population. According to these stories, Postyshev, disguised as a worker, went to various workers' quarters and asked for a meal. He was either refused or else given the common type of soup—*balanda*. He then visited the stores and learned that most common articles were unobtainable. Later, Postyshev returned to these districts and held Party meetings pointing out the shortages and drawbacks. As a result, the workers, so the story ended, received more food and commodities. Similar stories vere circulated about Postyshev's trips to the villages. They were all designed to idolize Stalin's plenipotentiary in the Ukraine, and to make him popular with the people.

Postyshev himself understood very well the value of popularity. He visited kindergartens and schools and saw to it that photographs, showing him in the midst of children, were frequently published in the daily press. The irresistible power of suggestion which this propaganda produced is demonstrated in a recent sketch of Postyshev.[2]

Not being able to feed and satisfy everybody, Postyshev took care to provide for the Soviet bureaucracy on which he had to rely. Special dining halls for officials of the Party and the administration were established in all the large Ukrainian cities. A former Soviet Ukrainian describes one such dining hall for Party officials in Pehrybyshcha:

> Day and night it was guarded by militia keeping the starving peasants and their children away from the restaurant; their terrible appearance alone could ruin the appetite of the "builders of socialism." In the dining room, at very low prices, white bread, meat, poultry, canned fruit and delicacies, wines and sweets were served to the district bosses. At the same time, the employees of the dining hall were issued the so-called Mikoyan ration, which contained 20 different articles of food. Around these oases famine and death were raging.[3]

There can be no doubt that the privileged class of Party officials and managers was enjoying the benefits of Postyshev's rule in the Ukraine.

Another slogan, devised to mitigate austerity and drabness in the Soviet upper class was: "abolish boredom." Party gatherings were to be regarded as social occasions, to be held in a friendly atmosphere, with tea or vodka served at the conclusion of business meetings. More gaiety was encouraged in public life. Following an article in *Pravda*, Western (bourgeois) dance music was allowed in the USSR. The foxtrot and the tango were heard in places of public amusement. Parties given by various departments of the Soviet government at the public expense became quite frequent.

This banqueting in the land of the dead was part of the setting for Postyshev's next move. While dissemination of the new "happy life" slogans was in full swing, and the city dwellers were smothering in a thick smoke of propaganda, the follow-

---
[2] *Soviet Political Personalities; Seven Profiles,* New York, Research Program on the USSR, 1952, pp. 7-12.
[3] Vysochenko, *op. cit.,* p. 19.

ing changes took place in the Soviet Ukrainian government. On March 1, 1933, *Visti,* the organ of the CC of the CP(b)U announced that:

1) P. P. Lyubchenko had been appointed first Deputy Chairman of the Council of People's Commissars of the Ukrainian SSR.

2) M. O. Skrypnyk had been relieved of his duties as Ukrainian Commissar of Education and appointed Chairman of the State Planning Commission of the Ukrainian SSR.

3) V. P. Zatonsky had been relieved of his duties as Commissar of Workers' and Peasants' Inspection and appointed to the post of Commissar of Education, formerly held by Skrypnyk.

4) V. K. Sukhomlin had been appointed Commissar of Workers' and Peasants' Inspection.

5) Ya. M. Dudnyk had been relieved of his duties as Chairman of the State Planning Commission and Deputy Chairman of the Council of People's Commissars of the Ukrainian SSR and appointed first Deputy Chairman of the State Planning Commission.

A few days later, *Visti*[4] carried news of more changes in the Soviet Ukrainian government:

1) The Central Committee of the CP(b)U has elected M. M. Popov[5] as its secretary, and placed him in charge of the Propaganda and Press Section of the CC of the CP(b)U.

2) The Presidium of the Ukrainian Executive Committe has announced the appointment of the former chief of the Propaganda and Press Section of the CC, CP(b)U, A. A. Khvylya,[6] to the post of Deputy Commissar of Education of the Ukrainian SSR.

3) A. A. Karpeko has been dismissed from his post as Deputy Commissar of Education of the Ukrainian SSR.

---

[4] *Visti,* March 3, 1933.

[5] M. Popov, a former Russian Menshevik, a member of the Communist Party since 1919, was one of the few high officials of the Party who, during his service in the Ukraine, became an adherent of the Ukrainian trend in the CP(b)U. He was also known as a historian of the CP(b)U, author of *Ocherki istorii KP(b)U* (A Sketch of the History of the CP(b)U), Kharkov, 1929.

[6] A. Khvylya acquired notoriety in 1925-29 as the chief Party spokesman against Khvylovy. A former Borotbist, who joined the CP(b)U in 1918, he was a prominent journalist. In several emigre sources his name is often incorrectly identified as a pseudonym of Musulbas (e. g. R. Smal-Stocki, *The Nationality Problem of the Soviet Union,* Milwaukee, 1952). Khvylya and Musulbas were two different men, both members of the CC, CP(b)U (cf. list of members of the CC, *Visti,* January 23, 1934). The confusion of their names probably resulted from a misreading of the Shumsky letter to the CC, CP(b)U, on February 3, 1927 *(Budivnytstvo radyanskoi Ukrainy,* I, 135). Majstrenko *(op. cit.)* gives separate profiles of Khvylya and Musulbas. Very little is known of Khvylya's early life (he was born in 1898 in Khotyn uezd) and his real name has not been discovered. D. Solovey, in an unpublished manuscript on the purge of Poltava (preserved in the Ukrainian Academy in the United States), offers a conjecture that Khvylya's real name was Olinter.

These changes were not merely a re-shuffle of the Soviet Ukrainian government—they foreshadowed a drastic crisis for the rulers of the Ukrainian SSR. An even clearer indication of this crisis was the announcement, made at the same time, of the uncovering of a major anti-Soviet conspiracy, which allegedly was active primarily in the Ukraine. As a result of this sensational disclosure by the OGPU, 35 men were sentenced to be executed as enemies of the state.[7] At their head was F. M. Konar (real name Palashchuk), a Western Ukrainian who had risen to be Deputy Chairman of the Commission of Agriculture of the USSR. The charge against Konar and the other men was that they had attempted to sabotage the agricultural effort in the Ukraine, the North Caucasus, and Belorussia. Konar and 34 associates were executed, 22 others were sentenced to 10 years, and 18 to 8 years in jail. For those who could read between the lines, the "conspiracy" of Konar had an obvious relation to the changes in the government: both were indicative of Postyshev's new course.[8]

This was one of the first times in the USSR that an old member of the Party and a high official, Ukrainian by birth, and responsible for Ukrainian agriculture, was tried by the OGPU and executed on charges of counter-revolution. This indeed was a *memento mori* given to the top Ukrainian Communists, as if to warn them that their Party record and standing would be of no avail, should they be accused of similar crimes.

The most significant change in the government was the removal of Skrypnyk from his post as Minister of Education. Yet he was replaced by another Ukrainian Communist, Zatonsky, and two former Borotbists, Lyubchenko and Khvylya, were elevated to responsible government posts. On the surface these moves did not portend an anti-Ukrainian course. Unless—was Postyshev selecting Ukrainians to purge other Ukrainians?

---

[7] "Povidomlennya OHPU" (An Announcement by the OGPU), *Visti*, March 5, 1933; "Ot kollegii OGPU" (From the Collegium of the OGPU), *Pravda*, March 12, 1933.

[8] During the trial of Rykov and Bukharin in 1938, the former Finance Minister of the USSR, G. F. Hrynko, a Ukrainian, testified that a "nationalist organization in the Ukraine was preparing an uprising against the Soviet government . . . to aid the partisan warfare, [the enemies] maintained liaison through Konar . . ." *Pravda*, March 4, 1938.

Chapter XII

Before the Final Assault

The Purge of Ukrainian Literature

The next objective to attract Postyshev's attention was Ukrainian culture, in particular literature. By 1938, the spirit of an independent search for cultural and literary modes of expression was all but suppressed by the earlier imposition of Party controls. Not only were several writers silenced and their ideas condemned and branded as counter-revolutionary (Khvylovy, Zerov, Pidmohylny, Ivchenko), but also all literary organizations and groups, such as "Hart," "Pluh," "Vaplite," Mars, New Generation, VUSPP, "Avant-garde," the Neoclassicists, "Lanka," "Prolitfront," had either been disbanded earlier or else dissolved, following the Party resolution on literature issued in April 1932.[1]

However, there were still among the living writers and critics those who in the past had led the movement of cultural regeneration in the Ukraine. Their earlier works were permeated with an anti-centralist, often anti-Russian, spirit and were rooted in the conviction that a spontaneous growth of socialist Ukrainian culture, linked with the past traditions of that country, was possible and desirable. In 1933 many of these writers seemed subdued to Party controls, although some of them still showed some resistance to the Soviet regimentation of literature, which showed itself with special prominence during the formation of the Soviet Writers' Union (1932–34). It was against these champions of the spiritual resistance in the Ukraine that Postyshev directed his attack. He began by destroying those who were already dead.

In Kharkov where Chernyshevsky and Artem streets meet there stood a small statue, commemorating the leading Ukrainian Communist (former Borotbist) and writer, Vasyl Ellan (Blakytny). It was erected, after the poet's death, in 1925. Blakytny, who died at the age of 32, had been the editor of *Visti,* and chairman of the proletarian literary organization "Hart." The statue was small and in the course of the years ordinary citizens had become indifferent to it, with the exception of a few writers and students who came there at times to pay homage to the deceased writer.

One May morning, early passersby noticed that the statue was badly damaged. It was reduced to a heap of rubble. During the day some people enquired as to the reason for this act of vandalism. The explanation given in the following day's papers was that the statue had been inadvertently damaged by a truck. As a result of the accident it was decided to remove the statue altogether and to re-erect it

---

[1] Cf. Luckyj, *op. cit.;* for the resolution on literature see *Pravda,* April 24, 1932.

in another place, to be decided upon by the city planning commission.[2] Needless to say, the Blakytny monument was never re-erected. The truck which destroyed it was, in all probability, sent expressly for that purpose by Postyshev.

Next on the list were the living representatives of the Ukrainian opposition to Party controls in literature. On May 12, the OGPU arrested the writer Mykhaylo Yalovy (nom de plume, Yulian Shpol), a former president of the Ukrainian literary group "Vaplite," and chief political editor of the Ukrainian State Publishing House. This was a signal that the core of the Ukrainian literary resistance to Moscow's policy, represented by former members of "Vaplite," was to be ruthlessly destroyed. The impact of this blow was felt particularly deeply by Mykola Khvylovy, the spiritual leader of "Vaplite" and its chief theorist. He considered himself morally responsible for the fate of his associates. Besides, Yalovy was a close personal friend of Khvylovy.

On May 13, 1933, Khvylovy invited some of his friends to breakfast at his apartment. A few moments after his guests had assembled, he asked to be excused, went to his study and shot himself. By the time his friends reached him he was dead. On his desk lay a letter, addressed to the Central Committee of the CP(b)U. In it he accused the Party of betraying the Revolution, and branded the terror which it used in the Ukraine as the beginning of a new *Thermidor*. He wished his suicide to be regarded as an act of protest against the tactics of the Party.[3]

It is no exaggeration to say that Khvylovy was the most colorful personality in Ukrainian literary life. He owed his reputation not only to the independence and integrity he showed in opposing the cultural policy of the Party in the Ukraine. He was also an outstanding writer and essayist, and had been a member of the CP(b)U since the days of the Revolution. His death, therefore, could not be ignored. On May 14, 1933, the official organ of the CP(b)U, *Visti*, carried an obituary of Khvylovy.[4] It ended with these words:

> At the moment when the masses of workers and collective farmers are fighting with enthusiasm in all fields of socialist construction, the revolutionary fervor of the writer Khvylovy has given out. In spite of our regard for Khvylovy as one of the outstanding Soviet writers who has greatly enriched Soviet literature, we cannot but deplore his thoughtless step.

---

[2] The incident is based entirely on the author's reminiscences. The search to find the information in the Soviet press proved fruitless.

[3] Khvylovy's letter has not been preserved. Its contents were related to the present author by two close friends of Khvylovy who read it. According to them, soon after Khvylovy's death the police entered his apartment and seized the letter together with other documents. The existence of such a letter is confirmed in the following publications: O. Han, *Trahediya Mykoly Khvylovoho* (The Tragedy of Mykola Khvylovy), Augsburg, Promotey, n. d.; O. Filomelya, *Ukrainsky litopys abo Kalendar istorychnykh podii* (A Ukrainian Chronicle or a Calendar of Historic Events), Winnipeg, 1950, pp. 41-42; S. Harmash, "M. Khvylovy i nasha doba" (M. Khvylovy and Our Epoch), *Nasha borotba* (Our Struggle), No. 2, 1946, pp. 48-53; "Spohady pro Mykolu Kulisha Antoniny Kulish" (Antonina Kulish's Recollections of Mykola Kulish), in Mykola Kulish, Tvory (Works), New York, 1955, pp. 416-18.

[4] *Visti*, May 14, 1933.

In spite of precautionary measures, Khvylovy's funeral turned into a spontaneous demonstration against Postyshev's regime. It was attended by writers, students, workers and trade union representatives, as well as by the printers, many of whom had known the deceased writer well.

The Central Committee of the CP(b)U was quick to brand such actions as hostile to the Soviet state. The secretary of the CP(b)U, Popov, publicly condemned Khvylovy's suicide as a "demonstration against the state."[5]

About the time of Khvylovy's death, another Ukrainian poet, Hirnyak, committed suicide. Professor Havryliv, of the Kharkov Pedagogical Institute, also took his own life. Some time later, another former member of "Vaplite," the writer Dosvitny, was arrested. During the next few months scores of Ukrainian writers and critics were rounded up by the OGPU. Some of them were sentenced to death and executed, a few committed suicide, and nearly 300 others were deported to concentration camps.

The Fate of the Historical School of M. Yavorsky

The greatest modern authority on Ukrainian history was Professor Mykhaylo Hrushevsky. His *Istoriya Ukrainy-Rusy* (History of Ukraine-Rus), mostly written before the Revolution, was an outstanding study of Ukrainian history, based on original sources, earlier works of Ukrainian historians, and Slavic historiography in general. Written in nine large volumes, Hrushevsky's work also represented the result of years of research, illuminated by competent scholarly analysis. It established the continuity of Ukrainian history, beginning with the earliest period, the ninth century, and it demonstrated the inter-relation of the political and social aspects of this history.[6] Hrushevsky was no Marxist. This, as well as the fact that he was the chairman of the Central Rada, the parliament of the Ukrainian People's Republic (1917–20), made his work unacceptable to the Soviet regime. Therefore, while tolerating further research conducted by Hrushevsky as a member of the Ukrainian Academy of Sciences, the Soviets encouraged another school of history, based on the Marxian approach. The latter was headed by a young Ukrainian scholar, Matviy Yavorsky,[7] who, in 1929,

---

[5] *Visti*, July 12, 1933.

[6] An abbreviated version of Hrushevsky's work was published in English: M. Hrushevsky, *A History of the Ukraine*, New Haven, Yale University Press, 1941.

[7] Matviy Ivanovych Yavorsky was born on November 15, 1885, in the village of Korchmyn, district of Rava Ruska, in Galicia. After receiving his education as a lawyer, he served in the Austrian army during the First World War. In 1918, still in the army, he reached Kiev where he established close contacts with Ukrainian political leaders. In November 1918, Yavorsky took part in the uprising against Hetman Skoropadsky; in 1920, together with the Borotbists, he joined the Communist Party. His work as a historian began in the early twenties. In 1928 he took part in the covention of historians in Berlin. (All these data are gathered from *Nauchnye rabotniki SSSR bez Moskvy i Leningrada*, Izd. Akad. Nauk, 1928, p. 507, and *Bolshaya sovetskaya entsiklopediya*, 1st ed., Vol. 65, Moscow, 1931, p. 328. Yavorsky's chief works are: *Narys istorii Ukrainy* (An Outline of the History of the Ukraine), Kiev, 1923; *Ukraina v epokhu kapitalizmu* (The Ukraine in the Era of Capitalism), Kharkov, Poltava, 1924-25; *Narysy z istorii revolyutsiinoi borotby na Ukraini* (Sketches in the History of the Revolutionary Struggle in the Ukraine), 2 vols., Kharkov, 1927, 1928.

became a full member of the Academy of Sciences. As the head of the Institute of History and chief editor of *Istoryk-Marksyst* (The Marxist Historian), Yavorsky organized extensive research into Ukrainian history. The fruits of this he presented at the First All-Union Conference of Marxist Historians, held in Moscow from December 28, 1928, to January 4, 1929.[8] At this conference Yavorsky and his pupils attacked the centralist Russian concepts of history which some Soviet historians had inherited from Imperial Russia. Yavorsky's arguments were so convincing that the foremost Soviet Russian historian of the time, M. Pokrovsky, whose authority was undisputed,[9] recognized the contribution of Ukrainian historians as of signal importance to Marxian historiography. In his final address to the conference, Pokrovsky made it clear to his Ukrainian colleagues that there was no room in Soviet historiography for the theories of the "one and indivisible Russia."

Pokrovsky's pledge was premature. His view of Soviet history did not coincide with Stalin's plans.[10]

In the Ukraine, the repudiation of the Marxian historical school of Yavorsky began soon after his return from the Moscow conference in 1929. He was first attacked in an article in the *Bilshovyk Ukrainy*.[11] Soon an outright smear campaign was started against Yavorsky. He was accused of having had dealings with Hetman Skoropadsky. An alleged former wife of Yavorsky published in the press some letters revealing the immoral character of this Academician and member of the Party.

Sometime in 1930, Yavorsky was expelled from the Party, dismissed from the Academy of Sciences, and exiled to a distant part of the USSR. It would seem, therefore, that by the time Postyshev began his purge of Ukrainian intellectuals, Yavorsky's fate was sealed. A similar fate was meted out to Professor Hrushevsky who, in 1930, was deported from the Ukraine. However, the final blow to Ukrainian historians was reserved for Postyshev. After all, Yavorsky's and Hrushevsky's ideas could be revived if the pupils of these historians were allowed to live and to

---

[8] *Trudy pervoi vsesoyuznoi konferentsii istorikov-marksistov* (Proceedings of the First All-Union Conference of Marxist Historians), 28. XII. 1928-4. I. 1929. Vol. I. Moscow, Komaka-demiya, 1930; see especially: pp. 36-40, 426-35, 436-59, 460-68.

[9] A. Avtorkhanov, *Pokorenie partii*, Chapter XII, *Istoricheskaya shkola Pokrovskogo* (The Historical School of Pokrovsky), *Posev*, No. 4, 5, 6, 1951.

[10] M. N. Pokrovsky died in 1932, and his school was later destroyed. See Avtorkhanov, *op. cit.* For Stalin's evaluation of Pokrovsky as historian see *Malaya sovetskaya entsiklopediya* (Small Soviet Encyclopedia), Vol. 8, 2nd ed., pp. 385-88.

[11] Yavorsky's views were declared un-Marxian and false. The following condensation may be found in *Bolshaya sovetskaya entsiklopedia*, 1st ed., Vol. 65, Moscow, 1931, p. 328: "In his works Yavorsky, screening himself behind Marxian phraseology, developed a nationalist-kulakist system of ideas. Its basic tenets were: a) an attempt to interpret the whole of Ukrainian history as a struggle of the people for a state of their own; b) the presentation of the Ukrainian bourgeoisie and the kulaks as a revolutionary force holding hegemony in a bourgeois-democratic revolution and a denial of the hegemony to the proletariat; c) the idealization of Ukrainian petty-bourgeois parties; d) the rejection of the historical preparation for the dictatorship of the proletariat and hence a denial of such a proletarian revolution in Ukraine."

carry on their work. It was decided, therefore, to annihilate whole groups of associates and pupils of the two famous historians.

In March 1933, Yavorsky was arrested (at the same time as Shumsky, Maksymovich, Solodub and other Ukrainian national Communists) and charged with belonging to an alleged Ukrainian underground military organization.[12] There were reports that, three or four years later, during mass executions of prisoners in the concentration camps, he was shot.[13] In his speech at the Twelfth Congress of the CP(b)U in January 1934, Postyshev listed the following professors of the All-Ukrainian Association of Marx and Lenin Institutes (VUAMLIN) as enemies of the state: Yavorsky, Richytsky, Chechel, Mazurenko, Holubovych, Khrystyuk, Romanyuk, Lyzanivsky, Trublaevych, Bilyk, Chichkevych, Bilash, Vikul, Fedchyshyn, Demchuk, Bon, Stepovy, Svidzinsky, Zozulyak, Oliynyk, Kuzmenko, Lozynsky, Chekhovych, Yurynets, Slipansky, and Vityk.[14] About the same time other associates of Yavorsky (Hurevych, Rubach) were also arrested. The VUAMLIN was dissolved in 1935 or 1936. Shlikhter, in a speech at the Thirteenth Congress of the CP(b)U, in 1937, declared that "in the former VUAMLIN the band of counter-revolutionaries, Trotskyites and nationalists made a nest for itself."[15] Thus ended the Marxian school of Ukrainian historians.

The Fate of the Historical School of Hrushevsky

Until 1931, the historical section of the Ukrainian Academy of Sciences was under the chairmanship and intellectual leadership of Professor Hrushevsky.[16] In 1931, after the trial of the so-called Union for the Liberation of the Ukraine (SVU), held during the previous year, a new "secret" organization, consisting of Ukrainian scholars and intellectuals, was uncovered. It was the so-called Ukrainian National Center (UNTs)[17] which was supposed to include nearly all the former political associates of Hrushevsky (Chechel, Holubovych, Khrystyuk, Shrah, Kosak). Hrushevsky himself was accused of being the head of this conspiratorial body.[18] Hrushevsky was not arrested, but was removed from the Ukraine to the vicinity of Moscow, where he was isolated from Ukrainian scholarship.[19] Here, while reporting regularly to the GPU, Hrushevsky continued to work on the history of the Ukraine in the eighteenth century, from time to time publishing the results of his research in the *Izvestiya* (News) of the All-Union Academy of Sciences.

---

[12] Polonska-Vasylenko, *op. cit.*, pp. 65-66.

[13] S. Pidhayny, *op. cit.*, pp. 57-60.

[14] *Visti*, January 24, 1934.

[15] *Visti*, June 5, 1937.

[16] Cf. Polonska-Vasylenko, *op. cit.*, pp. 81-84; also supplement No. 5, pp. 122-26.

[17] O. Buzhansky, "Za gratamy GPU-NKVD" (Behind the Bars of the GPU-NKVD), *Svoboda* (Liberty), No. 288-300, December, 1950; D. Solovey, *op. cit.*

[18] "Itogi i blizhaishie zadachi provedeniya politiki na Ukraine" (Results and Immediate Tasks of the Conduct of Policy in the Ukraine), *Pravda*, December 2, 1933.

[19] For more details, see the section of this study devoted to the Ukrainian National Center, pp. 89—90.

The year 1933 brought no relief to Hrushevsky. "At the beginning of the year," writes one of his former collaborators, "two learned associates of the historical section of the Academy of Sciences, H. Hlushko and S. Shamray, were arrested. After the first of August all the members of the historical section of the Academy were relieved of their duties and all research facilities connected with the history of the Ukraine or former projects of Hrushevsky, were abolished."[20]

Later, Hrushevsky was moved to Kislovodsk, where he died on November 25, 1934.[21]

The Bahaliy Institute for the Study of Slobidska Ukraine, although not directly within Hrushevsky's jurisdiction, was severely purged in 1933. One of its outstanding scholars, Professor Natalia Mirza-Avakiantz, was arrested and deported.

The End of the Historians of the CP(b)U

The purge of Ukrainian historians also affected official Party historiographers. The history of the CP(b)U and of the Ukrainian Communist movement represented an obstacle to Stalin's plans to extirpate the national spirit and tradition from the non-Russian Communist movements. First of all, the journals *Litopys Revolyutsii* (The Chronicle of the Revolution) and *Istoryk-Marksyst* (The Marxist Historian), devoted to study and research in Soviet Ukrainian history, were discontinued. A virtual blackout was imposed on all investigations in the fields of Ukrainian Communism. During the years 1933–53 not a single work on the history of the CP(b)U was published.

The first official historian of the CP(b)U and the author of many works on the history of the revolution in the Ukraine was M. E. Ravich-Cherkassky.[22] A former member of the Jewish Social-Democratic Party, *Bund*, Ravich-Cherkassky firmly believed that the national aspect of the Revolution in the Ukraine was of the greatest importance. He was a staunch opponent of the traditional Russian interpretation of Ukrainian history and approached the study of Soviet Ukrainian history deeply convinced that the Ukrainian state was not a gift of the Soviet regime, but a hard-won prerogative springing from the Ukrainian past. He wrote:

> Up to the present a notion persists, not only in the circles of the bourgeois Russian intelligentsia, but also to a certain extent among the Communists, a notion not very different from the one which holds that the Ukraine was invented by the

---

[20] O. M. "Ostanni roky zhyttya Mykhayla Hrushevskoho" (The Last Year in the Life of M. Hrushevsky), *Nashi dni* (Our Days), No. 3, Lviv, March, 1943.

[21] For a more detailed review of Hrushevsky's last years see the present author's article "The Last Days of Academician M. Hrushevsky," *Ukrainian Review*, No. 5, Munich, 1957, Institute for the Study of the USSR, pp. 73-83.

[22] Apart from the history of the Ukrainian Communist Party *(op. cit.)*, Ravich-Cherkassky edited the following books: *Revolyutsiya i KP(b)U v materialakh i dokumentakh* (The Revolution and the CP(b)U in Materials and Documents), I, Kharkov, 1926; *Pervoye maya: Yuzhno-russkie rabochie soyuzy* (The First of May: The South-Russian Workers Union), 1926.

52

Germans. Many members of the RCP, swayed by bourgeois prejudices, believe that the UkSSR and the CP(b)U are fictitious or else merely playing at independence. At best they concede that during the period of struggle against the nationalist Central Rada and Directory, it was imperative for the Communist Party and the Soviet government in the Ukraine to adorn themselves with defensive, national and independent colors. Now that the Soviet government in the Ukraine has been firmly established, they argue that the role of the UkSSR and the CP(b)U is finished.[23]

Ravich-Cherkassky viewed the Russian imperialist outlook with real apprehension. He held that the unfettered development of the Soviet Ukraine was of cardinal importance in the battle to win the other countries of Eastern Europe over to Communism. The historic mission of the Soviet Ukraine was to unite those parts of the country which were occupied by Poland, Rumania, and Czechoslovakia into one Soviet Ukrainian State. Such a "United Soviet Socialist Ukraine," he wrote, "will be a powerful factor in the social revolutionary movement among the Slavic states in Europe."[24]

Ravich-Cherkassky disappeared from political and scholarly life two years after Yavorsky. Following the pronouncement of the Central Committe of the All-Union CP(b), dated October 9, 1932, which concerned the counter-revolutionary group of Riutin, Ivanov and Galkin, Ravich-Cherkassky was expelled from the Party together with 24 others, including Zinoviev and Kamenev.[25] His subsequent fate is unknown.

Another historian of the CP(b)U, M. Popov, after enjoying a spell of popularity during Postyshev's regime, disappeared in 1937.

The purge of Ukrainian historians, including those who were exclusively concerned with the study of Ukrainian Communism, paved the way for the creation of the *Short History of the CPSU*. Having suppressed the early historiography of the Ukraine and of the CP(b)U, and having disowned Pokrovsky's[26] school of history, Stalin was ready to write his own version of the history of the USSR.

---

[23] Ravich-Cherkassky, *Istoriya* . . . p. 5.

[24] *Ibid.*, pp. 2-6.

[25] *Pravda*, October 11, 1932.

[26] The letter which Lenin wrote to Pokrovsky appears in the English translation of the latter's history (M. N. Pokrovski, *Brief History of Russia*, translated by D. S. Mirsky, London, 1933, Vol. I, p. 5.): Comrade Pokrovski, I congratulate you very heartily on your success. I like your new book, "Brief History of Russia," immensely. The construction and the narrative are original. It reads with tremendous interest. It should, in my opinion, be translated into the European languages.

I will permit myself one slight remark. To make it a text book (and this it must become), it must be supplemented with a chronological index. This is, roughly, what I am suggesting: 1st column, chronology; 2nd column, bourgeois view (briefly); 3rd column, your view, Marxian, indicating the pages in your book.

The students must know both your book and the index so that there will be no skimming, so that they will retain the facts, and so that they will learn to compare the old science and the new. What do you say to such an addition? With Communist greetings, yours, Lenin.

Before the Revolution of 1917, the Ukraine produced many outstanding writers (Shevchenko, Kulish, Franko, Lesya Ukrainka, Kotsyubynsky, Vynnychenko) and scholars (Kostomarov, Antonovych, Drahomanov, Zhytetsky, Potebnya, Hrushevsky). There had, however, been very little progress in philosophy.[27] Not only were there no prominent Ukrainian philosophers in the early twentieth century, but interest and training in this discipline had declined considerably.

The early twenties brought a new lease of life to philosophy in the Ukraine. This became evident not so much among the members of the Ukrainian Academy of Sciences as among the Marxian thinkers gathered in the Institute of Philosophy established as a branch of the VUAMLIN (All-Ukrainian Association of Marx and Lenin Institutes). The leading role in this institute was played by Professor Semkovsky, a former Menshevik who later became a member of the Party. Although a man of sound philosophical training and great erudition, Semkovsky did not have much understanding of the current problems of Ukrainian life and therefore failed to attract young Ukrainian thinkers. Instead, beginning with 1929, a new star was rising on the horizon—that of Volodymyr Yurynets (born in 1891), a pupil of Pokrovsky and Deborin.[28] A man of Western European education, a former student at the Universities of Vienna, Berlin and Paris, Yurynets had obtained his doctorate before the Revolution. In 1920 he was graduated from the Institute of Red Professors in Moscow and was sent, on Pokrovsky's recommendation, to lecture first at the Communist University for Toilers of the East and then at the University of Moscow. He was a man of many talents, interested not only in philosophy and mathematics but also in poetry and languages, several of which he spoke fluently. His study of Freud, written and published in German, was widely discussed in European philosophical journals of the twenties.

Around Yurynets there formed in the Ukraine a group of promising young philosophers (Demchuk, Stepovy, Paskel, Nyrchuk). In 1928, Yurynets, with the complete approval of the Party, was made a full member of the Ukrainian Academy of Sciences. With the help of his associates Yurynets published at that time several collections of philosophical writings and was an active contributor to the periodical *Prapor marksyzmu* (Banner of Marxism). One of his colleagues, Professor Nyrchuk, was nominated to the newly established chair of philosophy at the Kiev branch of VUAMLIN.

The work of the Ukrainian Institute of Philosophy was carried on in two fields: the history of philosophy in general and of Marxism in particular; and the

---

[27] The two best known Ukrainian philosophers of the past were Hryhoriy Skovoroda (1722-1794) and Pamfilo Yurkevych (1827-1894). "It is impossible to deny the weakness in the development of our theoretical philosophy," reports *Entsyklopediya ukrainoznavstva* (The Ukrainian Encyclopedia), ed. V. Kubijovych and Z. Kuzelya, Munich—New York, Vol. II, p. 718). The reasons for this, it suggests, may be found in the "absence of one's own state, lasting a long period of time, and in the resultant low material standard of the Ukrainian people for centuries."

[28] See *Literaturny yarmarok* (The Literary Fair), No. 5, Kharkov, 1929.

philosophy of Ukrainian history. Until 1933 conditions had been favorable for the inquiries conducted by the Institute. A drastic change occurred after Postyshev's arrival. The first victim of the new policy was Professor Nyrchuk. In March 1933, the Central Committee of the CP(b)U published the following declaration:

> The symposium "For Leninist Philosphy," issued by the Kiev branch of VUAM-LIN, contains a series of gross errors and distortions of Marxian-Leninist theory. The method used by the chief editor of the collection, Comrade Nyrchuk, that of copying entire passages from the classical works of Marxism without indicating the sources, of arbitrarily wrenching quotations out of their context and garbling them for his own purposes, is completely anti-Bolshevik and anti-Party.

As a result, the Central Committee resolved to

> deliver a severe reprimand to Comrade Nyrchuk, and to remove him from this command post on the ideological front. To reprimand the editorial board of the symposium. To instruct the Kiev Provincial Committee of the CP(b)U to organize an inspection of the activities of the entire group working under the leadership of Comrade Nyrchuk.[29]

The last paragraph of the resolution made it clear that the Party held the Institute of Philosophy and Professor Yurynets responsible for the failings of Nyrchuk.

On July 3, 1933, the secretary of the CP(b)U, Popov, delivered a direct attack on Yurynets in his speech before the Kharkov Party meeting.[30] Results speedily followed. On July 17, 1933, a Pronouncement by the Central Committee of the CP(b)U condemned Yurynets and his school. It read as follows:

> The Central Committee of the CP(b)U notes the extreme lack of Party spirit of V. Yurynets who, in his article, "On the Crisis of Contemporary Physics," and in his textbook on dialectical materialism, committed direct plagiarism from the works of many bourgeois authors (Jordan, Haas, Schrodinger) as well as Soviet authors (Maximov, Yegorshin)...
>
> The Central Comittee considers V. Yurynets an adherent of bourgeois-idealist philosophy and a philosophical supporter of Yavorsky's historical school... He furthered the idea of the "bourgeois-less character" of the Ukrainian nation and preached orientation toward Western Europe...

The Central Committee of the CP(b)U decided, therefore, to

> exclude V. Yurynets from the ranks of the Party, as one who adheres to bourgeois philosophy, supports the historical scheme of Yavorsky, a pseudo-scientist, and plagiarist.[31]

---

[29] *Visti*, May 10, 1933.

[30] M. Popov, "Pro natsionalistychni ukhyly v lavakh ukrainskoi partorhanizatsii ta pro zavdannya borotby z nymy" (On Nationalist Deviations in the Ranks of the Ukrainian Party Organization and on the Means of Combatting Them), *Visti*, July 12, 1933.

[31] The resolution of the CC CP(b)U dated July 17, 1933, *Visti*, July 22, 1933.

The charge of plagiarism was a familiar device for discrediting scholars in the eyes of the public.

After being expelled from the Party, Professor Yurynets and Nyrchuk were deprived of their chairs and both were later arrested. Professor Nyrchuk was chosen by the NKVD to head the fictitious Trotskyite-Nationalist Terrorist Bloc, which included several Ukrainian scholars, philosophers and intellectuals, all condemned for terrorist activities. The present author met several of them (M. Yuvchenko, P. Savchuk, Davydenko, Professor Ye. Shabliovsky, and I. Greenberg) in the Lukianivska prison in Kiev, early in 1936. According to these men, Nyrchuk, after being tortured by the NKVD, confessed to being a ringleader of the "Bloc."

The net result of these persecutions of Ukrainian philosophers was the annihilation of all independent thought among the Ukrainian Marxists. They were considered dangerous as idealogists of Ukrainian Communism, and as thinkers who were favorable toward Western European ideas.

Ukrainian Linguistics on Trial

The attack which Postyshev launched against Ukrainian linguistics was primarily directed against the Institute of Linguistics at the Ukrainian Academy of Sciences.

Even since 1917, work on the standardization of the Ukrainian literary language had been carried on by Ukrainian scholars, actively supported by those Ukrainian Communists who realized the importance of this task for the development of Ukrainian culture and literature. Skrypnyk, who in 1926 became Commissar for Education, was a real enthusiast in this cause and did a great deal to co-ordinate the work of Ukrainian linguists. Professor Sherekh, an authority on the Ukrainian language, describes the situation in the twenties in the following words:

> The centers formed or reactivated by the government for scholarly investigation of Ukrainian language problems were: The Ukrainian Language Institute of the Ukrainian Academy of Sciences, devoted to working out Ukrainian scientific and technical terminology, the Ukrainian language chairs at the Institutes of People's Education (Universities), and courses in Ukrainian, in particular the Central Course of Ukrainian Studies in Kharkov. The moving force behind this movement was the Commissariat of Education, headed first by Shumsky and then by Skrypnyk.[32]

In 1927, on Skrypnyk's initiative, for the first time a scholarly conference was convened, which devoted itself to the problem of the systematization of Ukrainian orthography. The Commission of Ukrainian scholars formed both from the Soviet Ukraine and abroad at this conference worked out a uniform Ukrainian orthography which replaced the two spelling systems used before (one in the

---

[32] Yu. Sherekh, "Pryntsypy i etapy bolshevytskoi movnoi polityky na Ukraini" (Principles and Stages of the Bolshevik Linguistic Policy in the Ukraine), *Suchasna Ukraina* (Contemporary Ukraine), June 29, 1952.

Soviet Ukraine, the other in the Western Ukraine and Bukovina). According to the new orthography, the Ukrainian transliteration of foreign words, in Sherekh's words, "broke away from the Russian tradition and approached that of Western Europe."[33]

This research in Ukrainian linguistics became an integral part of the policy of the CP(b)U, which was aimed at achieving cultural and linguistic self-expression within the framework of the Soviet Ukrainian state. After 1930, this policy was attacked by the All-Union CP(b). In the field of Ukrainian linguistics the new Postyshev line showed itself first of all in the assault on the Institute of Linguistics. The signal for it was given in an article published in *Pravda*. The author, B. Levin, charged that the Ukrainian Institute of Linguistics was a center of bourgeois nationalists and enemies of the people who wished to separate the Ukraine from Russia, to alienate the Ukrainian language from the "brotherly Russian tongue," and to bring Ukrainian closer to Polish and German. The article also named some members of the Institute—Olena Kurylo, Yevhen Tymchenko, Mykhaylo Dray-Khmara and Sheludko—as enemies of the Soviet state, thus sealing their fate.[34]

Following an intense campaign against the "bourgeois nationalist Ukrainian linguists," (mostly in the columns of the Party organ *Bilshovyk Ukrainy* and the linguistic journal *Movoznavstvo* [Linguistics]), the OGPU emerged as the supreme arbiter in this debate by arresting scores of Ukrainian linguists.[35] Among those who perished were such leading philologists of the day as Kurylo, Tymchenko, Sulyma, Synyavsky, Nakonechny, Nemchinov, Smerechynsky, and Dray-Khmara.

The End of a Theater

One of the few manifestations of pre-Revolutionary Ukrainian culture which the tsarist regime could not suppress was the theater. In the Ukrainian theater there survived a tradition of stubborn protest against oppression. In the nineteenth and early twentieth century this protest showed itself in the ethnographic and romantic melodramas from Ukrainian life which formed the repertory of the theaters of Sadovsky and Saksahansky. After the Revolution the role of this type of theater was exhausted and there followed a period of search for new theatrical forms. In the Soviet Ukraine two theatrical companies became prominent during the twenties. One was the Franko Theater (director and producer Hnat Yura) which continued to develop in the tradition of realism and did not experiment with new techniques. The other theater, formed by Les Kurbas (formerly of the *Molody Teatr*), was *Berezil*.

The talented producer Les Kurbas created in the *Berezil* a theater which reflected the latest Western European trends, above all expressionism. The function of the theater, according to Kurbas, was to disturb and stimulate the spectator,

---

[33] *Ibid.*, p. 10.

[34] B. Levin, "Kak orudovali burzhuaznye natsionalisty" (How the Bourgeois Nationalists Acted), *Pravda*, April 27, 1933.

[35] R. Smal-Stocki, *op. cit.*, *passim*.

not to tickle his palate. In order to perform this task, the theater had continually to employ new methods of dramatic expression. "No stabilization, no return to the old [forms] is possible," wrote Kurbas. "In our period of transition there is no style which can become stable."[36]

At the same time, Kurbas' theater provided scope for sharp criticism of the new Soviet philistinism and snobbery. This did not increase its popularity in many quarters, yet, owing to the support of Skrypnyk, *Berezil* became, in the late twenties, the most prominent Ukrainian theater. It received the title of "the first state academic dramatic theater."

Postyshev's direct attack on *Berezil* began on October 5, 1933, when Kurbas was asked to deliver a lecture on the theoretical and aesthetic principles of his theater in the Commissariat of Education. Following his expose, the Commissariat issued a resolution condemning Kurbas' views as "nationalist" and accusing *Berezil* of being linked with the "Vaplite" literary group and of perverting Soviet reality.[37] It also relieved Kurbas of his duties as the director of *Berezil*.

The last act of the Kurbas drama followed very soon. It was played by Kurbas in the best tradition of *Berezil*—courageously and with zest. From the accounts given by one of Kurbas' associates, an actor of the *Berezil* company, Yosyp Hirniak, we know of the last meeting between Kurbas and Postyshev. The dictator of the Ukraine attempted to win Kurbas over by every possible means of blackmail and persuasion, demanding that *Berezil* give up its principles and its criticism of the Party, and follow "socialist realism." In reply, Kurbas is supposed to have said that he would never betray the basic principle of his theater which was the unmasking of falsehood and evil, no matter what forms these might assume.[38]

Kurbas' intrepid stand cost him his career. He was arrested in November 1933, and deported to a forced labor camp, from which he never returned. *Berezil*, with its director and producer taken away, was subjected to further purges and renamed the *Shevchenko Theater*. Only after such repressive measures could Postyshev present "socialist realism" upon the Ukrainian stage, "socialist realism" represented by the plays of Korneichuk and glorifying Soviet rule in the Ukraine.

The Extent of the Purge

Postyshev seems to have acted with extreme thoroughness. He left nothing untouched; every field of cultural, scholarly or scientific endeavor in the Ukraine

---

[36] Kurbas, *op. cit.*, p. 162.

[37] "Postanova NKO Ukrainy pro kerivnytstvo teatru Berezil" (The Resolution of the People's Commissariat for Education on the Directorship of the Theatre *Berezil*), *Visti*, October 8, 1933.

[38] V. Khmuryi, Yu. Dyvnych, Ye. Blakytnyi, *V maskakh epokhy* (The Masks of an Era), Germany, 1938; also Yosyp Hirniak, "Birth and Death of the Modern Ukrainian Theater," in *Soviet Theaters; 1917-1941*, ed. M. Bradshaw, New York, Research Program on the USSR, 1954, pp. 250-338.

was affected by the purge. Here are some of the institutions which were investigated and "cleansed."

1) The Agricultural Academy (the director Sokolovsky, his deputy Slipansky, Academician Yanata, Professor Bilash, all perished in concentration camps).

2) The Research Institute of Soviet Construction and Law (the director Trublaevych, his deputy Tsarehradsky, and Professors Lozynsky, Romanyuk, Romanyshyn, Veretko, Chekhovych, Demchuk, Sarvan, Semenova, Nedbaylo, Pankyn, Poznyakovsky, Myroshnychenko, Li, Kulykov were all arrested and deported).

3) The Research Institute for the Deaf and Dumb (director Sokolyansky was arrested).

4) The Shevchenko Research Institute of Literary Scholarship (research associates V. Boyko, S. Demchuk, M. Panchenko, Ye. Shabliovsky, R. Verba, P. Kolesnyk, Yosypchuk, V. Koryak, Yu. Lavrynenko, V. Kubas, H. Kostiuk, V. Bobynsky, Yu. Savchenko, A. Paniv were all arrested and sentenced to long terms in concentration camps; director S. Pylypenko and research associates A. Richytsky, R. Shevchenko, K. Pivnenko, H. Protsenko, and S. Matyash were executed).

5) The Ukrainian State Publishing House (director Ozersky, editors Yalovy, Epik and many others were arrested).

6) The *Molody Bilshovyk* (The Young Bolshevik) Publishing House (director M. Hrytsay was arrested).

7) The *Rukh* (Movement) and *Knyhospilka* (Book-Union) Co-operative Publishing Houses were dissolved after several members of the staff were arrested.

The fine arts were not overlooked. The Ukrainian School of Painting, headed by Professor M. Boychuk, and most of the prominent painters of the day, V. Sedlyar, Padalka, Pavlenko, Shekhtman, Mizin, as well as the distinguished art critic Vrona, were silenced. They were accused of idealism, obscurantism, medievalism, nationalism and other sins.

The Ukrainian film industry was forced to follow a new policy in its productions. Famous Ukrainian films, produced by one of the best Soviet directors, the Ukrainian Dovzhenko, such as *Soil, Arsenal, Zvenigora*,[39] were withdrawn from circulation. Dovzhenko himself was sent to Moscow where he made films to suit the style of "socialist realism." Another promising director in the Ukraine, Kavaleridze, was also denied the opportunity to continue his own path. The loss of Dovzhenko, whose early films showed a promise of great and original art, was particularly grievous for Ukrainian cinematography.

[39] Lewis Jacobs (*The Rise of the American Film: A Critical History*, New York, 1939, pp. 322-23) has this to say about Dovzhenko: "His films have not had such advantages of widespread publicity and distribution as the other two directors [Eisenstein and Pudovkin] have enjoyed, but they are in many respects equally unique and valuable. To the structural contributions of his associates he has added a deep personal and poetic insight, which not only gives his films a mystical quality, but makes them utterly unusual ... So personalized are these pictures [*Arsenal, Soil*] that they achieve the emotional intensity of great lyrical poems; so concentrated, rich, and unexpected are their images that Dovzhenko, perhaps more than anyone else, can be called the first poet of the movies."

Chapter XIII

The Objectives of the Purge of the CP(b)U in 1933

On December 10, 1932, the Central Committee of the All-Union CP(b) resolved that a purge of the Party be carried out in 1933.[1] The most important features of the resolution were:

1) During the course of 1933 a purge of members and candidate members of the Party is to be conducted.

2) The admission of members and candidate members of the Party throughout the USSR, in the cities as well as in the villages, is to be halted on the day this resolution is published.

This communique alone did not provide a clue to the nature of the forthcoming purge. All the major Party purges of the past (1921, 1924, 1925, and 1929) had had in each case a different but specific purpose. In 1921, the purge was initiated to cleanse the Party of non-proletarian and criminal elements which had "accidentally" become members during the Civil War. In that purge 175,000 out of 600,000 Party members were cast out of the Party—almost 26 per cent.[2] The purge of 1924 was primarily directed against intellectually critical elements and against the recalcitrant new student generation, sympathetic to the Trotsky left opposition which was gaining strength at that time. In the following year the purge swept Trotskyite and leftist elements out of the village cells. In 1929 the purge chiefly affected the adherents of Bukharin. Now, in 1933, the purge once more had a specific purpose. In May 1933,[3] the Central Committee adopted a series of concrete directives for the execution of the purge and on May 22, 1933, Kaganovich revealed the Party's intention even more clearly in his speech to a Moscow Party meeting.[4]

According to him, there were five objectives in the current purge. The Party was to be cleansed of: 1) hostile class elements which had joined it by fraud; 2) open and hidden double-dealers; 3) those who broke the iron discipline of the Party; 4) degenerates, who had joined forces with the kulaks and the bourgeoisie; 5) bureaucrats, careerists, and self-seekers.

Directives more specifically concerned with the Ukraine came from Manuilsky, whom Trotsky once described as "the most repulsive renegade of Ukrainian

---

[1] Resolution of the CC All-Union CP(b), *Pravda*, December 11, 1932.

[2] L. Kaganovich, "O chistke partii" (On the Purge of the Party), *Pravda*, June 1, 1933.

[3] *Visti*, May 20, 1933.

[4] Kaganovich, *op. cit.*

Communism."[5] In his report before the Party organization in Kiev, delivered on May 28, 1933, Manuilsky supplemented Kaganovich's instructions.[6]

He pointed out the presence of undesirable elements in the CP(b)U and hinted that they were primarily those who came to the CP(b)U from other parties (Borotbists, Ukapists). "Here, in the Ukraine," said Manuilsky, "there are a number of institutions which have the elevated titles of academies, institutes and learned societies, which frequently harbor not socialist science but class-hostile ideology... The task of building Ukrainian culture is often entrusted to the double-dealers, men of-the hostile class... The national problem has been leased to former members of nationalist parties who failed to join organically with the Party."

He reminded the Ukrainian Communists that the only correct interpretation of the national problem in the USSR was that of Lenin and Stalin.

Manuilsky's words made it clear that as far as the CP(b)U was concerned, the purge was directed above all against the "nationalist deviationists."

In practical terms, the purge was aimed at Skrypnyk, the leader of Ukrainian Communist scholars and thinkers, at the former Borotbists and Ukapists and other "undesirable elements." The final objective of the purge was to make the CP(b)U entirely subservient to Moscow.

The extent of the purge in the Ukraine was indicated in Postyshev's speech before the November Plenum of the CP(b)U in 1933.[7] According to incomplete returns up to October 15, 1933, 27,500 members of the CP(b)U were expelled from the Party (23 per cent of the total membership). This general percentage was confirmed in 1934 by Sukhomlin, who told the Seventeenth Party Congress that in the four provincial Party organizations (Kiev, Odessa, Vinnitsa, Donets), 51,713 (out of a total of 267,907) members of the CP(b)U were purged.[8] In order to comprehend the magnitude of Postyshev's purge of the CP(b)U, it is necessary to bear in mind that most of those who were purged were not only expelled from the Party, but were arrested and liquidated.

[5] L. Trotsky, "Ob ukrainskom voprose" (On the Ukrainian Question), *Byulleten oppozitsii*, No. 77-78, 1939.

[6] D. Manuilsky, "Zavdannya chystky kyivskoi partorhanizatsii" (The Tasks of the Purge of the Kiev Party Organization), *Visti*, June 5, 1933.

[7] Postyshev's speech, *Pravda*, November 24, 1933.

[8] Kovalevsky, *op. cit.*, p. 150.

Chapter XIV

The Suicide of Mykola Skrypnyk

Not until the preparatory moves described above had been made, could Postyshev consider his chief objective: the destruction of the leader of Ukrainian Communism—Skrypnyk.[1] This was no easy matter. One can be sure that the Kremlin devoted a great deal of time to the planning of this campaign. Skrypnyk's popularity in the Ukraine was then at its peak. In any other but a totalitarian state it would have been almost impossible suddenly to undermine a man of such high reputation. In the Soviet Union, with complete control of the press and of all means of communication in the hands of the Party, this was possible.

The first salvo against Skrypnyk was fired by Manuilsky in the speech quoted earlier, which stripped the Ukrainian Communist leader of all honors and disclosed an alleged nationalist conspiracy among his subordinates. Much the same line was taken by Postyshev in his speech before the Plenum of the Central Committee of the CP(b)U on June 10, 1933.[2] He spoke of several workers in the cultural field who, apparently, had been uncovered as agents of foreign intelligence and enemies of the state, desiring to sever the ties between Russia and the Ukraine. All these men, charged Postyshev, were "hiding behind the broad back of the Bolshevik Skrypnyk." The Ukrainian nationalists, claimed Postyshev, had developed a whole series of pernicious ideas and doctrines (in philosophy—Yurynets, in literature—Khvylovy, in economics—Volobuyev, in linguistics—Krymsky and Tymchenko, in agriculture—Slipansky, in political theory—Shumsky) which were aimed at the abolition of the Soviet government in the Ukraine and the restoration of the capitalist regime. Skrypnyk, who not only abetted but in some cases actually defended such ideas, was therefore directly responsible for these deviations and was guilty of "serious errors."

Skrypnyk's reply to Postyshev before the Plenum of the Central Committee was never printed. Perhaps that fact alone, that the morning papers carried only Postyshev's accusations against Skrypnyk, showed how helpless the latter was. However, enough has seeped through of Skrypnyk's reply to Postyshev to show that the Ukrainian leader was not repentant. On the contrary, he defiantly rejected Postyshev's charge and delivered a lengthy speech accusing Postyshev of

---

[1] For biographical data see: "Moya avtobiohrafiya" (My Autobiography), in Skrypnyk, *Statti i promovy* (Articles and Speeches), Vol. I, Kharkov, 1930, pp. 5-17; *Entsiklopedichesky slovar russkogo bibliograficheskogo instituta Granat*, 7th ed. First and second fascicles of Part III, Vol. 41, supplement: "Deyateli Soyuza Sovetskikh Sotsyalisticheskikh Respublik v Oktyabrskoi Revolutsii," pp. 47-59; P. Fedenko "Mykola Skrypnyk," *Ukrainsky zbirnyk*, Munich, Institute for the Study of the USSR, No. 8, 1957, pp. 46-68.

[2] *Pravda*, June 22, 1933.

betraying the principles of internationalism and Leninism.[3] When these principles were faithfully adhered to, said Skrypnyk, the very same Ukrainian Communists who were now condemned, had been encouraged and regarded as indispensable. It was only because the most recent policy departed from these basic tenets of Communist doctrine that these people had come to be regarded as harmful.[4]

The impact of Skrypnyk's speech must have been great enough to make a unanimous decision by the Central Committee of the CP(b)U impossible. The Committee merely decided to ask Skrypnyk to submit a more detailed written exposition of his views to the Politburo of the CP(b)U. This he did, sensing that now the last battle between him and Postyshev was drawing near. We can only guess that in his stand before the Politburo Skrypnyk repeated his arguments, perhaps with greater force and determination. Yet his accusers refused to yield. They were determined to crush him, to force him to admit his mistakes, and thus to exonerate all their harsh measures. He was a stubborn old Bolshevik who would not play their game.

While the Politburo was deliberating over Skrypnyk (this lasted several weeks), Postyshev did his best to blacken Skrypnyk's name before the Ukrainian public. On June 14, before a Party meeting in Kharkov, Postyshev made a vitriolic attack on Skrypnyk in the latter's absence.[5] At the same time Khvylya, on Postyshev's orders, condemned Skrypnyk's activity as the former Commissar of Education and branded as "nationalist" his system of Ukrainian orthography,[6] which was replaced by a spelling system based on that of the "brotherly" Russian language.[7] On July 5, 1933, Panas Lyubchenko devoted his entire speech before the Plenum of the Central Committee of the Komsomol to the "unmasking" of Skrypnyk, undermining his prestige among the young Communists.

Seeing that the net was drawn closely around him, Skrypnyk, it was rumored, sought an interview with Stalin, but all his attempts to achieve this were unsuccessful. It was obvious that as far as Stalin was concerned, the fate of his old opponent on the national problem[8] was already sealed.

---

[3] This account is based on the verbal report of Skrypnyk's speech, given to the author by Ivan Kulyk, a prominent Ukrainian Communist, member of the CC of the CP(b)U, who heard Skrypnyk's defense.

[4] Skrypnyk's charges were confirmed by Postyshev in the latter's speech printed in *Pravda*, June 22, 1933. Answering Skrypnyk, Postyshev claimed that "the point is not that the situation has now changed. As has been said, earlier these men were suitable and now that the situation has changed they have become harmful."

[5] *Pravda*, July 3, 1933.

[6] Cf. Khvylya, *Vykorinyty, znyshchyty natsionalistychni korinnya na movnomu fronti* (To Uproot and Destroy the Nationalist Roots on the Linguistic Front), Kharkov, 1933.

[7] Cf. Yu. Sherekh, "Pryntsypy i etapy ..."; also R. Smal-Stocki, *Ukrainska mova v sovyetskii Ukraini*, Warsaw, 1936; Vasyl Chaplenko, *Bilshovytska movna polityka* (The Bolshevik Linguistic Policy), *Doslidy i materiyaly*, Munich, Institute for the Study of the USSR, Series II, No. 47, 1956, and, by the same author, "Shche pro natsionalno-movnu polityka bilshovykiv" (More about the National and Linguistic Policy of the Bolsheviks), *Novi dni* (New Days), Nos. 85-90, 1957.

[8] Stalin and Skrypnyk clashed over the nationality problem in the discussions at the Twelfth Congress of the Russian CP(b), in 1923.

On July 7, 1933, Skrypnyk took the stand before the Politburo of the CP(b)U. He read out the main theses of his view on the national problem. These were rejected unanimously. The members of the Politburo reminded Skrypnyk that he was there not to lecture to them but to admit his errors and to repent. He understood that what they wanted from him was unconditional surrender. Moreover, after his capitulation they would seek to use him as an example of the humiliated deviationist. Skrypnyk decided not to yield to these two demands. Realizing the hopelessness of his own position and seeing that the herd-like Central Committee was now ready to tear its old leader to pieces in order to please the new one, he made his decision. He would rather die than betray his belief and give himself up to be exhibited as a fallen Communist. He therefore told the Politburo that he needed more time to consider his final answer. This pleased his accusers who sensed the possible weakening of the defendant. When, at Skrypnyk's request, they adjourned the meeting until three o'clock in the afternoon, they felt that victory was within their grasp. For Postyshev, Skrypnyk's capitulation was of special importance; it would, as it were, legalize his regime and justify his use of terror. Without it, Postyshev's policy would appear to be blatant imperialism.

During the intermission, Skrypnyk went home to see his wife and son. Then he left for his office in the State Planning Commission. Locking himself in his room, he wrote a letter to the Central Committee of the CP(b)U, then took out the revolver which he had always carried since the days of the Civil War, and shot himself.

The news of Skrypnyk's suicide spread like lightning through the Ukrainian capital. The Central Committee and the Politburo were taken aback; they had not thought for one moment that Skrypnyk would choose this way out of his predicament. It was reported that, on hearing the news, Postyshev exclaimed: "Why ever did he do it?" Indeed, Skrypnyk had cheated him of an important victory.

On July 8, 1933, all the newspapers in the USSR carried an official obituary of Skrypnyk, issued by the Central Committee of the All-Union CP(b). This is what *Pravda* wrote:

> The CC All-Union CP(b) announces the death of a member of the CC All-Union CP(b), Comrade M. O. Skrypnyk, which was the result of suicide.
> Regarding the act of suicide as an act of faintheartedness particularly unworthy of a member of the CC All-Union CP(b), the Central Committee deems it necessary to inform members of the Party that Comrade Skrypnyk fell victim to the bourgeois-nationalist elements who, disguised as formal members of the Party, gained his confidence and exploited his name for their anti-Soviet, nationalist purposes. Having become entangled with them, Comrade Skrypnyk committed a series of political errors and upon realizing this he could not find the courage to overcome them in a Bolshevik manner and thus resorted to the act of suicide.

The Ukrainian *Visti* published, apart from the official obituary, a lengthy biography of Skrypnyk as well as condolences from the Central Executive Committee, the Council of People's Commissars and the Ukrainian branch of the All-Union Association of Old Bolsheviks.

Skrypnyk's funeral was held on July 8, at 2 p. m. Attendance was strictly limited. Apart from his closest relatives, only representatives of the Central Committee, the Trade Unions, and the writers' organizations were allowed to take part. The funeral cortege moved along Sumska Street, which was closed to pedestrians and all other traffic. At the same time, however, thousands of men and women were watching the procession from the windows and roofs of houses along that street. It was a spontaneous, silent manifestation of final respect paid by the Ukrainians to the man who had died defending their rights.[9]

The funeral orations were delivered by the chairman of the Ukrainian Central Executive Committee—Petrovsky, the Commissar of Education—Zatonsky, and the Commissar of Workers' and Peasants' Inspection—Sukhomlin.[10] All three speakers reproached Skrypnyk for having fallen victim to the nationalist conspiracy. "The nationalists," threatened Zatonsky, "who caught him in their net, will pay for it very dearly." These words sound particularly ironic if one bears in mind the subsequent fate of Zatonsky and Petrovsky. They were destined to inherit Skrypnyk's legacy of "nationalist deviation," and to become victims of Stalin's future purges of the Ukrainian Communists.

---

[9] The present author remembers very clearly how, immediately before the funeral, it was easy for anyone to enter the houses on Sumska and find a place at a window or on a balcony. All the doors were left open—a feeling of communal confidence and unity prevailed over everything else.

[10] *Visti*, July 9, 1933.

Chapter XV

A New Phase of Soviet Nationality Policy: The November Plenum of the CC CP(b)U

The General Situation

The November Plenum of the CC of the CP(b)U was held in an oppressive atmosphere. The Party itself was in the midst of a wholesale purge of "national deviationists" which, after Skrypnyk's death, became intensified. The country was still suffering from the effects of the widespread famine which, in the spring and summer of 1933, had swept millions of peasants to their graves. It was fortunate that the harvest of that year was good; it held a promise of relief from food shortages.

The November Plenum, held only four months after the last Plenum of the Central Committee, had the task of laying down and clarifying the new nationality policy of Stalin and Postyshev. It was imperative that by the time the next Party Congress convened in January 1934, the voices of all Ukrainian Communists should sound in unison. The atmosphere of terror and purge had to be cleared, and the confidence of the rank-and-file members of the Party had to be restored. The singleness of purpose and the unanimity so essential for the successful operation of the Soviet system had to be firmly established. Now that the chief opponents of Stalin's and Postyshev's policy in the Ukraine were either imprisoned or dead, the time was ripe for consolidation of the victory of the regime.

The Agenda of the Plenum

The chief problem before the Plenum was the national question. The very titles given to the speeches stressed that point. Kosior spoke on "The Results of and the Next Steps in the Application of the Nationality Policy in the Ukraine."[1] Lyubchenko's speech was entitled "Fire on the Nationalist Counter-Revolution and National Deviationists,"[2] while Postyshev's second address was on "The Soviet Ukraine—Indestructible Outpost of the Great USSR."[3]

Before these important pronouncements, Postyshev briefly reviewed the agricultural scene.[4] It was full of brilliant "achievements." The harvest, he claimed, had been gathered with the help of the 10,000 experienced Bolsheviks sent to the

---

[1] *Pravda*, December 2, 1933. For the resolution of the plenum see: *Pravda*, November 27, 1933.

[2] *Visti*, December 11, 1933; also *Chervony shlyakh*, No. 10, 1933.

[3] *Pravda*, December 6, 1933.

[4] *Pravda*, November 24, 1933.

66

villages to help the farmers, and the general picture was much brighter than the year before. This was chiefly due to the participation of cadres of experienced Bolsheviks, of workers from industrial areas, as well as of children, in harvesting the grain. Postyshev boasted that in 25 districts alone, over 550,000 children had been helping with the harvest. The independent farmer, Postyshev claimed, was losing ground, and over 80,000 farms had joined the kolkhozes in the previous ten months.

In the main, Kosior emphasised the cultural and educational achievements of the Soviet Ukraine, as well as her industrial progress. The resolution adopted by the Plenum after Kosior's speech read:

> On the basis of the Bolshevik industrialization and socialist transformation of agriculture, on the basis of the firm application of the general Party line and the waging of a ruthless struggle against opportunism and nationalism, it was possible to achieve the complete abolition of the former colonial position of the Ukraine and, interwoven with it, her cultural backwardness.

The resolution also stressed the growth of the Ukrainian proletariat and the strengthening of Soviet Ukrainian culture, which, it claimed, fortified the Soviet Ukrainian state.

How is one to interpret these claims? In one sense they were true. The cultural, scientific, and industrial achievements of the Ukraine were unquestionable. However, they were not at all the results of the new Party policy. They occurred in spite of it, not because of it, and neither Postyshev nor Kosior could lay claim to any credit for them.

The interesting question is why did they claim credit for them? How can we explain the tone of Ukrainian patriotism which pervaded the November Plenum? Why did Postyshev and his lieutenants speak so much about the great Soviet Ukrainian culture, about the Soviet Ukrainian state and her industrial might? There is only one possible answer. The ideas of a Soviet Ukrainian culture and state, fostered by Ukrainian Communists like Shumsky and Skrypnyk, Khvylovy and others, were so widely accepted by the public that it was impossible to uproot them. The murderers of Skrypnyk and Khvylovy decided, therefore, that their only chance of success was to hide themselves behind the ideas of the men they had destroyed and to masquerade as Ukrainian patriots. Otherwise their prestige among the Ukrainian workers and peasants might be undermined seriously. They had, therefore, assumed the role of defenders of Soviet Ukrainian independence. They did not hesitate to promote as their chief assistants Ukrainian Communists like Lyubchenko, Khvylya, Shlikhter, and Zatonsky in order to create the impression that their devastation of the Ukraine was for the sake of a brighter future and in the real interests of that country.

The CP(b)U and the Ukrainians Abroad

In order to reserve for themselves the right to be regarded as the sole protectors of Ukrainian independence and sovereignty, it was first necessary for Postyshev and his colleagues to repudiate and deny this right to anyone else. First of all they opened fire against the Ukrainian political parties abroad, especially those in the Western Ukraine, under Polish occupation. The aim was to show that the Ukrainian national forces which had emigrated after the fall of the Ukrainian People's Republic and which were continuing their activities abroad, as well as all other Ukrainian socialist, liberal or nationalist parties, could not claim to represent the Ukrainian people or to form a Ukrainian state. They were all, according to the Soviet version, agents and servants of foreign capitalist interventionists. A paragraph in the resolutions adopted by the November Plenum condemned the "interventionist campaign" conducted by all emigre and Western Ukrainian political parties.[5]

There is no doubt that the events of 1933 in Germany put the Soviet rulers on their guard. Hitler made no secret of his expansionist aims with regard to the Ukraine. "It must not be forgotten," said Kosior at the Plenum, "that the Ukraine occupies a forward position in the Soviet Union in relation to capitalist encirclement." Postyshev, too, stressed the "intense interest of international imperialism, especially that of Germany, in the Ukraine."[6]

A concerted effort was made by the principal speakers at the Plenum to establish the thesis that foreign imperialists and their servants, the Ukrainian nationalists, had succeeded in infiltrating the Soviet Ukraine. These enemies of the Soviet state, it was claimed, had penetrated the highest offices in the Soviet Ukrainian government and public life. "Nests of counter-revolutionary double-dealers," read the resolution, "were established in some People's Commissariats (Education, Agriculture, Justice), in institutions of learning (the All-Ukrainian Institute of Marxism and Leninism, the All-Ukrainian Academy of Sciences, the Shevchenko Institute, the Writers' Organization) and also in the district Party organs."[7]

Among the Ukrainian leaders abroad who were subjected to the severest attack were above all Andriy Livytskyi, the head of the Ukrainian People's Republic government in exile, as well as Volodymyr Vynnychenko, Mykyta Shapoval, Yevhen Konovalets, Isaak Mazepa, and Metropolitan Andriy Sheptytsky. A letter from Vynnychenko to the CC, CP(b)U, condemning terror in the Ukraine,[8] was read in support of these allegations.

Kosior furnished the Plenum with a detailed analysis of the alleged activities of these counter-revolutionary organizations in the Soviet Ukraine.[9] According to him the three main centers of subversion (apart from the SVU—the Union for the Liberation of the Ukraine) were: the Ukrainian National Center (UNTs:

---

[5] The resolution of the November Plenum, *Pravda*, November 27, 1933.

[6] *Pravda*, December 6, 1933.

[7] *Pravda*, November 27, 1933.

[8] Vynnychenko was a well-known Ukrainian writer and politician, who headed the anti-Communist Ukrainian government in 1917 and 1918. A copy of his letter to the CC of the CP(b)U is preserved in the archives of the Ukrainian Free Academy of Sciences in New York.

[9] Kosior's speech, *Pravda*, December 2, 1933.

Hrushevsky; Chechel; Shrah; Khrystyuk; Kosak; Yavorsky), the Ukrainian Military Organization (UVO: Maksymovych; Shumsky; Bilenky; Solodub—directed from abroad by Konovalets), and the All-Ukrainian Center of SR's. He further provided "evidence" of the dealings between the Ukrainian nationalists (Sushko and Yary) and the Nazis and revealed the plans which the latter had prepared for a German expansion into the Ukraine. "So you see, comrades," ended Kosior, "what kind of an 'independent Ukraine' this is—everything, from beginning to end has been sold and betrayed in advance to foreign capitalists."[10]

The "nationalist agents" in the CP(b)U who were arrested during Postyshev's regime (Shumsky, Maksymovych, Solodub, Yavorsky, Volokh, Yalovy, Richytsky, Avdienko, Sirko, Tur, and scores of others) were old Party members, representatives of three different trends of Ukrainian Communism—the Borotbists, the Ukapists, and the followers of Skrypnyk. A less numerous group of those who fell into disgrace were Communists from the Western Ukraine and the remnants of Hrushevsky's group of Social-Democrats. What Stalin and Postyshev were determined to destroy were the Soviet Ukrainian Communists of anti-Moscow orientation, not the mythical enemies from abroad. But the best way to discredit the Ukrainian Communists in the eyes of the public, and the best way to justify

---

[10] How fantastic the statements produced in support of the evidence fabricated by the GPU were may be seen from the following "confessions" of several witnesses in the trials as quoted in the above speech by Kosior:

Professor Vikul, accused of belonging to the Ukrainian National Center, testified that "beginning with 1927 the organization carried on work directed toward an armed uprising and intervention against the dictatorship of the proletariat in the Soviet Ukraine. This work was but one link in a chain of general plans of intervention against the Soviet Union. The political center of the organization, headed by Hrushevsky, made agreements as to common activities directed to overthrow the Soviet regime, with Russian Kadet circles, the Russian SR's, the Georgian Mensheviks, and the Belorussian nationalists."

Another defendant, O. Bukshovany, a Western Ukrainian Communist, was accused of being an agent of the UVO (Ukrainian Military Organization). "In the second half of February, 1933," he testified, "Bandrivsky informed me that Sushko (a well-known emigre leader of the OUN) had arrived in Berlin and that, together with Yary (another leader of the OUN), had talked with A. Rosenberg, a foreign affairs expert of the Hitlerite party and an advocate of intervention against the USSR. On the basis of this conversation, Sushko told me that Germany is following a sharp anti-Soviet course, is forming a coalition with Italy, England and France for the purpose of intervention against the USSR, and is exerting pressure on Poland to join the block. According to Sushko, Rosenberg believed that the UVO must undertake immediate action against the Soviet regime, since Hitler's coming to power and his aggressive course against the USSR have created favorable conditions for the setting up, with the help of intervention, of an independent Ukrainian state."

The defendant Pyrkhavka testified that "the Committee of the Ukrainian Socialist Revolutionary Party abroad, in Prague, fully concurs with the interventionist plans and conducts its activity jointly with Ukrainian fascists headed by Konovalets. Realizing that the local forces which could overthrow the Soviet regime and establish an independent Ukrainian state are inadequate, we also accepted the idea of intervention."

The defendant Kozoriz testified further that the interventionist plans for an "independent Ukraine" would mean division of the Ukraine between Poland and Germany. Thus the concept of an independent Ukraine, which might have had some appeal, was largely obscured.

the use of terror against them, was to associate them with foreign interventionists and nationalists.

A Definition of Nationalist Deviation

The November Plenum also served the purpose of making Skrypnyk the chief villain of Ukrainian nationalism. While in June,[11] and even shortly after his death, Skrypnyk[12] was described as having "committed errors," in November he was branded as a "nationalist degenerate" and the leader of the "nationalist deviation ... coming close to the counter-revolutionaries, working for the cause of intervention."[13] The resolution of the Plenum stressed that "unless the entire CP(b)U realizes the nature of the nationalist deviation headed by Skrypnyk, it is impossible to carry out the true tasks of Bolshevik Ukrainization and the international education of the masses."[14]

The speakers at the Plenum linked Skrypnyk's activities with the earlier deviation of Shumsky which, it was argued, had never been completely stamped out and had been continued by Skrypnyk. The constant reiteration of these charges in various speeches was aimed at creating the impression that Skrypnyk, the chief culprit, was caught red-handed as the master mind of nationalist counter-revolution.

What, then, was the complete synopsis of Skrypnyk's nationalist deviation provide by the November Plenum? It can be summarized in the following points:[15]

1) In his works and activities Skrypnyk betrayed Trotskyite, "Right-opportunist," and, above all, nationalist tendencies.

2) In works on Ukrainian history, Skrypnyk and his school idealized and glorified Ukrainian petty-bourgeois political parties, in particular those from the period of the Central Rada.

3) Skrypnyk advocated the separation of the Ukrainian language and culture from the Russian language and culture. In this and in his pro-Western orientation, he followed close upon the nationalist deviation of Shumsky and Khvylovy, which he continued.

4) Skrypnyk did not reject but on the contrary was in favor of the Latinization of the Ukrainian alphabet (cf. the nationalists Pylypenko, Kasyanenko and others) and in this way he deepened the gulf between Ukrainian and Russian culture.

5) Skrypnyk and his followers (Rubach, Sukhyno-Khomenko, Hirchak, Ovcharov) were of the opinion that there was a period in the history of the Revolution

---

[11] Postyshev's speech, *Pravda*, June 22, 1932.

[12] Popov's speech, *Visti*, July 12, 1933.

[13] Kosior's speech, *Pravda*, December 2, 1933.

[14] The resolutions of the November Plenum, *Pravda*, November 27, 1933.

[15] Cf. "Itogi ..." *Pravda*, November 27, 1933, and the speeches by Postyshev, Kosior, Popov, and Lyubchenko at the November Plenum.

when the CP(b)U had an incorrect attitude towards the national question in the Ukraine.

6) At the same time, they perverted the history of the CP(b)U, maintaining that the acceptance of the Borotbist and Ukapist platform by the CP(b)U was advisable.

7) Skrypnyk supported the forced Ukrainization of the non-Ukrainian proletariat in the Ukraine and through this stirred up national hostility between the working classes in the Ukraine and in Russia.

8) Skrypnyk upheld the struggle against imperialist Russian nationalism and encouraged local forms of nationalism (Ukrainian and others).

9) He regarded the Constitution of the USSR as insufficient because it failed to satisfy the needs of the national republics, and he fought for its modification.

10) Skrypnyk fought against the creation of the USSR as a single centralized federal state, with one foreign policy.

11) Skrypnyk and his school regarded the national question not as auxiliary to the class struggle of the proletariat, but as an independent and decisive factor in the struggle for the liberation of oppressed nations.

12) He belittled Lenin's theoretical teaching on the national question, and completely ignored Stalin's contribution to it.

13) He accused the All-Union CP(b) of inconsistency, diplomatic insincerity and of double book-keeping with regard to the national question.

14) Under Skrypnyk's auspices Ukrainian scholarship, literature, theater and art became permeated with nationalist theories which were aimed at the restoration of capitalism in the Ukraine.

15) Skrypnyk headed the nationalist conspiracy within the CP(b)U.

After such an analysis of Ukrainian nationalist deviation, proclaimed a "major threat to the Soviet state," the rulers of the Ukraine could unfold their own version of the theory of the "multi-national Soviet Union."

The Significance of the New Course in the Nationality Policy in the Ukraine

The November Plenum declared in its resolutions that "at the present time local Ukrainian nationalism represents the chief danger in the Ukraine."

This meant a most radical change in the Soviet nationality policy which, until then, had stressed imperialist Russian nationalism as the major threat to the Soviet state. The latter position, formulated by Lenin, was officially adopted by the All-Union CP(b) at the Twelfth and Sixteenth Party Congresses.[16] It was dictated

---

[16] "The chief danger at the present time is *great-power deviation* (italics in the original) attempting to alter the basis of the Leninist nationality policy and, under the flag of intervention, concealing an attempt of the moribund classes of the formerly dominant Great Russian nation to regain lost privileges." *Shestnadtsaty sezd VKP(b)* (Sixteenth Congress of the All-Union CP(b)), Moscow, 1931, p. 299.

It is interesting to compare the fate of the "great power" and "nationalist" deviationists. The former were especially numerous in the Ukraine, where many Russian Communists scorned

by historical developments in the non-Russian countries of the former Empire after the Revolution. These countries lived through a brief period of independence and their incorporation into the Soviet state could be achieved only after they were assured of the "right to self-determination." This concession to the non-Russian nationalities was granted not so much on principle as by necessity. Yet it was of the greatest practical importance for the political and cultural development of the non-Russian nationalities within the USSR, who tried to give this theoretical right some practical content. At no time prior to 1933 did the All-Union CP(b) dare to alter this tenet of the nationality policy, continuing, at least formally, to recognize the position adopted at the Twelfth Party Congress in 1923 ("all talk about the superiority of the Russian culture is nothing but an attempt to strengthen the domination of the Russian nationality")[17] as the correct one.

In the Ukraine, the CP(b)U declared that the chief obstacle to the solution of the national problem and the abolition of national inequality is the survival of Russian chauvinism, which has deep roots in the past.[18] Local nationalism was generally considered merely a reaction to Russian chauvinism.[19]

The new centralist course, set by Stalin, called for a change in the Bolshevik theory of the national question. It was Postyshev's task during the November Plenum to announce the reversal of the traditional Party point of view in the Ukraine. His statement must be regarded, therefore, as marking a turning point in the Soviet theory of the national question. It heralded a new wave of terror against "Ukrainian nationalism," which Postyshev so luridly painted in all its manifestations as the chief threat to the Soviet state.

That the new course in the nationality policy in the Ukraine was immediately interpreted as legalization of Russification may be seen from Popov's speech at the Plenum. In it he complained that the decision of the CP(b)U to publish two more newspapers in Russian[20] was taken in some quarters as a signal for an anti-Ukrainian course. Many others papers started publishing in Russian, and some papers in the Donets Basin became bilingual. This, of course, the Party could not officially approve. Popov, therefore, went on to declare that

"Ukrainization" and regarded the Ukraine as a province of Russia. One of the earliest Great Russian deviationists was the secretary of the CC CP(b)U, D. Lebed, the author of the "theory of the struggle of two cultures" which implied the dominance of Russian culture in the Ukraine. He was recalled from his post in Kharkov and sent to Moscow to become Deputy Chairman of the Council of People's Commissars. Another high official in the Ukrainian Commissariat of Justice, Malitsky, who opposed "Ukrainization" was also transferred from the Ukraine. None of the "Great Russian chauvinists" in the Party suffered the fate of the Ukrainian "bourgeois nationalists" who were arrested, shot, or driven to suicide.

[17] Leytes and Yashek, op. cit., p. 298.

[18] *XII sezd Rossiiskoi Kommunisticheskoi Partii (bolshevikov)* (The Twelfth Congress of the Russian Communist Party [Bolshevik]), Moscow, 1923, p. 446.

[19] Leytes and Yashek, op. cit., p. 296.

[20] Unfortunately, no stenographic report of this plenum has been published. For an account of Popov's speech see *Visti*, December 10, 1933.

the Party will mercilessly unmask all attempts to revise the decisions of the Twelfth and Sixteenth Party Congresses—attempts which are camouflaged by leftist phrases such as saying that the national question has outlived its usefulness, and that there is no longer any need for national republics.[21]

This only revealed that such "phrases" were now heard more frequently. To condemn them was necessary in order to keep the friendship of the Ukrainians who were still in the CP(b)U (Lyubchenko, Zatonsky, Khvylya, Chubar, Kotsyubynsky), without whose collaboration the new course of the All-Union CP(b) policy would be difficult to implement. Second, it exposed the double-talk of Popov and Postyshev. While in fact reversing the resolutions of the Twelfth and Sixteenth Congresses on the national question, they still continued to claim their adherence to them. After all, it was not they but those bad Ukrainian Communists who had changed the Leninist policy.

In summing up the November Plenum, it may be said that its resolutions lead us to the following conclusions:

1) The development of national consciousness and the economic and cultural growth of the national republics in the USSR prior to 1933 led to the formation of strong anti-centralist forces.

2) Stalin's main blow was delivered against the Ukraine which, because of its political, cultural, and geographic position, represented a serious threat to Soviet unity.

3) In order to conceal the real purpose of the purge and to make it acceptable to the people, the Party paraded under the slogans of Ukranian patriotism.

4) The task of the Plenum was to discredit once and for all the idea of an independent Ukraine.

5) To achieve this, Skrypnyk and his associates, as well as thousands of those arrested and deported on charges of nationalism, were declared to be instruments of foreign intervention.

6) Ukrainian nationalism was proclaimed the main threat to the Soviet state—a step which sanctioned the rule of terror in the Ukraine.

7) The debates of the Plenum showed that the new course revived the forces of Russification in the Ukraine.

8) The Plenum left no doubt that the new Party policy for the Ukraine was charted by Stalin,[22] who emerged as the immediate ruler of that country.

For Postyshev the Plenum marked the triumph of his regime, which now seemed firmly established.

---

[21] The resolutions of the November Plenum, *Pravda*, November 27, 1933, or *Visti*, November 26, 1933.

[22] M. M. Popov, in his speech (*Visti*, December 10, 1933) remarked that "our daily struggle with Ukrainian counter-revolution and nationalist deviation in the ranks of our Party, and particularly with the nationalist deviation headed by Skrypnyk, is guided by the direct leadership and assistance of the CC All-Union CP(b), and personally conducted by Comrades Stalin and Kaganovich."

Chapter XVI

Parade of the Victors and the Vanquished

The Twelfth Congress of the CP(b)U

Two months after the November Plenum, the Twelfth Congress of the CP(b)U was held in Kharkov January 18–22, 1934. *Pravda,* in a leading article, "To the New Victories of the Bolsheviks of the Ukraine" (January 18), stressed the "huge successes in all branches of life in the republic and the achievements of the new methods of management." This was the first time in four years that the CP(b)U had received any word of official recognition. The masters of the Kremlin were obviously pleased with the results of Postyshev's purges in the Ukraine.

The Twelfth Congress marked no new developments. Everything that had to be decided, had been decided previously at the November Plenum. The Congress itself served as an assembly of the "purged" CP(b)U and provided an opportunity for all the members to become thoroughly acquainted with the new Postyshev course. The significance of the Congress was made clear in the following ways:

1) It unanimously confirmed and approved the resolutions of the November Plenum, and thus legalized Postyshev's regime.

2) It revealed that the star of the first secretary of the CP(b)U, S. U. Kosior, was on the wane. The political report of the Central Committee of the CP(b)U was read to the Congress not by Kosior but by Postyshev,[1] which was indicative of the latter's ascendancy. The shift also meant that the apparatus of the CP(b)U was gaining the upper hand over its ideological leader. This change of emphasis in the Party command was further strengthened by Stalin at the Seventeenth Congress of the All-Union CP(b).

3) The Congress showed its profound reverence for and obedience to Postyshev. According to *Pravda,* as soon as Postyshev's name was mentioned by the first speaker, H. Petrovsky, "all rose and applauded."

4) The most characteristic feature of the Twelfth Congress was its spirit of servility to Stalin. This was particularly obvious in the resolutions of the Congress[2]

---

[1] "Sovetskaya Ukraina na novom podeme" (The Soviet Ukraine in a New Advance), *Pravda,* January 24, 1934; *Visti,* January 24, 1934. Postyshev's supremacy over Kosior was largely due to his "apparatus"—the men he brought with him from Moscow or found ready to serve him in the Ukraine. One heard a great deal about "Postyshev's men," just as one heard of "Kaganovich's men" or "Ordzhonikidze's men," all of them being, of course, "Stalin's men." Obviously, Postyshev, much more than Kosior, had learned from Stalin the secret of success.

[2] *Pravda,* January 23, 1934.

and the article "The Bolsheviks of the Ukraine—to the Central Committee of the All-Union CP(b) and to Stalin."[3] Here the obsequiousness of the Party organization in the Ukraine reached staggering proportions. Among the epithets given to Stalin in the report of the Twelfth Congress we find the following: "the greatest man of our time," "the beloved leader and teacher of the proletariat of the world," and "our great, beloved Stalin." The sentimental and turgid verbiage of the report was a true mirror of the new ruling bureaucracy in the Soviet Ukraine.

How was it possible that the same CP(b)U which had received Postyshev so coolly in 1933 now wildly cheered him? The purge of the Party in 1933 alone cannot explain this. The reason is to be found in the new balance of forces within the CP(b)U as it was established by Postyshev. While it would be true to say that from 1917 to 1933 the most influential group, although not on every occasion, was composed of the Ukrainian Communists from Skrypnyk's camp, strengthened by the Borotbists and Ukapists, now, after Skrypnyk's fall, their opponents in the CP(b)U, the Russophile centralist group, came to the fore. The representatives of "Russian great power chauvinism"[4] who formed the majority of delegates at the Congress felt that Postyshev's new policy offered them an amnesty. The fall of Skrypnyk, their greatest enemy, gave them a new lease on life. They offered, therefore, their unquestioned support to the new protector of Russian chauvinists and opportunists in the Ukraine, and the resolutions of the Twelfth Congress expressed a vote of complete confidence in Postyshev and approved, or rather applauded, his policy set out during the November Plenum. The only new decision of the Congress concerned the transfer of the Ukrainian capital from Kharkov to Kiev. This was done in order "to bring the government of the Ukraine and its central Party apparatus close to the major agricultural areas in the Right-Bank Ukraine, and also to speed up national cultural construction and Bolshevik Ukrainization, based on industrialization and collectivization."[5] The move was planned for the fall of 1934.

Having fulfilled the purpose of their existence (to endorse Postyshev and to glorify Stalin), the delegates to the Twelfth Congress dispersed to prepare for another spectacular puppet show—the Seventeenth Congress of the All-Union CP(b).

The New CP(b)U

What effect did Postyshev's policy have on the national Ukrainian cadres in the CP(b)U? By "national cadres" we mean all those Ukrainian Communists (the ex-Borotbists, ex-Ukapists, and Skrypnyk's group) who while subscribing to internationalism believed in the right to national self-determination. For them, true internationalism meant the end of national oppression everywhere. Any attempt

---

[3] "Bolsheviki Ukrainy—TsK VKP(b), tov. Stalinu," *Pravda*, January 20, 1934.

[4] Cf. Leytes and Yashek, *op. cit.*, pp. 293-303. In the history of the Party, the following members were branded as Russian chauvinists by the CP(b)U in the pre-Postyshev era: Dashkovsky, Lebed, Larin, Mashkin, Malitsky, Antonov-Ovseyenko, and Muravev.

[5] *Pravda*, January 22, 1934.

to abrogate national rights was viewed by them as a betrayal of the Revolution. It is important to bear in mind that this national trend in the CP(b)U did not only include Ukrainians. Apart from such prominent Ukrainian Communists as Skrypnyk, Shumsky, Khvylovy, Kulish, Lyubchenko, Kotsyubynsky, it counted among its supporters several Jews (Yakir, Ravich-Cherkassky, Kulyk, Lifshits, Feldman, Hurevych), Russians (Popov, Volobuyev, Shvedov), Germans (Shlikhter, Bon, Yohansen), Poles (Skarbek, Shmayonek, Kvyatek), and members of other nationalities.

It would be false to suggest that all these men were liquidated by Postyshev, although many of them were purged. Many of those who were retained in the CP(b)U became, as a result of the purges, loyal supporters of the new policy, while others (Zatonsky, Lyubchenko, Khvylya) were won over by receiving the posts formerly occupied by their rivals. Could it be possible that pursuit of personal gain blinded these men so much that they failed to grasp the nature of Postyshev's policy? Did they not realize that, as representatives of an independent tendency in Ukrainian Communism, they themselves might, in turn, come under attack from the ruling centralist clique?

There is good reason to believe that the Ukrainian Communists who remained were not blind to the facts, but that they regarded the situation in 1934 as not entirely hopeless for their cause. They took up Postyshev's challenge, confident that they would be better trustees of the Ukrainian Communist ideas than Skrypnyk had been in the past. They, therefore, participated actively in the reformed Central Committee, and were nourished by the pious hope of all fellow-travellers that a day would come when their point of view would find more sympathy in the Kremlin than the words of its own emissaries to the Ukraine.

The most gifted of these Ukrainian Communists, Panas Lyubchenko, succeeded in obtaining nomination as the Chairman of the Council of People's Commissars. Of the twelve members of the Politburo of the CP(b)U (Demchenko, Zatonsky, Sukhomlin, Chubar, Chuvirin, Kosior, Petrovsky, Sarkis, Yakir, Balitsky, Khataevich, Postyshev) only the last three were outspoken enemies of the Ukrainian Communists.

The Ukrainian group also had four (Shlikhter, Lyubchenko, Chernyavsky, Popov) out of five candidate members in the Politburo. It appeared therefore, that the Ukrainian Communists were not defeated; they still had numerical preponderance. This view proved to be quite illusory, and not very long afterwards all of them paid for this dream with their lives.

The new Politburo did not completely stem the growth of Ukrainian culture and literature. The forces of Ukrainian Communism revived after the blow they suffered in 1933. Moreover, they were strong enough to corrupt even men like Postyshev. For failing to hold the resurgence of these forces, Postyshev as well as all the prominent members of the Ukrainian government and the CP(b)U itself fell into disfavor in 1937.

Three days after the end of the Twelfth Congress of the CP(b)U, the Seventeenth Congress of the All-Union CP(b), known in official Soviet history as the "congress of the victors," was convened in Moscow. In his lengthy report to the Congress, Stalin repeated the conclusions he had reached at the January Plenum of the Central Committee of the All-Union CP(b).[6] They could be summarized in two points: 1) the USSR had been transformed from an agricultural into an industrial country, while agriculture itself had become mechanized and collectivized, 2) the socialist system had become dominant throughout the entire economy of the country. This led Stalin to remark that the USSR had "already entered into the period of socialism."[7]

It is outside the scope of the present study to scrutinize this contention. Let the economists and the historians pass judgement on whether Stalin's achievement should be called socialism, state-capitalism, or something else. Only after such an analysis will it be possible to say whether this claim to victory was justified.

There is no doubt, however, that the Seventeenth Congress marked a true victory for Stalin as far as his own position of power was concerned. This victory can be attributed to the following measures, taken previously, which were openly or tacitly approved by the Congress:

1) The liquidation of all opposition within the All-Union CP(b) with the help of a central Party apparatus—the new Stalinist bureaucracy.

2) The liquidation of all national deviations within the local republican branches of the All-Union CP(b), one of the most dangerous of them being Skrypnyk's group in the CP(b)U.

3) The designation of national deviation rather than Russian chauvinism as the chief threat to the Party, and the Soviet state. This marked a victory for the Russian centralist elements in the All-Union CP(b).

4) The centralization of the Soviet economy.

5) The successful terrorization of the peasantry and the working class. The peasants were chained to the collective system and the workers to the Stakhanov system.

The victory of the Stalinist oligarchy was confirmed in Stalin's own words. He told the Congress that this victory "did not just happen of itself," but was won by the Party. Its "power and authority," he admitted, "have grown to an unprecedented degree; now everything, or almost everything, depends upon it."[8]

---

[6] Cf. "Itogi pervoi pyatiletki" (Results of the First Five-Year Plan), *Pravda*, January 10, 1933.

[7] *XVII sezd VKP(b)* (Seventeenth Congress of the All-Union CP(b)), Moscow, 1934.

[8] *Ibid.*, p. 33.

The delegates to the Congress must have realized very well to just what an "unprecedented degree" the power and authority had increased. The new Party bureaucrats were only able to express their most fervent gratitude to their new leader. Following his speech they tried to outdo each other in glorifying bureaucratic absolutism and its creator, Stalin.[9] In voicing their adulation of the man whom Trotsky described as "the second-rate figure of the proletarian revolution,"[10] they pledged themselves to carry out faithfully anything their new master might decree.

---

[9] See, in particular, the speeches by Molotov and Kuybyshev (on the Second Five-Year Plan), and Kaganovich (on organization of the Party and the State).

[10] *Byulleten oppozitsii*, No. 46, December 1935.

PART TWO

The Consolidation of Stalinism in the Ukraine

Chapter I

Two Documents

In the struggle against his opponents, Stalin and his aides in the GPU-NKVD used the grossest fabrications and falsifications to produce faked evidence against the accused. The story of this forgery, which began in the early thirties and culminated in the well-known Moscow trials (1936–38), has been analyzed by many Western journalists, writers and scholars.[1] Two prominent defendants, Trotsky and Sedov, have themselves given their own interpretations of the trials and confessions.[2]

In all this voluminous literature, the nature of the accusations and the trials in the Ukraine is not discussed. This is all the more regrettable since the trials in the Ukraine which took place before the Moscow trials occupy a special place in the history of Soviet falsification and deserve careful scrutiny. In the ensuing pages an attempt will be made to study some aspects of the Ukrainian trials.

The first big political trial in the Ukraine was held in 1921. The defendants were a group of Ukrainian Social Revolutionaries, headed by Vsevolod Holubovych, a former member of the Central Rada, delegate of the Rada to the Brest-Litovsk peace conference, and onetime Prime Minister of the Ukrainian People's

---

[1] Nathan Leites and Elsa Bernaut, *The Ritual of Liquidation: The Case of the Moscow Trials*, Glencoe, The Free Press, 1954. Friedrich Adler, "Moskovsky protsess vedm" (The Moscow Witch Trial), *Sotsialistichesky vestnik*, No. 18-19, 20, 1936. A. Avtorkhanov, *op. cit.* Max Schachtman, *Behind the Moscow Trial, the Greatest Frame-up in History*, New York, Pioneer Publishers. *The Case of Leon Trotsky; Report of Hearings on the Charges Made Against Him in the Moscow Trials by the Preliminary Commission of Inquiry*, John Dewey, Chairman, Carleton Beals (resigned), Otto Ruehle, Benjamin Stolberg, and Suzanne LaFollete, New York, Harper Bros., 1937. Arthur Koestler, *Darkness at Noon*, London, Cape, 1941. George Orwell, *Animal Farm*, London, 1946. Victor Serge, *The Case of Comrade Tulayev*, New York, 1950. Josef Czapski, *Na nieludzkiej ziemi* (In an Inhuman Land), Instytut literacki, Paris, 1949. Ivan Bahriany, *Sad hetsymansky* (The Orchard of Gethsemane), 1950.

[2] L. Trotsky, *Moya zhizn*, II, Bereg, 1930; *Prestupleniya Stalina* (Stalin's Crimes), 1937; "Rech k amerikanskim rabochim" (A Speech to the American Workers), *Byulleten oppozitsii*, No. 54-55, March 1937; "Novaya moskovskaya amalgama" (A New Moscow Amalgam), *ibid.*; also *Byulleten oppozitsii* No. 62-63, 1938 (Trotsky's comments on the International Commission of Leon Sedov, *Livre rouge sur le proces de Moscou*, Paris, published in German under the title *Rotbuch über den Moskauer Prozess*; "Moskovskie protsessy—sud nad oktyabrem," *Byuelleten oppozitsii*, No. 52-53, 1936.

Republic.[3] Like the trial of the Russian Social Revolutionaries which took place a year later (1922) in Moscow, the Ukrainian trial was conducted without forgery or fabrication.

To compromise the former Social Revolutionaries, the victorious Bolshevik Party did not condescend to extorting or forging the evidence of the accused. The Moscow trial of the Russian Social Revolutionaries, in particular, was conducted in an atmosphere of unrestrained fair play.[4] Prominent Western lawyers and leaders of the Second International (Vandervelde, Liebknecht, and Rosenfeld) were invited to participate in the defense council. The defendants in both trials (Moscow and Kiev) bore themselves with dignity and spoke courageously, at times even quite outspokenly, in their own defense.

The Bolsheviks could afford to treat their conquered opponents with magnanimity. They did not ask for their heads;[5] on the contrary, they let them feel their helplessness and then released them. This is precisely what happened to Holubovych and his colleagues. Shortly after serving a mild sentence, Holubovych was appointed to a highly responsible government post, chairman of the Supreme Economic Council of the UkSSR, which he occupied until 1931. Another defendant, Professor S. Ostapenko, became one of the chief contributors to the government-sponsored periodical *Chervony shlyakh*, and professor at the Institute of National Economy in Kiev. Ivan Lyzanivsky, who was tried at the same time, later obtained the post of director of the *Rukh* publishing house.

It may, indeed, be said that the confidence which the Bolsheviks had in their victory and the support of the people which they had succeeded in obtaining by the highsounding promises of the Revolution were so great that neither lies nor force were necessary in combatting their opponents. Not until the people began to feel that they had been betrayed by the Bolsheviks and that the promises of the Revolutions were not being fulfilled did the Party resort to falsehood and fabrication. Through these devices it attempted to convince the people whose confidence it had lost.

The nationality policy pursued by Skrypnyk and approved by the Party up to 1929 offered an amnesty to former leaders of Ukrainian anti-Soviet parties as long as they were ready to collaborate with the Soviet Ukrainian regime. After 1930, Stalin's new course in the nationality policy made it necessary to remove from their posts all those who had once taken part in the creation of an independent

---

[3] D. Manuilsky and S. Dukelsky (ed.), *Delo chlenov Tsentralnogo Komiteta Ukrainskoi Partii Sotsyalistov-Revolutsionerov Golubovicha, Petrenko, Lyzanivskogo, Chasnyka, Yaroslava i dr.* (The Case of Holubovych, Petrenko, Lyzanivsky, Chosnyk, Yaroslav and Other Members of the Central Committee of the Ukrainian Party of Socialist-Revolutionaries), Stenographic Report, Kharkov, 1921.

[4] Cf. E. Kuskova, "V Yevrope li my" (Are We in Europe), *Novoe russkoe slovo* (The New Russian Word), December 6, 1952.

[5] It is true that Shumsky asked the penalty of death for Holubovych, yet this demand was made in sheer retaliation for a similar request which Holubovych had made when Shumsky was tried in 1919 (Cf. *Budivnytstvo radyanskoi Ukrainy*, I, pp. 134-35).

Ukraine. It was impossible to do this legally, especially as most of them had a long record of loyal work for the Soviet regime. These men could only be arrested and tried on false charges.

The first such attempt was made in the Ukraine in 1930, at the trial of the so-called Union for the Liberation of the Ukraine (SVU). During this trial, organized primarily to discredit certain scholars and intellectuals connected with the Ukrainian People's Republic,[6] the methods of fabrication and intimidation used later at the Moscow trials were given their first full-dress rehearsal. After this successful experiment the GPU created a new fictitious conspiratorial organization—the Ukrainian National Center (UNTs). The arrests which followed the "uncovering" of these two organizations removed many former leaders of the Ukrainian People's Republic, most of whom were not members of the Party. The same Ukrainian SR's who, in 1921, had received mild sentences and were subsequently released, were re-arrested on much more serious charges ten years later, and were all liquidated. After the arrival of Postyshev the attention of the Soviet police was primarily directed at the Ukrainian Communists, "the counter-revolutionaries with Party membership cards in their pockets."

The second phase in the story of Soviet incriminations is eloquently told by two "documents" which were described as "circulars of the Ukrainian underground." The first of these was made public by Popov in his speech at the November Plenum,[7] the second by the chief of the Ukrainian GPU, Balitsky, at the Twelfth Congress of the CP(b)U.[8]

Here are the most important parts of the first "document" as revealed by Popov. "I have now in front of me," said Popov, "a most interesting circular issued by the Ukrainian counter-revolutionaries. It made its way to the editorial office of *Komunist* by accident. It describes in detail the methods of struggle against the Soviet government. Here is the political platform of these counter-revolutionaries." The alleged document read as follows:

> Hitler's seizure of power showed the Ukrainian national-socialists the concrete path towards liberation from Muscovite occupation...
> Working deep in the underground we must be extremely careful, resilient, tenacious, shrewd, and more able than anyone else to exploit the situation to our advantage, especially since we possess continuity in our purpose and a more practical sagacity. In case of danger we should re-arm, disperse into single units, and, if this is insufficient, use all means to save the whole while sacrificing the parts. The main areas of our activity must be as follows: the workers' milieu in large industrial areas; technical and engineering personnel; the village (the kolkhoz, the sovkhoz, and the individual farm); the centers of technical agronomy; the industrial managers; co-operators; teachers; city proprietors; and lastly—those Communists who are sympathetic with us...

[6] Cf. Kovalevsky, *op. cit.*, pp. 72-108; Solovey, *op. cit.*, pp. 119-125; Smal-Stocki, *op. cit.*, pp. 102-103; Chamberlin, *op. cit.*, p. 57.
[7] *Visti*, December 10, 1933.
[8] *Visti*, January 21, 1934.

Collectivization, having destroyed the basis of agriculture, has forced out from the villages the most talented and cultured elements, which have taken refuge primarily in heavy industry. These elements, deprived of the right and opportunity to show their creative initiative in agriculture ... are the most suitable material for propagating our ideas ...

While working among non-Ukrainians, it is necessary to avoid the nationalist point of view; we must realize that the Ukrainian state cannot be built up by the forces of Ukrainization alone ...

In our illegal activities, it is imperative to disguise our thoughts by suitable words when addressing public meetings. The Communist slogan, "we create a Ukrainian culture national in form and socialist in content," we must change in practice to "socialist in form and national in content," meaning by "socialist form" this smoke-screen which should enable us to fight our enemies.

The GPU chief, Balitsky, revealed the following "document" proving Ukrainian conspiracy, which, according to his account, had fallen into his hands by accident:

Our program must be a compromise between the program of Hitlerism and that of the Ukrainian peasants ...

Social classes and a Ukrainian aristocracy must exist ... I am not a reactionary, but the nation should be heterogeneous ... The working class must be linked with the craftsman ... Industry must be denationalized. Real property should be reinstated ... The present moment calls for a consolidation of forces here and abroad ... Our present task consists in uniting all national forces—from the peasants to the socialists.

There followed directives for underground activities:

1) The underground headquarters should establish close contact with the agents abroad and with the interventionists.

2) It must preserve strictest conspiracy.

3) It must prepare the fighting cadres for the future war.

4) It must establish close contact with the anti-Communist underground in Georgia, Belorussia and the other republics of the Soviet Union.

The first thought which occurs after examination of these sensational "documents" is this: Which anti-Soviet center of Ukrainian resistance could have been responsible for their content? Neither Popov nor Balitsky gave a clear answer to this question. There were theoretically two possible sources from which these "documents" could have emanated: 1) the Ukrainian emigre parties abroad, 2) the alleged nationalist underground in the Soviet Ukraine.

Let us first survey the emigre Ukrainian political scene. It consisted of the following major political groups:

1) The Ukrainian Socialists, supporting, on the whole, the Ukrainian government in exile of the Ukrainian People's Republic headed by Andriy Livytsky.

The chief Ukrainian Socialist parties were the Social Democrats, the Social Revolutionaries, and the Social Radicals.

2) The Ukrainian National Democrats (UNDO), the most influential group in the Western Ukraine.

3) The Ukrainian Nationalists (OUN) headed by Yevhen Konovalets, ideological followers of fascism.

4) The Ukrainian Monarchists (USKHD, later SHD), followers of Hetman Pavlo Skoropadsky.

5) Small groups of Ukrainian ex-Communists (the Communist Party of the Western Ukraine, the Galician group, "Sel-rob,") which showed an anti-Soviet orientation after the liquidation of Shumsky's deviation in the CP(b)U.

There was no shred of understanding between these groups; on the contrary, they were all extremely hostile to each other. Therefore, it would be inconceivable that the secret "documents" could have been dictated by a coalition of these groups.

Which of these separate groups could have been responsible for the "underground circulars?" The first paragraph of the circular mentioned by Popov excludes the possibility that the three mentioned groups could have issued it. The Socialists, the Democrats, and the ex-Communists were openly anti-fascist and anti-Hitler. They were also sharply opposed to the Nationalists and on no occasion did any of them assume the appelation "national-socialists," mentioned in Popov's speech. This term was also avoided by the Nationalists, and a careful check of their literature shows that it did not appear in any of their writings. Although the Nationalists often borrowed their theory from the arsenal of fascism, they could not be described as mere dupes of Hitler. What makes it improbable that they were responsible for the circular is the appeal to the Soviet workers, and the ex-Communists. Such an orientation was foreign to the Ukrainian Nationalists (OUN).

Popov's "document" remains, therefore, full of inner contradictions and does not correspond to the program of any single Ukrainian emigre group.

The authenticity of the "document" produced by Balitsky is also extremely doubtful. It contains what may best be described as the "restoration program" for the Ukraine. Yet the principles of the restoration, (the denationalization of industry, the return of the Ukrainian aristocracy and of real property, the heterogeneity of the nation) could hardly come from a single political party. What makes the whole program particularly questionable is the phrase "I am not a reactionary but I think that the nation should be heterogeneous." This personal form of address would hardly occur in a political program; it is more likely to have come from the report of a Soviet agent on a visit to one of the Ukrainian emigre groups. There is good reason to believe that such agents operated quite successfully.[9]

Is it possible that these secret "documents" originated in the Soviet Ukraine? In answering this question one must rather rely upon one's judgment of Soviet reality than on the speculative evidence for or against such a possibility. It is as difficult to imagine that the Ukrainian Communists (Skrypnyk, Shumsky, Khvylovy) were capable of being nationalist agents as it is difficult to believe that men like Bukharin, Trotsky, or, for that matter, Beria were tools and dupes of foreign agents. All evidence based on an analysis of their outlook and activities as well as on the opinions of all those in the West who wrote on the Soviet trials supports the view that the Soviet charges in the Ukraine were a part of the "greatest frame-up in the world." The "documents" of Popov and Balitsky have no relation to the historical situation in the Soviet Ukraine and are the products of the GPU and its masters.

Why, then, were they made public and in this particular form? Simply because it was necessary to evoke the specter of a wide Ukrainian conspiracy, involving all parties and groups, in order to dispose of anyone whom the GPU wanted to destroy. Popov's and Balitsky's "programs" supplement each other. The first is more general and "suited" to the "national deviationists" in the CP(b)U, the second, more specific in its formulation, was "suited" to those who did not fit the first category. Both postulate a conspiracy to overthrow the Soviet regime in the Ukraine, to separate the Ukraine from Russia, and to restore capitalism. These were the charges made against all those Ukrainian Communists and non-Communists who perished in 1932–34. The "documents" were invented in order to furnish "evidence" that these charges were true.

---

[9] Cf. *Ukrainsky derzhavnyk, kalendar-almanakh* (Ukrainian Statesman: calendar, almanac), (1942), Berlin, pp. 74-79. Yaroslav Kutko, "Pekelna mashyna v Rotterdami" (The Time Bomb in Rotterdam), *Narodnya volya* (The People's Will), September 25, 1952.

Chapter II

Ways and Means of Terror

Alleged Underground Organizations in the Ukraine, 1930—33

If there were "circulars emanating from the Ukrainian nationalist underground," there must have been an underground. According to the reports in the Soviet press and the statements by Party leaders, many such underground organizations existed in the Ukraine, but absolutely none of them actually existed in the form in which they were alleged to exist. They were all invented; not one of them was real. Their invention may have been based on men who could have created them, but in the form in which they were "uncovered" they were all mythical. It is important to understand the problem, since it helps us to understand the nature of the Soviet regime in the Ukraine. Soviet sources mention the existence of fourteen such organizations in the years 1930–37, of which three were "uncovered" before 1932 while the others were liquidated between 1932 and 1937. Soviet publications[1] make mention of the following organizations. (The last date following the name of the organization is that of its liquidation.)

1) The Union for the Liberation of the Ukraine (SVU-Spilka vyzvolennya Ukrainy)—1930;

2) The Union of Ukrainian Youth (SUM-Spilka Ukrainskoi molodi)—1930;

3) The Ukrainian National Center (UNTs-Ukrainsky natsionalny tsentr)—1931;

4) The Union of the Kuban and the Ukraine (Soyuz Kubani i Ukrainy)—1929–32;

5) The All-Ukrainian SR Center, or, Organization of the Ukrainian SR's (Vseukrainsky eserivsky tsentr—orhanizatsiya ukrainskykh eseriv)—1933;

6) The Counter-Revolutionary Sabotage Organization (led by Konar)—1933;

7) The Ukrainian Military Organization (UVO-Ukrainska viyskova orhanizatsiya)—1933;

8) The Polish Military Organization (POW-Polska organizacia wojenna)—1933;

9) The All-Ukrainian Borotbist Center (Vseukrainsky borotbystsky tsentr)—1928–35;

10) The Ukrainian White Guard Terrorist Center (Ukrainsky tsentr bilohvardeytsiv-terorystiv)—1934;

[1] See the following newspapers and periodicals for 1930-39: *Pravda, Izvestiya, Visti, Bilshovyk, Bilshovyk Ukrainy, Komunist.*

85

11) The Terrorist Group of Professor Zerov (Terorystychna hrupa profesora Zerova)—1935;

12) The Bloc of Ukrainian Nationalist Parties (Blok ukrainskykh natsionalistychnykh partiy)—1932–36;

13) The Trotskyite Nationalist Terrorist Bloc (Trotskistsko-natsionalistychny terorystychny blok)—1935;

14) The Ukrainian Trotskyite Center (Ukrainsky trotskistsky tsentr)—1936;

15) The National Fascist Organization of the Ukraine (Natsionalistychna fashystivska orhanizatsiya Ukrainy)—1935–37.

The most striking feature of all these "underground" organizations was that their alleged existence was not supported by any documentary evidence. Apart from the two "documents" discussed in the previous chapter, the GPU-NKVD produced no other evidence.[2] The only evidence of the existence of these conspiracies was the charges made by the Soviet authorities and the confessions of the alleged members of these organizations during their trials. Those interested in the validity of confessions obtained at Soviet trials may be referred to the large body of literature which is available on the subject, especially to the study of the Moscow trials edited by John Dewey.[3] The conclusion arrived at by most Western students of the problem involved is that the presentation of evidence at the trials had little or no relation to truth, and that the trials were not conducted in accordance with established juridical procedures.

The lack of published documentary evidence bearing on the programs and aims of the liquidated organizations is significant. It is in itself indicative of the fictitious nature of these conspiratorial bodies.

It may be difficult to understand how any government could insist on the existence of fabricated networks of fictional organizations with thousands of alleged members who paid for these accusations with their very lives, and all without any protest from public opinion. If one recalls the famous case of Beyliss[4]

---

[2] At the trial of the Union for the Liberation of the Ukraine (1930) the prosecution produced a letter allegedly written by the prominent Ukrainian emigre, Professor Levko Chykalenko, to the chief defendant, Professor Yefremov. Professor Chykalenko at the time denied in the Ukrainian press (*Dilo* [Action], Lvov) that he had ever written the letter. We may, therefore, conclude that this letter falls into the same category as the circulars revealed by Popov and Balitsky. A defendant in the trial of the SVU, K. Turkalo, who is now an emigre, reports in his account of the proceedings that the existence of such a letter was admitted by the accused, Academician Yefremov, but denied by another accused, Hermayze. When, during the intermission, Hermayze asked Yefremov why the latter had testified as he did, the answer he received was "That's what I wrote down and now it is too late to deny it" ("Sorok pyat" [The Forty-Five], *Novi dni*, No. 34, 1952, p. 5.).

[3] *The Case of Leon Trotsky; Report of Hearings on the Charges Made Against Him in the Moscow Trials by the Preliminary Commission of Enquiry*, New York, Harper Bros., 1937.

[4] Beyliss, a Jew, was accused of the ritual killing of a Christian boy, A. Yushchinsky. The trial was held in October 1913 in Kiev. After persistent attempts by the tsarist prosecution to convict Beyliss, the latter was exonerated.

in tsarist Russia, or the *affaire Dreyfus* in France, one must concede that, horrible though these false incriminations of innocent people were, they were nevertheless uncovered and rectified, largely through the efforts of the independent press and of the general public both in Russia and in France. The government of autocratic tsarist Russia was responsive to public opinion. But in the Soviet Union the people had no means of expressing their views. The most elementary right of comment on the actions of their government was denied them.

Secure in its absolute and unquestioned authority, the Soviet government could, therefore, perpetrate the worst crimes, organize enormous travesties of justice, and sentence hundreds of thousands of people to death on the basis of faked evidence, without the slightest criticism or opposition from public opinion.

In the great Soviet political trials of the thirties, three main phases may be clearly discerned:

1) Official announcement of the uncovering of a counter-revolutionary plot and organization;

2) Mass arrests of people who are branded in the press as nationalists, Trotskyites, or enemies of the people;

3) Parade of the accused on trial, ready to confess to any crimes.

This pattern alone, as well as the absence of any fair method of investigation, trial, or defense, and the fact that no true documentary evidence was published, deprived such trials of all appearance of justice. It is also noteworthy that of the fourteen "underground" organizations uncovered by the NKVD, only one (The Union for the Liberation of the Ukraine) was given a public trial. The other trials were held in secret. While it would be wrong to assume that forged evidence is less likely to be presented at public than at secret trials, the fact that thirteen "underground organizations" in the Ukraine were disposed of without a public hearing is of some significance.

Our conclusion, therefore, must be that in the form in which they were "uncovered" the "nationalist underground organizations" in the Ukraine were purely mythical, invented by the Soviet authorities for reasons we have discussed earlier.

Does this conclusion mean that there was no resistance to the Soviet regime in the Ukraine? Certainly not. The resistance was widespread and fierce, sometimes flaring up in peasant rebellions, but it was not carried on through underground organizations only. It was a spontaneous resistance by the people against their oppressors and it was not controlled from abroad. No emigre group claimed responsibility for the direction of this resistance.[5] No recent refugees (since 1943) from the Soviet Ukraine have declared that in the thirties they received orders from abroad.

Apart from the spontaneous resistance of the Ukrainian people there was also wide-spread and well-organized resistance to Moscow's policy in the Ukraine by Soviet Ukrainian writers, scholars and intellectuals, encouraged in their con-

---

[5] The claims made by some Ukrainian Nationalists are discussed later.

tribution to independent Ukrainian culture by Ukrainian Communists like Skrypnyk. There is little doubt that it was this resistance which irked the Kremlin most. It was finally destroyed after the participants had been falsely accused of collaboration with foreign interventionists and "underground" organizations.

Having denied the existence of the alleged underground organizations, is it possible to dismiss them entirely? In spite of their unreality, there must have been some purpose in inventing each one of them, as far as the NKVD plans were concerned. We shall attempt, therefore, to analyze them on the basis of their membership and ideology, not in relation to the Ukrainian resistance but to the policy of the Kremlin. Perhaps, after all, the various groups which were liquidated had some significance in this respect.

The Union for the Liberation of the Ukraine. The uncovering of this alleged organization, which was followed by the arrest of prominent Ukrainian scholars and intellectuals, coincided with the beginning of Stalin's supremacy. In April 1929, the Sixteenth Party Conference adopted Stalin's "optimum variant" in the fulfillment of the Five-Year Plan.[6] In order to make the realization of this "optimum variant" possible, it was necessary to make certain preparations. The ground was cleared for the introduction of the "optimum variant" by mass arrests of its alleged opponents. Apart from "saboteurs," scores of intellectuals were also arrested.

Kharkov, the capital of the Ukraine, witnessed, in 1930, the sensational trial of forty-five persons accused of belonging to the Union for the Liberation of the Ukraine and its affiliate, the Union of Ukrainian Youth.[7] The trial lasted from March 9 to April 20.

The defendants were mostly prominent Ukrainian leaders of the pre-revolutionary and revolutionary periods. They were the former Social-Democrats, Social-Federalists, Social-Revolutionaries and politicians who were not Party members, former leaders of the Ukrainian People's Republic.[8] There were some younger men among the group, too, mostly pupils of the older generation. At the time of their arrest the leaders of the group occupied prominent posts in learned institutions and universities. After seeing the collapse of their dreams of an independent Ukraine in 1919, they did not emigrate, but stayed on and devoted themselves to scholarship. All of them were prominent in the cultural life of the

---

[6] *Short History of the CPSU(b),* pp. 282-83.

[7] Cf. Solovey, *op. cit.,* M. Kovalevsky, *Ukraina pid chervonym yarmom* (The Ukraine under the Red Yoke), Warsaw, 1936; K. Turkalo, "Sorok pyat," *Novi dni,* November, December, 1952, and January, February, March, 1953. L. Akhmatov, "Za radyansku literaturu" (For a Soviet Literature), *Chervony shlyakh,* No. 4, 1930, pp. 151-157. M. Skrypnyk, "Kontrrevolyutsiyne shkidnytstvo na kulturnomu fronti" (Counter-Revolutionary Sabotage on the Cultural Front), *Chervony shlyakh,* No. 4, 1930, pp. 138-50. N. Pavlushkova, "Moye slovo pro protses SVU ta SUM'u" (My View of the Trial of SVU and SUM), *Novi dni,* Nos. 49, 50, 51, 1954; V. I. Hryshko, "Istoriya moyei SVU" (The History of My SVU), *Ukrainsky Prometey* (The Ukrainian Prometheus), Nos. 7-28, 1955. *Spilka vyzvolennya Ukrainy; stenohrafichny zvit* (The Union for the Liberation of the Ukraine: Stenographic Report), Kharkov, 1930.

[8] Cf. John S. Reshetar, Jr., *op. cit.*

Soviet Ukraine. Among them were the well-known scholar and literary historian, Academician Serhiy Yefremov; the historian, Yosyp Hermayze; the literary critic, Andriy Nikovsky; the writer, Lyudmyla Starytska-Chernyakhivska; the writer, Mykhaylo Ivchenko; the linguist, Hryhoriy Holoskevych and several other associates of the Academy of Sciences in Kiev. None of them were Marxists, and to charge them merely with having been previously engaged in active support of Ukrainian independence would have been insufficient to discredit them before the public and to impose long-term sentences on them. They were, therefore, accused of being counter-revolutionaries, and of plotting to overthrow the regime. Two students at Kiev University, M. Pavlushkov and B. Matushevsky, were also sentenced for alleged anti-Soviet activities. The main purpose of the trial was to destroy and to discredit the old generation of Ukrainian democrats and to put a end to their influence on Ukrainian youth. But the organization had never existed in terms of the purposes of which it was accused.

The Ukrainian National Center. Like the first group, the Center comprised former active participants in the Ukrainian independence movement, and like the first group, its existence was mythical in terms of the purposes of which it was accused. According to official Soviet accounts and to reminiscences of one of the survivors, the Center was headed by the former chairman of the Central Rada, Professor Mykhailo Hrushevsky, while most of the members were former Ukrainian SR's.[9]

Among the members of the Center were: a professor of law, M. Shrah; the historian, P. Khrystyuk; the former Minister of Communications in the government of the Ukrainian People's Republic and the author of a well-known book on construction, then a professor at Kharkov Construction Engineering Institute and Kharkov Institute of Construction Technology, M. F. Chechel; a former general in the Ukrainian Galician Army, H. Kosak; the former Prime Minister of the Ukrainian People's Republic, V. Holubovych; a professor of law, V. Mazurenko; the director of the publishing co-operative *Knyhospilka*, I. Lyzanivsky (the last three were prominent SR's); and D. Koliukh, a Social-Democrat, formerly Minister of Supply in the government of the Ukrainian People's Republic, then chairman of the union of Ukrainian consumer co-operatives.

Apart from these men who were the alleged ringleaders of the Center, thousands of other and little-known intellectuals, workers, teachers, and peasants were arrested on the same charges. Neither the accounts by Postyshev and Kosior nor the reminiscences of Buzhansky tell us anything about these unknown rank-and-file members of the Center, except that they mention that they were numerous. According to Kosior, the Center had its men in the CP(b)U, Mykhaylo Levytsky being one of them.

The reason for destroying the men allegedly implicated in the Center was the same as in the case of the Union for the Liberation of the Ukraine. The new course

---

[9] Postyshev's speech at the Twelfth Congress of the CP(b)U, *Visti*, January 24, 1934. O. Buzhansky, *op. cit.*

of Soviet policy, initiated by Stalin, made it imperative to remove all former members of the Ukrainian republican democratic government. The group gathered around Professor Hrushevsky had come back to the Soviet Union in 1924 with their leader. Their return was undertaken with the approval and assurances of the Soviet government. The rulers of the USSR in 1924 (Trotsky, Rykov, Bukharin), as well as the Soviet Ukrainian leaders (Shumsky, Chubar, Zatonsky, Skrypnyk), allowed Hrushevsky and his group into the Soviet Ukraine under the condition that they would occupy themselves with scholarship alone. They were given all necessary facilities to continue their researches and, for their part, Hrushevsky and his colleagues never renounced their right to maintain freedom of thought and criticism within the limitations of the Soviet constitution.[10] The contribution made by this group to the development of Soviet Ukrainian culture and scholarship was generally acknowledged and was in line with the cultural policy of the twenties. It was Stalin's new course which called for a radical change in the attitude to them.

The Union of the Kuban and the Ukraine. Although there is no mention of this organization in the Soviet press, post-war emigre sources provide information to the effect that the Soviet authorities charged that such an organization existed.[11] Semen Pidhayny testifies in his reminiscences that in 1933 he was sentenced to eight years in a concentration camp for belonging to it, adding that it was purely "mythical."

Why should the NKVD invent the Union of the Kuban and the Ukraine?

The Kuban region comprises the North-Caucasian territories and borders on the Ukraine. The population of the area was 2.7 million in 1937,[12] of whom almost a million were Ukrainians.[13] Apart from ethnic ties there are also historical links between the Ukraine and the Kuban. After 1775, the remnants of the Ukrainian Zaporozhian Cossacks were settled in the Kuban.[14] Linguistically and culturally the people of the Kuban felt strong bonds with the Ukrainians. During the 1917 Revolution, when in all the Ukrainian border lands (Galicia, Bukovina, Transcarpathia) there was a desire to unite, there was also a powerful Ukrainian

---

[10] Cf. M. Hrushevsky, "Vidkryty lyst holovi Rady Narodnikh Komisariv Ukrainskoi Sotsyalistychnoi Radyanskoi Respubliky Kh. H. Rakovskomu" (An Open Letter to the Chairman of the Council of People's Commissars of the Ukrainian Socialist Soviet Republic, Kh. H. Rakovsky), *Boritesya-poborete* (Fight and You Will Conquer), Vienna, No. 10, 1921, pp. 1-8; "Zapyska zakordonnoi delehatsii UPSR dlya providnykiv Rosiyskoi Komunistychnoi Partii pro vidnosyny Ukrainy i Sovetskoi Rosii 19. VII. 1920" (A Note by the Foreign Delegation of the UPSR to the Leaders of the Russian Communist Party Concerning Relations between the Ukraine and Soviet Russia, July 19, 1920), *Boritesya-poborete*, No. 4, 1920, pp. 59-63 (the note is signed by M. Hrushevsky and O. Zhukovsky); Mykola Shrah, "Slova i dila sotsyalistiv v natsionalnii spravi" (Words and Deeds of the Socialists Concerning the National Problem), *Boritesya-poborete*, No. 2, 1920, pp. 18-49.

[11] Semen Pidhayny, *op. cit.*, also his *Islands of Death*, Toronto, Burns, McEachern, 1953.

[12] *Bolshaya sovetskaya entsiklopediya*, XXXV, 1937, p. 361.

[13] *Entsyklopediya ukrainoznavstva* (The Ukrainian Encyclopedia), Munich, New York, 1949, I, p. 29.

[14] *Ibid.*, I, 459-65.

movement in the Kuban. After 1923 the Kuban was not included in the Ukrainian SSR and, having been made a province of the RSFSR, it lost direct contact with the Ukraine. However, this did not put a halt to Ukrainian cultural and social life there. During the twenties, the Ukrainians in the Kuban showed signs of significant cultural and educational growth. The early Soviet nationality policy did not arrest this development. Many Ukrainian schools were established in the Kuban and a Ukrainian Pedagogical Institute was formed in the provincial capital of Krasnodar, and a Pedagogical Technical School in Poltavskaya. Ukrainian educational institutions in the Kuban were administered by the Ukrainian Commissariat of Education in Kharkov, headed by Skrypnyk. The Resolution of the CP(b)U on the "Results of Ukrainization," issued in 1926, stressed the need for further cultural work among the Ukrainian minority in the RSFSR.[15] This referred, above all, to the Kuban.

Stalin's new policy made no provision for furthering the growth of the Ukrainian Kuban. On the contrary, it was sharply opposed to it, having revived the policy of Russification and centralization. The Kuban intelligentsia was to share the fate of the Ukrainian intelligentsia; it was earmarked for destruction as one of the centrifugal forces in the USSR.

The Kremlin's campaign against the Kuban region started in the Ukraine. In December 1929, at the time of the arrests of the Ukrainians accused of participating in the Union for the Liberation of the Ukraine, many Ukrainian students and professors of Kuban descent (Ivan Teliha, Vera Hubaylo, Orel) were also detained. They were not charged with belonging to the Union for Liberation; their case was separate. The arrests of the Ukrainians from the Kuban region continued in the early thirties. Early in 1933 the following prominent Kuban leaders fell victim to the NKVD: the old Bolshevik, Yuriy Sambursky, who was the envoy plenipotentiary of the Ukrainian SSR in Moscow and was responsible for the Ukrainian minorities in the RSFSR; Semen Pidhayny, a young scholar working in one of the museums in Kharkov; most of the professors in the Pedagogical Institute in Krasnodar and the Pedagogical Technical School in Poltavskaya (Ivan Shalya, P. Horetsky, Petro Hrebinnyk, Shchepotev). According to one source, the staff and students of the Pedagogical Technical School were deported, together with the 30,000 inhabitants of the Poltavskaya *stanitsa* (Cossack settlement) in October 1932.[16] Many teachers of the Ukrainian elementary schools in the Kuban perished in the so-called "Kuban Operation" in 1932–33.[17] Russian replaced Ukrainian as the language of school instruction.

[15] Leytes and Yashek, *op. cit.*, pp. 293-303.

[16] Fedir Rogiles, "Z nahody 17 richya znyshchennya stanytsi Poltavskoi" (On the Seventeenth Anniversary of the Destruction of the Poltavska Settlement), *Vilna Kuban* (The Free Kuban), Toronto, No. 2, December 1949; H. Kubanska, *Ternystym shlyakhom, spohady* (Along a Thorny Path-Recollections), Winnipeg, 1948; D. Solovey, *op. cit.*

[17] Vadim Denisov, "Massovye aktsii KRU i SPU NKVD" (The Mass Actions of the KRU and SPU of the NKVD), *Narodnaya Pravda*, No. 9-10, September, 1950, pp. 29-30. H. Kubanska, *op. cit.*, p. 56; Solovey, *op. cit.*, pp. 227-28. Pidhayny, *Ukrainska inteligentsiya na Solovkakh*, pp. 53, 69.

The Union of the Kuban and the Ukraine, which, according to one of its alleged members who survived, was fictitious, was created in order to justify the use of terror in implementing Stalin's new policy of Russification and centralization.

The All-Ukrainian SR Center (Organization of the Ukrainian SR's)—1933. The uncovering of this organization was first reported by Kosior at the November Plenum. He described it as having been "detected only recently," and mentioned the well-known SR, Pyrkhavka, as one of its members, who apparently revealed the contact between this organization and the emigre group of the Ukrainian Party of Social Revolutionaries in Prague. Although this organization was also mentioned in the speeches of Postyshev, Popov, and Balitsky, no further details were made public. Thus far we have been unable to find any information concerning the SR Center in emigre sources.

The significance which this organization had for the NKVD may be surmised only through a process of deduction. The Ukrainian Social Revolutionaries, led by M. Shapoval and N. Hryhoriiv, had a well organized party headquarters in Prague where they also published their journal *Nova Ukraina* (The New Ukraine). Although the activities and publications of these SR's provided a strong antidote to Soviet propaganda, they became less effective as the Soviet Ukraine showed evidence of greater cultural achievements. In the twenties a drive against the SR literature was directed by such weighty Soviet Ukrainian publications as the magazines *Chervony shlyakh* (The Red Path) and *Zhyttya i revolyutsiya* (Life and Revolution), the publishing houses *Rukh* (Movement), *Knyhospilka* (Book-Union) and DVU (the Ukrainian State Publishing House), which for the first time in Ukrainian history issued complete editions of Ukrainian classical literature, the scholarly publications of the Ukrainian Academy of Sciences, and Hrushevsky's famous journal *Ukraina*. However, in the early thirties, when nearly all these publications had been either discontinued or radically changed as to content, there was a danger of immeasurably increased success for emigre SR propaganda. It was necessary, therefore to compromise the Ukrainian SR's abroad in the eyes of the Soviet Ukrainian public. This was most easily achieved by branding them as spies and interventionists.

Accordingly, Pyrkhavka confessed that "the Prague SR Committee has reported that it is in full agreement with interventionist plans and is working towards that goal together with the Ukrainian Fascists, headed by Konovalets." Moreover, the "underground" Organization of the Ukrainian SR's, he added, had "decided that the local forces were inadequate to overthrow Soviet rule and establish an independent Ukraine. Therefore it adopted an interventionist policy." In this way the emigre SR's were linked with Ukrainian fascists and foreign interventionists, and at the same time it was emphasized that the forces favorable to the idea of establishing an independent Ukraine were insignificant. The SR Center in the Ukraine was created in order to justify the arrests of former SR's and anyone connected with them.

The Ukrainian Military Organization—1933. Postyshev's charges against the "Ukrainian nationalists," who had allegedly infiltrated the management of the kolkhozes, Ukrainian literature, and the CP(b)U, were made public soon after his arrival in the Ukraine and were embodied in the resolutions of the Plenum of the CP(b)U in Kharkov, in February 1933.[18] Soon afterwards the anti-nationalist witchhunt assumed gigantic proportions; the purges that followed we have described earlier. At the November Plenum the charges against the nationalists were intensified. They were now regarded not as mere deviationists, but as counter-revolutionaries and agents of foreign intervention, working secretly for the separation of the Ukraine from the rest of the USSR.

In his speech before the November Plenum, Kosior mentioned that "early in 1933, a Ukrainian Military Organization was uncovered; it was headed by Maksymovych, Shumsky, Bilenky, Solodub and others, and was financed by Polish landlords and German fascists."[19] Postyshev confirmed the existence of this mythical organization in his speeches before the Twelfth Congress of the CP(b)U and the Seventeenth Congress of the All-Union CP(b).

According to Kosior and Postyshev, apart from Maksymovych, Shumsky, Bilenky, and Solodub, the following members of the Ukrainian Military Organization had been apprehended: the historian, Yavorsky; the deputy Commissar of Education and chief of the Propaganda section of the CC CP(b)U, Yuriy Ozersk (pseudonym of Zebnytsky); the sociologist, Professor Lozynsky; the deputy Commissar of Agriculture, Konyk; the economist and former official of the Commissariat for Foreign Affairs, I. Petrenko, and his successor, Tur; the author of the novel *The Blue Blood,* the writer, M. Kozoriz; an active member of the KPZU, O. Bukshovany, who in 1933 was recalled to Kharkov from Berlin and subsequently arrested; Skrypnyk's personal secretary, Esternyuk; and an official of the Commissariat of Education, a former active Communist agent in Czechoslovakia, Badan.

After Skrypnyk's suicide, when news of a "nationalist conspiracy" was publicized widely in the Soviet Ukrainian press, the public was expecting the unmasked nationalists to be secret but confirmed enemies of the Soviet state. How surprised they were when they learned from the proceedings of the November Plenum that these archenemies of the Soviet regime were their own Communist officials and prominent Ukrainian scholars and writers. All of them represented the independent trend in Soviet Ukrainian social and cultural life, which had no place in Stalin's plans. In order to justify the mass extermination of the Ukrainian Communist opposition to Moscow Communist centralism, it was necessary to ask for an indictment on a charge of high treason. It was, therefore, quite logical to the NKVD, although fantastic to the general public, that the underground military organiza-

---

[18] The resolution of the Plenum, *Pravda,* February 6, 1933.
[19] *Pravda,* December 2, 1933.

tion should be headed by the leaders of the former opposition within the CP(b)U, Shumsky and Maksymovych.

The Polish Military Organization (POW). The activity of this mythical organization is connected primarily with the person of Skarbek, a Ukrainized Pole who occupied several posts in the CP(b)U at different times as chairman of the provincial Trade Union Council, chief of the cultural and propaganda section of the Kiev Provincial Party committee, secretary of the Chernigov provincial Party committee, and secretary of the CP(b)U in the Marchlewski Polish national district.

The Soviet Ukrainian press and Kosior's speech at the November Plenum contain several sharp attacks on Skarbek who was described as the leader of the POW, an organization in the service of Polish landowners and Ukrainian nationalists.

The charges against the POW and the subsequent liquidation of Skarbek and the Polish Communists reveals a little known aspect of the change in the nationality policy in the Ukraine. It would be a mistake to think that the new course was directed only against the Ukrainians; it affected all other non-Russian nationalities in the USSR and national minorities within the Ukrainian SSR.

Under Skrypnyk's guidance the Soviet Ukrainian policy towards national minorities in the Ukraine had followed a distinctly liberal line. All non-Ukrainian nationalities had schools and newspapers in their own languages. Special Bulgarian, German, Russian, Moldavian, and Polish national self-governing districts were established in the Soviet Ukraine.[20] They continued to flourish until 1933 when on Postyshev's orders they were liquidated. Especially severe was the abolition of the Marchlewski Polish district in the province of Zhytomir as described below. All Polish schools as well as the Polish Pedagogical Institute were closed down. The Polish district ceased to exist.

These measures, consistent as they were with the new Kremlin policy, were also dictated by the fact that after 1933 Poland had come to be regarded by the Soviet government as the springboard of German aggression against the USSR. Postyshev described Poland, together with Germany, as displaying an interest in the Ukraine on the side of international imperialism. Similarly, Kosior painted a dark picture of Poland's designs and "imperialist appetite." The Ukrainian nationalists in Galicia had, according to this version, "completely sold themselves to the Polish landowners"; those of them who visited the Soviet Ukraine did so on Polish intelligence orders. Analysing the "confession" of Kozoriz, the writer, Kosior described in detail Poland's participation in the imperialist plans against the USSR. According to him, Poland was to receive the Right Bank Ukraine as a reward for her services to the Western European powers. Kosior, in addition, tried to find support for these charges in the Polish press, primarily in the editorials

[20] Cf. *Sotsyalistychna Ukraina*, Kiev, 1937, pp. 151, 153; M. Vasylenko, "Polsky natsionalny rayon im. Markhlevskoho" (Polish National Markhlevsky District), *Radyanska Ukraina* (Soviet Ukraine), 1930, No. 8-9.

of the *Robotnik,* organ of the Polish Socialist Party, and in an article by Leon Wasilewski in the *Polish Ukrainian Bulletin* in which the latter pleaded for a more tolerant Polish policy toward the Ukrainians.[21] The resolutions of the November Plenum lashed out against the "Ukrainian bourgeois nationalists, in the service of Poland."[22]

The intensified propaganda against Poland was accompanied by a revision of Soviet policy regarding the Polish minority in the Ukraine. It was decided to liquidate the Polish Marchlewski district, which was then viewed as a potential anti-Soviet base for Polish operations. In order to justify the liquidation of this ethnic group, a step no less inhuman than the treatment meted out to the national minorities in Poland, the NKVD invented the Polish Military Organization. Its members were revealed to be all the prominent cultural and social leaders of the Marchlewski district, headed by Skarbek, a devoted Polish Communist.

The Polish Military Organization was accused of having ties with the Ukrainian Military Organization. This fantastic charge was made in order to implant in the public mind the idea of a massive encirclement of the USSR by enemy forces who formed one grand alliance. Poland was represented not only as a hostile power, but as an active participant in aggression against the USSR, through underground channels.

The All-Ukrainian Borotbist Center (1928–35). Up to the end of 1933 no open charges of having betrayed the Soviet state for their former political ideals were made by the Party chiefs or the press against the former Ukrainian Borotbists. Many of them, however, were arrested on different charges. By 1933 only a few leading Borotbists were left in the Soviet government. They were: Panas Lyubchenko, Hryhoriy Hrynko, and Andriy Khvylya. The last-named left the party of the Borotbists[23] in 1918 and joined the CP(b)U two years before the merger of these two parties.

The first passing reference to the Borotbists as a party of "Ukrainian nationalists" was made by Balitsky, during the Twelfth Congress of the CP(b)U in 1934.[24] However, this mention had at that time little bearing on the general picture of Ukrainian counter-revolution as presented by the purgers. The Borotbists were spared an all-out attack for another two years.

It was in January 1936 that Postyshev, in his lengthy report to the Plenum of the CC CP(b)U branded the former Borotbists as double-dealers and counter-revolutionaries.[25] He declared that the former Borotbists, as well as the Ukapists, who merged with the CP(b)U in 1925, "not only failed to dissolve in our Bolshevik

[21] Postyshev's speech, *Pravda,* December 6, 1933.
[22] Kosior's speech, *Pravda,* December 2, 1933; *Pravda,* November 27, 1933.
[23] Cf. Majstrenko, *op. cit.*
[24] *Visti,* January 21, 1934.
[25] P. Postyshev, "Pidsumky perevirky partiynykh dokumentiv u KP(b)U ta zavdannya partiynoi roboty" (Results of the Verification of Party Documents in the CP(b)U and the Tasks of Party Work), *Bilshovyk Ukrainy,* No. 3, 1936.

melting pot and become Bolsheviks, but they actually came to the CP(b)U keeping intact their own position and continuously conducted counter-revolutionary and perfidious activities aimed at undermining the Party and Soviet rule."[26] To illustrate his point, Postyshev read excerpts from some "confessions" by former Borotbists. In one of them, M. Poloz, a member of the CC CP(b)U, and Ukrainian Commissar of Finance, revealed that "our [Borotbist] activity within the Party was guided by the high-flown slogan which became popular at the last Borotbist Congress: We shall merge with the Bolsheviks and submerge them."[27] Another prominent former Borotbist, later the rector of Kiev University, Semen Semko, was supposed to have said that the only intention which the Borotbists had in joining the CP(b)U was "to wrench power from the hands of the Bolsheviks."[28] Surveying the past of the Borotbist "double-dealers," Postyshev came to the conclusion that, after failing to seize power at the time of Shumsky's deviation (1926–28), the Borotbists expanded their activities in three directions: 1) surrounding Skrypnyk with their men and thus creating a legal base for their anti-Soviet work; 2) forming an underground Borotbist organization—an illegal base for their activity; 3) strengthening their influence in such organizations as the Union for the Liberation of the Ukraine and the Ukrainian National Center. This, concluded Postyshev, was made clear by the documents seized in the underground Borotbist organization.[29]

The only "documents" produced by Postyshev were the confessions of the accused Borotbist defendants. The former Borotbists Kost Kotko (Mykola Lyubchenko), the journalist and writer, and Lukashenko corroborated Postyshev's charges of the existence of an underground organization. According to Lukashenko, it was formed in 1926 and included the following ex-Borotbists: Shumsky, Poloz, Maksymovych, Solodub, Prykhodko, Yalovy, Ozersky, Polotsky, Semko, Kulish, Nikolenko, Chernyak, and Levytsky.

Up to 1930, this Borotbist underground organization aimed at uniting the forces of resistance and maintaining close contact with other illegal groups, like the one headed by Hrushevsky (testimony of Shelest). From 1930 to 1933 the organization prepared itself for an armed uprising against the Soviet government in the Ukraine (testimony of Yalovy). The armed uprising which was being prepared in conjunction with the Ukrainian Military Organization was forestalled by the "uncovering" of the latter.

Therefore, the Borotbist underground organization continued singlehanded to perpetrate acts of terror against Soviet rule. According to Postyshev's account, it was finally uncovered in 1934–35. Its leadership at that time consisted of Semko, Polotsky, Mykola Lyubchenko, Kudrya, Kovaliv, Kulish and Epik.[30]

---

[26] P. Postyshev, "Pidsumky . . ." op. cit.
[27] The author of the slogan was the Borotbist writer, Vasyl Ellan (Blakytny).
[28] Postyshev, "Pidsumky . . ." op. cit.
[29] Ibid.
[30] Ibid.

How much truth was there in Postyshev's story of a Borotbist plot? The historical background of the Borotbists[31] given by Postyshev is basically true, although somewhat exaggerated. The confessions of Semko and Poloz correspond to historical fact. In merging with the CP(b)U the Borotbists were hoping to retain their original platform—the national independence of the Soviet Ukraine. They made no secret of it, and their attitude was tolerated by the Bolshevik Party and by Lenin[32] who needed the co-operation of the Borotbists to ensure the success of the Soviet government in the Ukraine. The position of the Borotbists was, therefore, not a conspiracy; it was a recognized form of opposition. Similarly, the "deviation" of Shumsky was a movement headed by the Borotbists and their sympathizers. It was not, however, a test of strength between the Bolsheviks and Borotbists, but was an expression of Ukrainian protest against the centralist and Russifying tendencies of the CP(b)U.

It is, however, most unlikely that the ex-Borotbists would attempt to form an underground organization, though they had had a great deal of experience in underground work during 1917–19. In 1928 they possessed enough power in the state apparatus of the Ukrainian SSR to exert their pressure on the political, social and cultural development of the country. The charge that the Borotbists were preparing an armed insurrection in 1930–33 may be rejected outright. Because of their past experience they realized very well that such a venture would be doomed to failure. Nor were the Borotbists implicated in any of the peasant uprisings in 1932–33.

One question which remains is why the Borotbist Center was first mentioned as being uncovered in 1936? Why was the accusation against the Borotbists not made earlier, let us say in 1933?

In 1933 the Postyshev regime still needed the services of Borotbists like Lyubchenko, Khvylya, Hrynko. Therefore it purged the Borotbists not as Borotbists, but as members of the Military Organization, or simply as enemies of the state and fascists. This was done, in spite of Balitsky's statement in 1934 that a Borotbist conspiracy already existed. By 1936 the reign of terror in the Ukraine had come to an end and the country was an obedient vassal of the Kremlin. There was no longer any need to countenance the domination of the Ukraine by the ideals of Ukrainian patriotism, which men like Lyubchenko, Hrynko and Khvylya had provided from 1933 to 1936. The time was ripe for the destruction of the last vestiges of Ukrainian opposition and those who had supported it. The mythical Borotbist underground was created in order to facilitate the destruction of the last of the Borotbists.

The implication of the Borotbists in the anti-Soviet underground was not in itself sufficient. The Soviet fabricators proceeded to the last chapter of the revised

---

[31] Cf. Majstrenko, op. cit.

[32] Lenin, Stati i rechi ob Ukraine (Articles and Speeches Concerning the Ukraine), Partizdat TsK KP(b)U, 1936, p. 334.

history of Borotbism. In 1938, a leading article in *Bilshovyk Ukrainy*[33] accused the Borotbists of being, from the beginning of their existence (1918), agents of Ukrainian nationalism and foreign imperialism. It described the split in the Ukrainian Party of Social Revolutionaries in 1918 and stated that this led to the creation of the Borotbist Party as "a Jesuit maneuver of the Ukrainian-nationalist counter-revolution."[34] In this way the Borotbists, the co-founders of the Ukrainian SSR, were branded agents of foreign interventionists.

The Soviet perversion of Borotbist history and ideology shows that Borotbism (Ukrainian Communism) was deeply rooted in the Ukraine and that it had continued to represent a vital force in the politics of that country until 1938. It was not destroyed until its adherents had first been liquidated as nationalists and fascists, and then finally as Borotbists—members of the nonexistent underground Borotbist Center.

The Ukrainian White Guard Terrorist Center (December, 1934). On December 18, 1934, the Soviet press carried the following report of the verdict passed by the Military Court on the members of the Ukrainian White Guard Terrorist Center:

> From December 13 to 15 the visiting session of the Military Board of the Supreme Court of the USSR in Kiev, presided over by Comrade V. V. Ulrikh, and consisting of Comrades N. M. Rychkov and A. D. Goryachev, examined the cases of 1) A. V. Krushelnytsky, 2) Yu. A. Bachynsky, 3) I. A. Krushelnytsky, 4) T. A. Krushelnytsky, 5) R. F. Skazynsky, 6) M. M. Lebedynets, 7) I. R. Shevchenko,[35] 8) A. Yu. Karabut, 9) P. I. Sidorov, 10) V. A. Mysyk, 11) V. I. Levytsky, 12) A. I. Skrypa-Kozlovska, 13) H. M. Kosynka-Strilets, 14) D. N. Falkivsky, 15) M. H. Oksamyt, 16) A. H. Shcherbyna, 17) I. P. Tereshchenko, 18) K. S. Bureviy, 19) L. B. Kovaliv, 20) P. F. Helmer-Didushok, 21) A. F. Vlyzko, 22) A. I. Finitsky, 23) E. K. Dmitriev, 24) A. A. Bohdanovych, 25) P. I. Butuzov, 26) I. M. Butuzov, 27) V. V. Pyatnytsya, 28) Ya. P. Blachenko, 29) H. K. Stupin, 30) D. I. Polevy, 31) I. O. Khoptyar, 32) P. N. Boretsky, 33) L. I. Lukyanov-Svechezarov, 34) H. N. Protsenko, 35) K. I. Pivnenko, 36) S. Ya. Matyash, 37) A. K. Lyashchenko.
>
> All of them were accused of organizing acts of terror against officials of the Soviet government. The Court established that the majority of the accused had arrived in the USSR from Poland, some from Rumania, with the intention of organizing acts of terror on the territory of the Ukrainian SSR. Most of the accused were apprehended with revolvers and hand grenades. Guided by the resolution of the Presidium of the Central Executive Committee of the USSR dated December 1 of this year and articles 54–8 and 54–11 of the Penal Code of the Ukrainian SSR, the visiting session of the Military Board of the Supreme Court of the USSR sentenced: 1) R. F. Skazynsky, 2) I. A. Krushelnytsky, 3) T. A. Krushelnytsky, 4) M. M. Lebedynets, 5) I. R. Shevchenko,[35] 6) A. Yu. Karabut, 7) P. I. Sidorov, 8) H. M. Kosynka-Strilets, 9) D. N. Falkivsky, 10) M. H. Oksamyt, 11) A. H.

---

[33] "Burzhuazni natsionalisty-lyuti vorohy narodu" (The Bourgeois Nationalists—Fierce Enemies of the People), *Bilshovyk Ukrainy*, No. 7, July, 1938, p. 43.

[34] *Ibid.*

[35] The initials were transposed; it should read R. I. Shevchenko.

Shcherbyna, 12) I. P. Tereshchenko, 13) K. S. Bureviy, 14) A. F. Vlyzko, 15) E. K. Dmitriev, 16) A. A. Bohdanovych, 17) P. I. Butuzov, 18) I. M. Butuzov, 19) V. V. Pyatnytsya, 20) Ya. P. Blachenko, 21) D. I. Polevy, 22) I. O. Khoptyar, 23) P. N. Boretsky, 24) L. I. Lukyanov, 25) K. I. Pivnenko, 26) H. N. Protsenko, 27) S. Ya. Matyash, 28) A. K. Lyashchenko—to be shot.

Their property is to be confiscated.

The sentences have been carried out.

The Military Board of the Supreme Court of the USSR has decided to submit the cases of A. V. Krushelnytsky, Yu. A. Bachynsky, V. A. Mysyk, V. I. Levytsky, A. I. Skrypa-Kozlovska, L. B. Kovaliv, P. F. Helmer-Didushok, A. I. Finitsky, and H. K. Stupin for further investigation because of new circumstances.

In order to grasp the significance of this sentence and of the charges contained in it, it is necessary to survey briefly the circumstances which led to this trial.

On December 1, 1934, L. V. Nikolaev, a young engineer, a member of the Party and of the Leningrad District Committee of the All-Union CP(b), killed S. M. Kirov, the secretary of the Leningrad District Committee and a member of the Politburo of the All-Union CP(b), in the waiting room of the Committee Headquarters.

The next day, *Pravda* published the following report of the shooting:

The Central Committee of the All-Union CP(b) deeply regrets to inform the Party, the working class, the toilers of the USSR and of the entire world that on December 1, in Leningrad there fell, by the treacherous hand of an enemy of the working class, the prominent worker in our Party ... the secretary of the Central and Leningrad Committees of the All-Union CP(b), a member of the Politburo of the CC All-Union CP(b), Comrade Sergei Mironovich Kirov.

The special meeting of the Presidium of the Central Executive Committee of the USSR which was held on the same day adopted the following decisions:

1) To authorize the judiciary to speed up the investigation of cases pertaining to the preparation or perpetration of terrorist acts.

2) To instruct the tribunals not to stay the execution of the more severe penalties pending an appeal for clemency on behalf of the offenders, since the presidium of the Central Executive Committee of the USSR cannot consider these intercessions.

3) To instruct the organs of the NKVD to execute the more severe sentences for the above mentioned offences immediately after the verdicts have been handed down.[36]

This was the notorious "law of December 1, 1934," which countenanced the terror conducted by the NKVD in all parts of the country as a reprisal for Kirov's murder. The practical application of this drastic new law affected the Ukraine to such an extent that a detailed discussion of the murder of Kirov is included in an Appendix Note, pages 149-51.

---

[36] *Pravda*, December 4, 1934.

Official evidence for the existence of the White Guard Terrorist Center in the Ukraine consisted of 1) the published sentence promulgated by the Military Tribunal in Kiev, 2) the 37 victims of the trial, and 3) the "confession" of the poet Vlyzko, as reported in a speech by Postyshev.[37]

The text of the sentence asserted that the majority of the accused had come to the Ukraine from abroad and that they had been caught red-handed, in possession of arms. Of the 37 accused, at least 20, according to the verdict, had come from abroad. This may not sound unlikely to one not familiar with the names of the accused. In reality, however, 23 of the defendants were widely known writers, cultural and social workers in the Ukraine (M. M. Lebedynets, R. I. Shevchenko, V. A. Mysyk, V. I. Levytsky, H. M. Kosynka, D. N. Falkivsky, M. H. Oksamyt, A. H. Shcherbyna, I. P. Tereshchenko, K. S. Bureviy, L. B. Kovaliv, A. F. Vlyzko, D. I. Polevy, I. O. Khoptyar, P. N. Boretsky, H. N. Protsenko, K. I. Pivnenko, S. Ya. Matyash, A. K. Lyashchenko, Ya. P. Blachenko, A. Yu. Karabut, A. I. Finitsky, and V. V. Pyatnytsya). With the exception of M. Lebedynets, who was in the Soviet diplomatic service and had therefore travelled abroad quite frequently, and the young deaf-and-dumb poet Vlyzko, who had paid a short visit to Germany in 1929 or 1930, not one of the remaining accused had travelled abroad.

Only seven of the entire group were Galicians who had come to live in the Soviet Ukraine. Who were they, and under what circumstances had they come to the Soviet Ukraine? P. F. Helmer-Didushok was an old Ukrainian Social-Democrat, who, as an officer of the Austrian army, had been taken prisoner by the Russians before the Revolution. During the Revolution he took an active part in Ukrainian political life. He was a member of the Ukrainian delegation, headed by Professor Hrushevsky, to the Second International. After 1920 he accepted the Soviet regime and remained in the Ukraine. Yu. A. Bachynsky, a journalist and Social-Democrat, was a member of the Ukrainian National Council in Galicia in 1918 and later the Ukrainian envoy in Washington.[38] He became a loyal supporter of the Soviet regime and was legally admitted to the Ukraine in the early thirties. A. V. Khrushelnytsky, a writer, formerly Minister of Education in the government of the Ukrainian People's Republic (1919), later lived in Galicia and edited a pro-Soviet literary journal, *Novi shlyakhy* (New Paths). Early in the thirties he went over to the Soviet Ukraine, convinced of the bright future of that country. His wife, a daughter, and two sons accompanied him. Both his sons were co-defendants in the same case as their father and both were executed. R. F. Skazynsky and A. I. Skrypa-Kozlovska were in the same category as the Krushelnytskys.

This survey of the accused shows the falsity of the official charges that the majority of the defendants had crossed the Soviet frontier armed to the teeth, in order to carry out acts of terror.

---

[37] P. Postyshev, "Puti ukrainskoi sovetskoi literatury" (The Paths of Soviet Ukrainian Literature), *Pravda*, June 10, 1935.

[38] Cf. Julian Batschinsky, "Memorandum to the Government of the United States," 1919 (Columbia University Library).

Finally, there is one valuable piece of evidence which helps to expose the brand of justice meted out to the Ukrainian "White Guard terrorists." It was written by B. Podolyak,[39] who met K. I. Pivnenko, one of the accused, in November 1934. At that time, Pivnenko told the author that he had been arrested, together with two other Ukrainians, H. N. Protsenko, and S. Ya. Matyash, earlier in the year, but had subsequently been released on condition that he and his friends would leave the Ukraine. However, Podolyak added, the murder of Kirov had upset the plans made in preparation for the journey east. Shortly after his interview with Pivnenko, the three accused were re-arrested and executed.

The above evidence suggests that the White Guard Terrorist Center never existed, and that the members of the Ukrainian group were not responsible for the crimes attributed to them. They were innocent persons, victims of Soviet mass terror.

The Terrorist Group of Professor Zerov. In January 1936, a secret trial was conducted in Kiev. The accused were allegedly members of a "terrorist-nationalist" group headed by the famous Ukrainian literary critic, poet and professor of literature at Kiev University, Mykola Zerov.[40] Apart from Zerov, the following Ukrainian writers and intellectuals were included in the group: Pavlo Fylypovych, a poet and literary critic; Ananiy Lebed, a professor of literature; Mykhaylo Dray-Khmara, a poet and literary historian; Marko Vorony, and another professor, a friend of Zerov, whose name was not disclosed (in all probability Professor Viktor Romanovsky).[41]

Toward the end of the trial the case of Dray-Khmara was taken up by the Special Council of the NKVD, which, on March 28, 1936, sentenced Dray-Khmara to five years forced labor for "counter-revolutionary activity." He served his sentence in the camp in the Kolyma region. The last news of him was received in September 1938.[42]

The Soviet press made no mention of the trial of the "Zerov group." Postyshev and other Party leaders also kept silent about it. Our only sources therefore are the eyewitness accounts which have appeared in the press since 1943.[43]

---

[39] B. Podolyak, "Zhertvy hrudnevoi tragedii" (The Victims of the December Tragedy), *Moloda Ukraina* (Young Ukraine), No. 1-2, 1953. B. Podolyak is the pseudonym of the present author.

[40] Zerov was born in 1890. In Soviet Ukrainian literature he occupied a distinguished place as the leader of the Neoclassicists. He was the author of several volumes of literary criticism, *Nove ukrainske pysmenstvo* (Modern Ukrainian Literature), 1924, *Do dzherel* (To the Sources), 1926, and of collections of poetry *(Kamena,* 1924; *Sonnetarium,* 1948). Zerov was also an accomplished translator of classical Greek and Roman poetry *(Antolohiya rymskoi poezii* [An Anthology of Roman Poetry], 1920) as well as of the French Parnassians, and of Russian and Polish poets.

[41] Cf. H. Kostiuk, "Ukrainski pysmennyky to vcheni v bilshovytskykh tyurmakh i taborakh" (Ukrainian Writers and Scholars in Bolshevik Prisons and Camps), *Krakivski visti* (Cracow News), November 14, 1943.

[42] Yuriy Klen, *Spohady pro neoklasykiv* (Reminiscences of the Neoclassicists), Munich, 1947, pp. 33-48.

[43] H. Kostiuk, *op. cit.* S. Pidhayny, *Ukrainska inteligentsiya na Solovkakh.*

According to Lebed, whom the present author met in a concentration camp, Zerov and his group were accused of espionage (Article 54, Sections 6, 8, and 11 of the Penal Code of the Ukrainian SSR), of terrorist acts against Soviet Ukrainian Party leaders (Postyshev, Petrovsky) and of belonging to an illegal organization.[44] In support of the first charge, it was stated that in December 1934, Zerov and his friends had attended a memorial service for the Ukrainian writers who had been executed earlier in the month. Following the requiem, Zerov was supposed to have formed a group devoted to the idea of avenging the deaths of the executed writers.

The members of Zerov's alleged group came from three different, although related, strata: 1) the Neoclassicist poets, whose chief theorist was Zerov. Maksym Rylsky, Mykhaylo Dray-Khmara, Pavlo Fylypovych, and Yuriy Klen belonged to this school of poetry; 2) the so-called HUKUS, a linguistic circle of graduate students and University lecturers devoted to the study of the Ukrainian language. It was created in 1924 and included Kost Dovhan, Hryhoriy Levchenko and others, and was indirectly supervised by Zerov; 3) the Higher Literary Seminar, presided over by Zerov, who devoted a great deal of time to it. This literary laboratory produced several promising literary scholars. All three circles were founded with the approval of the authorities and were devoted to literature and scholarship alone. It was no secret that neither Zerov nor his students subscribed to Marxian theory. The fact that these groups represented centers of objective, scholarly research, and of pro-Western orientation in Ukrainian literature and criticism was enough to inspire charges of counter-revolution against them and to destroy some of the most cultured and talented men in the Soviet Ukraine. Their tolerant, liberal and pro-Western outlook could not be tolerated in the new course set by Stalin.[45]

Alleged Underground Organizations in the Ukraine, 1935—38

The Bloc of Ukrainian Nationalist Parties (UKP, the Borotbists, USD, USR, UVO)—1932–36. While uncovering various "underground" organizations in the Ukraine the Soviet authorities from time to time made an attempt to link them all up into one big conspiracy. The first hints of the existence of such a "bloc" were contained in speeches by Postyshev and Kosior at the November Plenum. The first concrete charge was made by Balitsky in his review of the "achievements" of his department (NKVD) before the Twelfth Congress of the CP(b)U in 1934. Balitsky disclosed that a "bloc of Ukrainian nationalist parties, UKP's, the Borotbists, the SR's, the SD's, the UV's and others,"[46] had been uncovered. During the next few years, hundreds or even thousands of former members of these parties were arrested, but no special amalgamated "bloc" appeared in the trials. It was

---

[44] H. Kostiuk, *op. cit.*

[45] Cf. Petrov, Viktor, "Ukrainska inteligentsiya—zhertva bildshovytskoho teroru" (The Ukrainian Intelligentsia—Victim of Bolshevik Terror), *Ukrainska literaturna hazeta* (Ukrainian Literary Gazette), No. 1, 2, 3, 4, 5, 6, 1955; No. 1, 2, 4, 5, 6, 7, 1956.

[46] *Visti,* January 21, 1933.

in January 1936, that Postyshev, in his address before the Plenum of the CP(b)U,[47] finally confirmed the existence of such a bloc, embracing all parties and diversionist groups and including Skrypnyk's group within the CP(b)U. Postyshev quoted at length the "confession" made by Professor Demchuk, which declared:

> The Ukrainian Military Organization could not have undertaken such wide organizational and political work in the Soviet Ukraine if it had not found suitable conditions there, i.e. powerful support from other counter-revolutionary, nationalist organizations and groups ...
>
> All these groups, e.g. the former Borotbists, former members of the UKP, USD, USR and UVO created one nationalist bloc.[48]

According to Postyshev, this bloc was not a mere union of associated partners; it had a directing center to which all the groups were subordinated. The Borotbist representatives in the bloc were Poloz, Solodub, Slipansky, Yalovy, Vrona, Nikolenko; the Ukapists were represented by Richytsky, Avdienko, Drahomyretsky and Kyyanytsya, and the Ukrainian Military Organization by Baran and Levytsky.

The Soviet accounts of the leaders of the bloc varied from time to time. Sometimes it was charged that Hrushevsky's group had the leading role in the bloc (1933), at other times it was the Borotbist group (1936).

What purpose, after all, was served by the invention of the Bloc of Ukrainian Nationalist Parties? No matter how incredible the charges made against various people accused of participation in underground activities might have been, they had to have about them an air of plausibility. Even if the charges were difficult to believe, they had to be within the limits of the possible. Skrypnyk could be accused of being a nationalist, but he could hardly be accused of being a fascist.

Therefore, a special technique of guilt by association had to be developed. Hence, even if people were not accused of being fascist, they were put on the same level as fascists if their organizations formed a bloc with fascist organizations. The professional NKVD man, Balitsky, must have grasped the usefulness of the idea even in 1934, but it was not until two years later that the Party politicians allowed him to put his plans into practice. This, in our opinion, explains the creation of the Bloc of Ukrainian Nationalist Parties.

The Trotskyite Nationalist Terrorist Bloc. It has already been mentioned that in 1935–36 the NKVD was busy creating a Ukrainian Trotskyite Nationalist Bloc, allegedly headed by Professor Nyrchuk.[49] The Soviet press contained only two references to Professor Nyrchuk as one of the founders of the Bloc. The first was the reprimand handed down by the CC CP(b)U on May 8, 1933.[50] Nyrchuk was mentioned for the second time in the resolution of the Kiev Party Committee issued in late August 1936, following a speech by Postyshev. It stated that

---

[47] Postyshev, "Pidsumky ..." *Bilshovky Ukrainy*, No. 3, 1936.
[48] *Ibid.*
[49] See above, pp. 54-6.
[50] *Visti*, May 10, 1933.

"Ukrainian Trotskyites, headed by Kotsyubynsky, Holubenko, Loginov, Nyrchuk, and others, formed a counter-revolutionary Trotskyite-Zinovievite nationalist bloc."[51]

There is no evidence to suggest that such a bloc existed in the Ukraine, although this possibility cannot be altogether excluded since certain conditions, favorable to the development of such a body, did certainly exist. As early as 1923, when Trotsky first found himself in opposition to the centralist trends in the Russian CP(b), he grasped the significance of the national problem in the USSR.

From Trotsky's autobiography, published in 1930,[52] it is clear that in 1923, during the conflict in Georgia between the Georgian opposition led by Mdivani on the one hand and Stalin and Dzerzhinsky on the other, Trotsky was on the side of the Georgians. He branded Stalin's policy as a "callous and insolent great-power oppression." At the Twelfth Congress of the Russian CP(b) in 1923, Trotsky moved an amendment to Stalin's proposed resolution on the national question. Looking back at this incident in 1930, Trotsky wrote: "I wanted a radical change in the nationality policy ... in regard to small, weak, and backward peoples."[53] Trotsky's later pronouncements on the national question were made in the same tone.[54]

It was to be expected that Stalin's opponents in the non-Russian republics of the USSR would automatically become sympathetic to Trotsky. This did actually happen in many instances. Thus it is known that Khvylovy showed obvious Trotskyite sympathies; many of his closest friends and associates (D. Feldman, Ya. Lifshits, and Victor Serge) were followers of Trotsky.

According to the testimony of Rappoport-Darin quoted by Postyshev, "in 1933–34 the Trotskyite organization formed a bloc with the organizations of Ukrainian national deviationists. At the end of 1931 Kotsyubynsky[55] told me that in all propaganda work we must bear in mind the peculiarities of the Ukraine. In the Ukraine, he said, we not only cannot bypass the national question, but we must also clarify our own attitude toward this question."[56]

---

[51] *Pravda*, August 23, 1936.

[52] Trotsky, *Moya zhizn* (My Life), Riga, Bereg, 1930.

[53] *Ibid.*, p. 222.

[54] Cf. L. Trotsky, "Ob ukrainskom voprose" (On the Ukrainian Question), *Byulleten oppozitsii*, No. 77-78; 1939; Nezavisimaya Ukraina i sektantskaya putanitsa" (The Independent Ukraine and the Sectarian Muddle), *Byulleten oppozitsii*, No. 79-80, 1939; "Demokraticheskie krepostniki i nezavisimost Ukrainy" (Democratic Slave-Owners and the Independence of the Ukraine), *ibid.*

[55] Yuriy Kotsyubynsky was the son of the well-known Ukrainian novelist, Mykhaylo Kotsyubynsky. He became a member of the Party in 1913 and in 1918 he was a member of the Bolshevik government in the Ukraine. Later, he was Soviet envoy to Poland whence he was recalled in 1931. In that year he was appointed Deputy Chairman of the Council of People's Commissars in the Ukraine and in 1934 he was re-elected a member of the CC CP(b)U. He was arrested in 1935 and was believed to have been executed without trial.

[56] Postyshev, "Pidsumky ..." *Bilshovyk Ukrainy*, No. 3, 1936.

There are many other references in the Soviet press to the Trotskyite National-ist Bloc.[57]

A report of Postyshev's speech in *Pravda* on January 14, 1935, mentions the activities of Ukrainian Trotskyites in Kiev and Kharkov universities, the publishing house of the *Soviet Ukrainian Encyclopedia*,[58] and in the Institute of People's Education in Lugansk (Tsykin, Deyneka).[59]

In December 1934, *Pravda* reported the unmasking of a Trotskyite bloc in the University of Dnepropetrovsk (Komarovsky, Brokhin, Kaplun, Yahnetyn-skaya, Karpenko, Davydenko).[60] It was further alleged that this group maintained contact with "Vinokur, Chichkevych, Hurevych and others."

Did these groups, allegedly discovered in 1934, have any relation to Professor Nyrchuk and the Trotskyite bloc of 1936? Probably none. Both "underground groups" (1934, 1936) were created for purposes known only to the NKVD. Those accused of being members were tried *in camera* and received a sentence of three to five years by the verdict of the so-called Special Counsel *(Osoboe Soveshchanie)*. The subsequent fate of Professor Nyrchuk is unknown. Perhaps his reason failed, or perhaps, having fulfilled his function for the NKVD, he was shot or deported to a concentration camp. To the NKVD this was of minor importance. What was important was that by playing the part of the leader of the Trotskyite bloc, he had helped to destroy many innocent Ukrainian scholars and intellectuals whom the NKVD had been ordered to find guilty.

The Ukrainian Trotskyite Center (1936). The problem of Ukrainian Trotsky-ism is a topic in itself. There is no doubt that the Trotskyite opposition must have had centers in the Ukraine too. It was strongest during the years 1924–27. It is also undeniable that Ukrainian Trotskyism had, as Postyshev said, "its own specific character."[61] The activity of the Ukrainian Trotskyites began to decline after 1929. It may be assumed that by 1933 there were no more centers of Trotskyite opposition. Yet it was precisely then that the "Trotskyite underground" became a necessary part of Stalin's plans to terrorize the country. In order to destroy all the former followers of Trotsky it was necessary to apprehend them while they were engaged in a widespread Trotskyite, underground conspiracy. If such an underground conspiracy did not exist, it had to be invented. At first the NKVD invented the Ukrainian Trotskyite Nationalist Bloc which we have already discussed. The liquidation of this bloc was completed by the end of 1936.

Soon afterwards a new Trotskyite organization in the Ukraine was uncovered. The drive against it began as early as 1935, with the arrest of Zinoviev, Kamenev, Bakaev, Yevdokimov, Fedorev and other "Trotskyites." From later pronounce-

---

[57] *Pravda*, December 14, 1934.

[58] *Soviet Ukrainian Encyclopedia* was a pet project of Skrypnyk, planned as an exhaustive reference work. It never appeared in print, although the first three volumes were ready for publication.

[59] *Pravda*, December 14, 1934.

[60] *Ibid.*

[61] Postyshev, "Pidsumky ..." *op. cit.*

ments by Postyshev[62] it is clear that the Ukrainian Trotskyites, Yu. Kotsyubynsky, Rappoport-Darin, Naumov, and several others must have been arrested about the same time, in 1935. Thus, although the Ukrainian press carried no reports of these arrests, it may be assumed that the invention of the "Ukrainian Trotskyite Center" goes back to 1935. When Postyshev, in his 1936 speech, officially mentioned the existence of the Center, thousands of Ukrainian workers, peasants and intellectuals had already been arrested on charges of being Trotskyites.

As the epic of the Ukrainian Trotskyite Nationalist Bloc was nearing its end, allegations of a new organization were emerging, this was the Ukrainian Trotskyite Center, headed by Yuriy Kotsyubynsky. On the horizon in Moscow there rose the first shadows of the big trials. A new wave of arrests, which flooded the Ukraine in 1936, called for a fresh exploit by the NKVD—the revelation of a "Trotskyite Center."

The Ukrainian Trotskyite Center was linked to all three Moscow trials.

During the trial of the so-called "Trotsky-Zinoviev Terrorist Center" (August 19–24, 1936), the Ukrainian problem aroused little attention. Apparently the organizers of this trial still found it difficult to establish ties between Zinoviev (who was always violently anti-Ukrainian)[63] and the Ukrainian deviationists and Trotskyites. It is also possible that at that time (1936) the nature of the Ukrainian Trotskyite Center was not yet clearly defined. This is especially obvious from Postyshev's speech, and from the text of the sentence passed on Zinoviev and Kamenev. The sentence mentioned that

> the prosecution has also established that the Trotsky-Zinoviev Center was at the same time ... preparing terrorist acts against Comrades Postyshev and Kosior, with the help of the Ukrainian terrorist group, acting under the leadership of the Trotskyite Mukhin. His case has been taken under separate advisement.[64]

Why was only Mukhin's group mentioned when previous revelations of Ukrainian Trotskyism contained the names of Kotsyubynsky, Loginov, Holubenko, Rappoport-Darin, and others? All these names were disclosed by Postyshev in January 1936, and in the article in *Bilshovyk Ukrainy*.[65] This can only be explained by the assumption that final plans for the invention of the Ukrainian-Trotskyite Center had not been completed.

The attack on the Center did not begin until after the first Moscow trial. Commenting on the trial, the resolution of the Kiev Provincial Party Committee, following the report by Postyshev in August 1936,[66] stated that

---

[62] *Ibid.*

[63] Cf. Postyshev, "Pidsumky," *op. cit.* Also Zinoviev's speech at the Presidium of the CC All-Union CP(b) in 1927.

[64] *Pravda*, August 24, 1936.

[65] "Nazavzhdy sterty z lytsya zemli zgrayu fashystskykh ubyvts" (To Wipe the Gang of Fascist Murderers from the Face of the Earth Forever), *Bilshovyk Ukrainy*, No. 8, 1936.

[66] *Pravda*, August 23, 1936; also *Bilshovyk Ukrainy*, No. 8, 1936.

the Trotskyite and Zinovievite conspirators paid special attention in their counter-revolutionary plans to the Ukraine. They were closely allied with the Ukrainian nationalists and their friends ... preparing to separate the Ukraine by force from the Soviet Union. Ukrainian Trotskyites, headed by Kotsyubynsky, Holubenko, Loginov, Nyrchuk, and others, organized the counter-revolutionary Trotsky-Zinoviev bloc, planning to assist the bands of German and Polish fascist interventionists to occupy the Ukraine and preparing terrorist acts against the leaders of the Party and Soviet government ...

The entire Party organization in the Ukraine must draw a stern lesson from the laissez-faire and criminal slackness which had occurred in Dnepropetrovsk where Trotskyite double-dealers worked in the district organizations until quite recently; and in Kharkov, where a counter-revolutionary group was active in the steel-casting section of the locomotive factory under the very noses of the City and District Party Committees; in the "Bolshevik" factory in Kiev; in the leather industry; in the Ukrainian Leather Trust; as well as in Odessa and the Donbas. The Party must forestall any repetition of similar incidents.

This resolution shows how widespread were the arrests in the Ukraine, conducted in connection with the Trotskyite Center. Trotskyism was no longer limited to university professors and graduate students—it was now infecting workers and managers in the industrial centers of the Ukraine. It also indicates that those who arranged the Moscow trial had decided to link the Ukrainian Trotskyites to the other Trotskyites, stressing the alliance between the former and the Ukrainian nationalists.

The second Moscow trial of the "Anti-Soviet Center" of Pyatakov, Radek, Sokolnikov and others took place January 24–30, 1937. The chief defendant, Pyatakov, made the following confession:

> At that time [1931–32] I was occupied with re-establishing the old Trotskyite contacts. I concentrated on the Ukraine. When I talked to Loginov in Berlin, we agreed on the creation of the Ukrainian Trotskyite Center ...
>
> First of all, we re-established our Ukrainian ties. These were—Loginov, Holubenko, Kotsyubynsky, Lifshits. We first came to an agreement with Loginov, and then with the others, as to the formation of a Ukrainian quartet.[67]

Later in the trial Pyatakov described how Trotskyite groups had been formed in Kharkov, Dnepropetrovsk, Odessa, Kiev, the Donbas and in other cities in the Ukraine, which were directly subordinated to the parallel center in Moscow.[68]

The testimonies of Radek, Pyatakov, and Loginov further stressed the wide activities of the Ukrainian Trotskyites, and branded them as allies of the Ukrainian nationalists. The emphasis of foreign intervention aimed at separation of the Ukraine from Russia was a new note in the Moscow trials.

This problem of the separation of the Ukraine and of the dismemberment of the USSR with the help of foreign intervention became the crucial issue of the

---

[67] *Pravda*, January 24, 1937.
[68] *Ibid.*

third Moscow trial (against Bukharin, Rykov, and others) held March 2–15, 1938. Yet the leading role was reserved not for the Ukrainian Trotskyites, but for the Ukrainian fascists, discussed in the next section. The Ukrainian Trotskyites had to retire to the background.

In conclusion, it is worth glancing at the central figure of alleged Ukrainian Trotskyism, Yuriy Kotsyubynsky. In all probability he was arrested before the trial of Zinoviev. However, Kotsyubynsky did not figure personally in any of the trials. Why was Loginov and not Kotsyubynsky the chief witness to Ukrainian Trotskyism in Pyatakov's trial? There is no answer to this enigma. It is possible, however, to venture an explanation of Kotsyubynsky's absence from all the trials. He was an old Bolshevik with long service in the Party, and in the highest and most responsible position. When he was arrested by the NKVD, which he himself had helped to create, he must have had no illusions about his end. Is it possible that, realizing his helplessness, he refused to break under the interrogating technique of the NKVD, refused to sign "confessions" or to supply lists of his co-workers in the "underground"? The fact that in all likelihood he had to be quietly disposed of in the cellars of the NKVD would seem to confirm this view. But the truth of what actually happened to Yuriy Kotsyubynsky will only be known some time in the future. After the liquidation of the Ukrainian Trotskyite Center, the stage was set for the next victim of the insatiable NKVD—the prime minister of the UkSSR—Panas Lyubchenko.

The National Fascist Organization of the Ukraine (1935–37). The second half of 1937 saw the final annihilation of the last Borotbists and of the national Communist cadres in the CP(b)U and the Soviet Ukrainian government. The bloody purges of that period were accompanied by disclosure of a new "underground" organization: The National Fascist Organization of the Ukraine. The first news of this organization was published on September 18, 1937, in *Pravda*.[69] A brief report from Kiev read as follows:

> The active members of the Kiev organization, devoted to the discussion of the results of the plenum of the CC CP(b)U, met September 15–16. The secretary of the CP(b)U, Comrade S. Kosior, delivered an address on the band of bourgeois nationalists uncovered in the Ukraine. In the discussion the active members sharply criticized the People's Commissariat of Education, and the work of Comrade Zatonsky . . .
>
> Comrade Zatonsky admitted that he had failed to unmask them. However, he did not say how he had rid the People's Commissariat of Education of bourgeois nationalists. This is understandable—Comrade Zatonsky could not say anything. The meeting unanimously sent its greetings to Comrade Stalin.

This laconic report referred to a most dramatic episode in Soviet Ukrainian history. The last sentence is especially characteristic of the climate of the time. What deep irony it contained! Here were the active Ukrainian Party members

---

[69] "Sobranie aktiva kievskoi partorganizatsii" (A Meeting of the Active Members of the Kiev Party Organization), *Pravda*, September 18, 1937.

assembled in the Ukrainian capital at a time when almost the entire Soviet Ukrainian government and the entire Central Committee (62 members and 40 candidate members) together with its Politburo (11 members and 5 candidate members) had been arrested as the leaders of a "bourgeois nationalist organization," and the others were already doomed. And they unanimously sent their greetings to Stalin.

The *Pravda* report mentioned neither the composition nor the nature of the new counter-revolutionary organization. It has, unfortunately, proved impossible to obtain the Kiev papers of the relevant period. We do not know, therefore, if a more detailed account of the "bourgeois nationalist band" described by Kosior was ever published. However, even if it was, it could not have been more extensive than the account given by the "leader" of this "secret organization," H. Hrynko, at the trial of Bukharin and Rykov. This report, issued first by the prosecution on the eve of the Bukharin-Rykov trial,[70] and virtually confirmed in the Procurator's summary after the trial,[71] read as follows:

> It has been established in the course of investigation that the "Right-Trotskyite bloc" united in its ranks the underground, anti-Soviet groups of Trotskyites, Right-wingers, Zinovievites, Mensheviks, SR's and bourgeois nationalists of the Ukraine, Belorussia, the Central Asiatic republics, Georgia, Armenia, Azerbaidzhan and the Maritime Provinces.

What was the alleged purpose of this alleged union of anti-Soviet organizations?

According to the same source, apart from espionage, sabotage, diversion, terror and provoking an enemy attack on the USSR, the aim of this united front was "the separation from the USSR of the Ukraine, Belorussia, Georgia, the Central Asiatic republics, Armenia, Azerbaidzhan and the Maritime Provinces." In such a broad program there was room for the Trotskyites, the Bukharinites, and the bourgeois nationalists. The fact that it was difficult to include in this the Mensheviks, the SR's or the Zinovievites did not deter the NKVD. What was important was that a broad union of all enemies of the Soviet state should be created.

What was the origin of the National Fascist Organization of the Ukraine?

The answer was given at the Rykov-Bukharin trial by the only "representative" and "leader" of this organization, Hryhoriy Hrynko:

> I joined the Communist Party as a member of the Borotbists—a Ukrainian nationalist organization. A considerable part of the Borotbist core, Shumsky, Poloz, Blakytny, Lyubchenko, and myself, after joining the CP(b)U, preserved and even increased our bourgeois nationalist positions ...
>
> The first stage [of our development] was in 1925–26. This was the so-called period of Shumskism. Even at that time Shumskism was, in fact, a program of separation of the Ukraine from the USSR ...

---

[70] *Pravda*, February 28, 1938.
[71] *Pravda*, March 3, 1938.

After the rout of this nationalist organization only fragments of it were left. But around 1929, a nationalist organization was revived in Moscow; it consisted of Shumsky, myself, Poloz, Maksymovych, Solodub and several others. This organization adopted an approach to its program and tactics which was different from that used in the first period.

[During the first period] we thought it was impossible that the evolution of the NEP would end in what we hoped for. On the other hand, we saw no power in Europe with which we could ally ourselves in order to take more determined steps forward...

The situation changed in the second period. This was the period of the unfolding socialist offensive, when the position of the capitalist elements in the country was seriously undermined; the evolution of the NEP in the direction of capitalism was now out of the question ...

In that period, the Ukrainian nationalist organization adopted the political attitude of the right, that is of the struggle against industrialization and collectivization ...

The Ukrainian nationalist organization ordered its members to gather their forces for active struggle, chiefly against collectivization, but also including the organization of uprisings. In that struggle we were already being assisted by some circles of a state hostile to the Soviet Union. These allies helped us. In order to sustain partisan warfare they intensified the transference to the Ukraine of diversionists, Petlyurian emissaries, arms, etc. Liaison was maintained by Konar and Kotsyubynsky ...

This period ended early in 1933 with the arrest of the entire group. I was the only one not arrested at that time.[72]

The only survivor of the organization described no activity by this body for the next two years. During that time the NKVD was busy inventing and destroying other "underground" organizations. However, he himself, he testified, had carried on intensive subversive activity, while he was People's Commissar of Finance of the USSR.

At the end of 1932, in my nationalist work I established treasonous contact with Mr. N. We met in my office where Mr. N. came on matters connected with a German trade concession ...

During the second half of 1933, Mr. N. told me openly that the German fascists wished to co-operate with the Ukrainian nationalists on the Ukrainian problem. In reply I agreed to co-operate with Mr. N.... Later, in 1933–34, I had several meetings with Mr. N.... Before he left the USSR, he introduced me to Mr. M. with whom I continued my contacts...[73]

At the beginning of 1935 I learned from Lyubchenko that a national fascist organization had been created in the Ukraine.[74]

This last information supplied by Hrynko helps to date the beginning of the alleged national fascist organization, which apparently was assured of comprising

---

[72] *Pravda*, March 4, 1938.
[73] *Pravda*, March 3, 1938.
[74] *Pravda*, March 4, 1938.

the remnants of the Borotbists. Its alleged aim was to separate the Ukraine from the USSR, and it hoped to receive help through

> military intervention of the forces with which I [Hrynko] was in personal contact. It also tried to contact the Right-Trotskyite bloc and establish relations with military conspirators.[75]

What was Hrynko's relation to the new organization? According to his testimony, he "agreed to join it [in order] to keep in touch with the Right-Trotskyite center, with governmental circles of some enemy states, and to help Lyubchenko in the expansion of the organization in the Ukraine." Further, he testified that:

> At the time I joined this organization [1935], it crystallized as a national fascist organization. Lyubchenko told me about the center of this organization in the Ukraine, which was made up of Lyubchenko, Porayko, and others. He told me that the center was discussing the problem of what character the Party organization and the Ukrainian state should assume. According to Lyubchenko, the organization chose to create a centralized party modelled on the national-socialist party. If successful, the organization foresaw the creation of a bourgeois Ukrainian state modelled on the fascist state.

Further, Hrynko testified that when the Right-Trotskyite center was informed of this intention by the Ukrainian fascists, Lyubchenko and others, it expressed its full approval. The tentacles of this Ukrainian fascist group, he added, reached even farther. With the help of Lyubchenko, it had also penetrated the army and established close liaison with military conspirators—Yakir and Gamarnyk.

How could these Ukrainian fascists' plans be reconciled with the bargain which Trotsky had made (according to Radek's and Rykov's[76] testimony) with the foreign interventionists, whereby territorial rights in the Ukraine were to be conceded to them? This difficult problem was happily solved. "Pyatakov and Gamarnyk told me," confessed Hrynko, "that Trotsky had come to an agreement [with the Ukrainian fascists] whereby compensation for the [territorial] loss to the Ukraine would be given in military aid for our struggle against the Soviet government."

The organ of the CP(b)U, *Bilshovyk Ukrainy,* commented:

> The national fascist spies, Lyubchenko, Hrynko, Khvylya and others, established ties with Yakir, Gamarnyk and Rykov for common action, in order to fulfill the desires of Trotsky and the foreign intelligence services: to destroy the Soviet government in the USSR and to establish a fascist dictatorship.[77]

---

75 *Ibid.*
76 For Radek's trial: *Pravda,* January 24, 1937; for Rykov's trial: *Pravda,* March 5, 1938.
77 "Vyrok vykonano" (The Verdict Has Been Carried Out), *Bilshovyk Ukrainy,* No. 3, 1938.

It is important to analyze this confusion of accusations, schemes and plots in order to establish some coherence in the official charges, based on the testimony cited above. The following pattern emerges:

1) The origin of the National Fascist Organization of the Ukraine goes back to the earliest history of the Borotbists and their merger with the CP(b)U.

2) Having passed through the phases of Shumskism (1925–28), participation in the Ukrainian nationalist UVO organization (1929–33) and individual diversionist action (1933–35), the remnants of the Borotbists in 1935 created a new organization—the National Fascist Organization of the Ukraine, in alliance with other Ukrainian nationalists.

3) The aim of these organizations was to commit diversionist and terrorist acts, to provoke a war, to help bring about foreign intervention, to separate the Ukraine from the USSR, and, finally, to convert the Ukraine into the colony of a capitalist state.

4) These aims were shared by the Right Trotskyite Center with which the Ukrainian organization was associated.

5) According to Soviet sources,[78] the National Fascist Organization of the Ukraine was headed by the following: Panas Lyubchenko, head of the Soviet Ukrainian Government, member of the CC and Politburo of the CP(b)U, and co-author of the new constitution of the UkSSR; I. V. Porayko, member of the CC, CP(b)U; H. F. Hrynko, People's Commissar of Finance of the USSR; V. P. Zatonsky, People's Commissar of Education of the UkSSR, member of the CC and the Politburo of the CP(b)U; Andriy Khvylya, Deputy Commissar of Education and chief of the Arts Section of the People's Council of Commissars of the UkSSR, member of the CC, CP(b)U; M. M. Popov, member of the CC and the Politburo of the CP(b)U and historian; Kileroh, Chief of the Publication and Propaganda Section of the CC, CP(b)U; Yanovsky, director of the Ukrainian State Opera in Kiev.

6) The majority of the members of Soviet Ukrainian government, of the CC, CP(b)U, and several prominent Soviet Ukrainian writers (I. Kulyk, V. Koryak, I. Mykytenko, I. Kyrylenko, B. Kovalenko, P. Kolesnyk and others) who had helped to purge Ukrainian literature in 1932–33, were also accused of belonging to this organization.

One does not have to search far for the reason for inventing this organization. Its purpose was to provide an excuse for a final purge of all independent Ukrain-

---

[78] Apart from the sources mentioned above, the following articles in *Pravda* contained information about the Ukrainian Nationalist Organization: "Kto khozyainichaet v muzeyakh Ukrainy" (Who is the Boss of the Museums in the Ukraine), *Pravda*, September 25, 1937; "Kak ochishchali ukrainsky yazyk" (How They Purified the Ukrainian Language), *Pravda*, October 4, 1937; "Prestupnaya bespechnost Poltavskogo gorkoma" (The Criminal Carelessness of the Poltava City Committee), *Pravda*, October 10, 1937; "Russko-ukrainsky slovar i yego sostaviteli" (The Russian-Ukrainian Dictionary and Its Compilers), *Pravda*, December 29, 1937; "Toptanie na meste" (Marking Time), *Pravda*, January 3, 1938.

ian Communists, and of all officials of the government and the Party who might oppose the Stalinist regime. The charge on which these men were tried before they were liquidated had to be very serious. Hence the accusation of fascism.

The indictment which was levelled at the accused group was so composed that it left no doubt upon one score: there was no difference between the Borotbists, Ukrainian nationalists, the followers of Skrypnyk, and the fascists.

In 1937, when the centralist course adopted by Stalin had been firmly established, it was possible, indeed imperative, to point to the danger of dismemberment of the USSR, and thus to add a sense of urgency to the instinct for self-preservation of the builders of the new Russian empire. At the same time, the idea of an independent Ukrainian state was to be utterly discredited. Hence the charge that the Ukrainian fascists had "sold their territorial rights" to foreign imperialists before they had even gained control of the territory. To complete this sinister Ukrainian conspiracy, the NKVD provided a link with the archenemy of Stalin—Trotsky. This set the scene for the last big act of terror in the Soviet Ukraine.

We have tried to peer through the smoke screen which Stalinist terrorism laid over the Ukraine in 1930–38, by analyzing in some detail the nature of the Ukrainian "underground" organizations "uncovered" and liquidated during that time. It is certain that the survey presented here is incomplete. There must have been several other conspiracies, invented and "uncovered" by the NKVD, apart from the "underground" organizations outlined above.

Our examination of all the available evidence has led us to regard all these charges as fabricated and the organizations themselves as largely fictitious, created in order to justify the plans for destroying the leaders of Ukrainian political and cultural life.

However, at the same time, it is obvious that these attempts by the NKVD to invent and to destroy Ukrainian anti-Soviet conspiracies were themselves a reaction to Ukrainian resistance to the Soviet regime. Behind the invention, therefore, there lay hidden the elemental forces of the Ukrainian people and their political and cultural leaders.

It is quite possible that our attempts to straighten out the tangle of the Ukrainian "underground" have not always been successful, and that there may still be some confusion in the reader's mind. The involved, cryptic reports on these matters in Soviet sources may be partly responsible for this failure. Yet only when the methods and objectives of the purges have been analysed and the motives behind them laid bare can we attempt to understand the peak of tragedy reached by the Soviet Ukrainian Republic in the years 1937–38.

Chapter III

The Fall of Postyshev

The Official Data

On March 19, 1937, *Pravda* carried this brief news item: "Comrade P. P. Postyshev has been elected acting secretary of the Kuibyshev Provincial Committee of the All-Union CP(b)."

On the following day *Pravda* offered additional information on the dictator of the Ukraine:

> *Kiev, March 19.* A plenum of the CC, CP(b)U was held on March 17. The plenum of the CC, CP(b)U listened to a report by Comrade Kosior on the plenum of the CC, All-Union CP(b) and considered several matters. In connection with the departure of Comrade Postyshev to a new post, the plenum of the CC, CP(b)U relieved him of his duties as second secretary of the Central Committee. Comrade M. M. Khataevich was elected second secretary of the CC, CP(b)U.

That was all. The disappearance from the Ukrainian political arena of its dominant personality cried for a more detailed explanation. Its absence would in itself suggest that the removal of Postyshev had a deeper significance.

Two months after the departure of Postyshev, the Thirteenth Congress of the CP(b)U severely censured the man who, at the last Congress of the CP(b)U, had been offered the deepest adulation and hero-worship.[1] The charges were made, curiously enough, by a rank-and-file member of the Party, Nikolenko,[2] who said that

> the situation, which had nothing in common with Bolshevism, reached its apogee when the Kiev Party organization was under the leadership of Comrade Postyshev. "Postyshev's instructions," "Postyshev's appeals," "Postyshev's kindergartens," "Postyshev's presents," etc. Everything began and everything ended with Postyshev.[3]

According to other charges, Postyshev was guilty of "lack of Party vigilance," and of "supporting the Trotskyites, the nationalists and the Bukharinites in the Kiev Party organization."

---

[1] *Visti*, June 3, 1937.

[2] Nikolenko was a Kiev party member who was a notorious squabbler and denouncer. In 1936 Postyshev recommended that she be excluded from the Party. Her expulsion was confirmed by the CC CP(b)U, but she appealed against it to the CC All-Union CP(b). During the February-March plenum of the All-Union CP(b) Stalin pardoned her, reinstated her in the Party, and later used her in denouncing Postyshev.

[3] "XIII sezd KP(b)U. Preniya po dokladu S. Kosiora" (The Thirteenth Congress of the CP(b)U: Discussion of the Report by S. Kosior), *Pravda*, May 30, 1937.

The chief speaker at the Congress, S. Kosior, who a year later was destined to follow in the footsteps of Postyshev, reminded the audience of the "dangers of nationalism." He stated that the CP(b)U had relaxed its vigilance, and allowed itself to be infiltrated by nationalists and Trotskyites. The Party organization in Kiev was particularly affected. "Here, the Trotskyites especially have dug themselves in," said Kosior. "They have seized control of important posts. The former secretary of the Kiev Committee, Comrade Postyshev, must bear the greatest blame."[4]

Having accused Postyshev of nationalism and of Trotskyism, the Kremlin decided to give him an opportunity to "correct his errors." We learn this from the January Plenum of the CC All-Union CP(b), held in 1938, which discussed "errors of Party organizations while excluding the Communists from the Party, the formal-bureaucratic attitude to the appeals of those excluded from the All-Union CP(b), and the means of overcoming these drawbacks."[5]

In the course of the discussion A. A. Andreev devoted much attention to the Ukraine. In order to illustrate the wrongdoings inside the CP(b)U, he quoted several cases which had occurred during Postyshev's period. This was not sufficient to expose the former dictator of the Ukraine. Therefore, Andreev cited some recent examples of the latter's misbehaviour. In his function as acting secretary of the Kuibyshev Party Committee, Postyshev, he alleged, had displayed gross egotism, "anti-Party twists," and "repressions of members of the Party."

The resolution of the plenum declared, among other things, that "the time has come to unmask and expose as careerists those Communists who are trying to gain advantage by the exclusion of others from the Party."[6]

It is not known if Postyshev was given an opportunity to defend himself. None of his speeches were printed after the plenum. Soon afterward he was deprived of his membership in the Central Committee and of his candidate membership in the Politburo of the CC All-Union CP(b).[7] After his return to Kuibyshev he received a final blow: he was expelled from the Party. Following this, all track of Postyshev was lost.

There are several versions of Postyshev's end; Avtorkhanov maintains that he was executed.[8] This is also accepted by A. Svetlanin.[9] However, one of the readers of *Sotsialistichesky vestnik*, writing under the initials B. N. O., reports that: "Postyshev fell into disgrace, was expelled from the Party, but was not officially arrested. He died of tuberculosis in the Kremlin Sanatorium."[10] Yet

---

[4] "KP(b)U v borbe za sotsialisticheskuyu Ukrainu" 'The CP(b)U in the Struggle for a Socialist Ukraine), *Pravda*, May 29, 1937.

[5] *Pravda*, January 19, 1938.

[6] *Ibid.*

[7] *Ibid.*

[8] Avtorkhanov, *op. cit., Posev*, December, 1950, p. 14.

[9] *Sotsialistichesky vestnik*, No. 3, 1949, p. 48.

[10] *Sotsialistichesky vestnik*, No. 8-9, 1949, p. 164.

another version of Postyshev's death, based on rumors which circulated in the Kiev prisons during the Yezhov period and an account by an inmate of the concentration camps, states that Postyshev was put in prison, where he died of tuberculosis.[11] Another story of Postyshev's end comes from A. Gaev, in a study of Postyshev.[12] Gaev, who had an opportunity to meet Postyshev personally, writes that "his death was reported by only one newspaper. Only *Vechernyaya Moskva* (The Evening Moscow), buried on the last page with reports of fires, criminal offences and street brawls, printed the fact that P. P. Postyshev, former member of the CC All-Union CP(b), has died after a long illness in the Kremlin hospital." Unfortunately, the author indicates neither the date of Postyshev's death nor the issue of the Moscow paper. On the basis of other evidence, which will be discussed later, it is probable that this last version of Postyshev's death is the most accurate. His death must have occurred some time in the autumn of 1939.

Three Versions of Postyshev's Fall

It is impossible to establish the real reason for the eclipse of Postyshev's star; all that can be offered is an analysis of the various hypotheses advanced to explain it. There are three of these: the official version given by the Party; one by Gaev; and one by Avtorkhanov.

Let us first examine the official Party version. From the previous pages of this study it is clear that Postyshev was the most devoted liquidator of Trotskyites, Bukharinites and the Ukrainian national opposition within the CP(b)U. He was the faithful executor of Stalin's orders, Stalin's most trusted man in the Ukraine. He was the creator and enforcer of the new imperialist, centralist and Russifying policy in the Ukraine. In view of this, the official charges of liberalism and lack of vigilance had no relation to the truth. For the crimes which Postyshev did commit in the Ukraine he could not, of course, be tried by the Party, since he had committed them on its orders. It would be equally false to assume that Postyshev could, as was charged, have elevated himself too high in the Party hierarchy, and been blinded by self-conceit. A faithful *apparatchik,* he reflected only some of the glitter which shone from his master. The list of Postyshev's wrongdoings in Kuibyshev is also unconvincing. In any case, his fall dates from his transfer from the Ukraine. His work in Kuibyshev was already a kind of punishment. The official version of Postyshev's fall may, therefore, be rejected.

According to Gaev, the reason for Postyshev's decline lay in his popularity, in the rise of his prestige, and in "his simplicity and open-heartedness." This seems a somewhat subjective judgment. However, Gaev's opinion that a year before his fall Postyshev had begun to show a certain hostility toward the Party bureaucracy and to develop a critical sense, deserves further attention. This new

---

[11] "O sudbe P. Postysheva" (The Fate of Postyshev), *Vestnik instituta po izucheniyu istorii i kultury SSSR,*" Munich, I, 1951, p. 145.

[12] [A. Gaev], *Soviet Political Personalities: Seven Profiles,* New York, Research Program on the USSR, 1952.

characteristic was, as we shall see, in line with Postyshev's policy in the Ukraine in 1936.

The third explanation of Postyshev's fall comes from Avtorkhanov. It is the most convincing of all. According to Avtorkhanov, Postyshev fell because of the political situation in which he found himself in the Ukraine and because of conflicts within the top strata of the All-Union CP(b) which came to a head in the fall of 1936. But having pointed out these very important reasons, Avtorkhanov neglected to provide all the possible arguments in their favor. This gap we shall try to fill.

Postyshev and the Ukrainian Situation

Avtorkhanov thinks[13] that in the fall of 1937 Postyshev had shown sympathy for the Ukrainians when, at the time of the final liquidation of the CC CP(b)U, he had sided with Kosior, Lyubchenko, Zatonsky, Petrovsky and Demchenko against Molotov, Khrushchev and Yezhov. This was true, with one important correction. Postyshev had already fallen; he had already been expelled from the Central Committee and was doing penance in Kuibyshev.

The rest of the "Ukrainian trouble" which contributed to Postyshev's fall lies elsewhere. It must be sought first of all in the specific atmosphere of the Ukraine to which Postyshev, in spite of rigorous Party training and orders from Moscow, must have succumbed. Postyshev, having sent to their doom hundreds of thousands of Ukrainians who had lived for this new Ukrainian society, and having paralyzed the Ukrainian trends in the CP(b)U, failed to destroy the idea of a Ukrainian state with its historical, cultural, social and economic peculiarities. Gradually and unconsciously Postyshev had become a captive of the Ukraine. This is why, in 1936, he began to show a lively interest in Ukrainian history and culture, and in the preservation of Ukrainian cadres in the CP(b)U.[14] Postyshev began to ridicule those Party chiefs who thought that "Ukrainianization is limited to mastering the Ukrainian language." He expressed the daring opinion that "it is imperative that a member of the Party have a thorough knowledge of the history, the economics, the culture of the Ukraine, and the history of the CP(b)U, so that all the members of the Party should be able to understand the processes of the construction of Soviet Ukrainian culture now being accomplished."[15] This, obviously, did not please the Kremlin. Postyshev had not been sent to the Ukraine to deliver speeches in defense of Ukrainian culture and history, or to use his authority to compel new cadres of the CP(b)U to study them. It is also possible that, as Gaev contends, Postyshev became aware of the alien and critical mood of the Ukraine, which could not be dispelled by terror. And, after all, his mailed fist, which destroyed thousands, had failed to destroy the CEC or the CC of the CP(b)U. This alone was enough to incur Stalin's displeasure.

[13] Avtorkhanov, *op. cit., Posev,* December 1950, pp. 14-15.
[14] Cf. Postyshev, "Pidsumky ..." *Bilshovyk Ukrainy,* No. 3, 1936; also Postyshev's speech, *Pravda,* December 9, 1936.
[15] Postyshev, "Pidsumky ..." *Bilshovyk Ukrainy,* No. 3, 1936.

The second reason for Postyshev's downfall was, according to Avtorkhanov, the purge of all secretaries of Party organizations and heads of governments of the republics in the USSR which began in the fall of 1937. This purge, in turn, was the result of widespread opposition to Stalin which appeared openly during a plenum of the CC All-Union CP(b) in November 1936, when the fate of Bukharin and his group was also decided. "After a three-day discussion," writes Avtorkhanov, "the question of Bukharin and Rykov was put to a secret vote. The results of the voting were: less than a third of the members of the Central Committee voted for the resolution of Yezhov [and Stalin, condemning Bukharin and Rykov]; the majority voted against the resolution or turned in blank votes. The resolution, which was basically approved by the Politburo, was, most astonishingly, defeated. The highest executive organ of the Party thus expressed a vote of non-confidence in Stalin and his lieutenant in the NKVD, Yezhov."[16] Avtorkhanov lists Postyshev as one of those who voted against Stalin. Following the unexpected vote, Stalin, according to Avtorkhanov, accepted the decision of the majority of the Central Committee and published, in *Pravda* and *Izvestiya* a few days later, an announcement from the Procurator's office that it had suspended its investigation of Bukharin and Rykov because of lack of evidence.[17]

A year later, contends Avtorkhanov, in the fall of 1937, out of 140 members and candidate members of the CC All-Union CP(b), only 15 men remained free, eight of whom were in 1946–47 members of the Politburo. This was how Stalin had implemented the decision of the Central Committee.

Does this interpretation by Avtorkhanov correspond with the truth? As a general picture of developments in 1936–37 it is correct, but it is highly inaccurate in detail. It is not surprising, of course, that Avtorkhanov's memory, which had retained so many facts, had become somewhat hazy in matters of dates and chronology. While there is little doubt that Postyshev's fate was affected by the conflict within the All-Union CP(b) which resulted in the prosecution of Rykov and Bukharin, the account of this conflict contains serious errors and inaccuracies.

The plenum of the CC All-Union CP(b) to which Avtorkhanov referred as having taken place in 1936 was actually held early in 1937, probably February 25 to March 5.

In view of the scarcity of official sources, I feel justified in presenting here another version of the plenum.

The Vorkuta Version

This version is based on several accounts by people whom the present author met in 1940 in the camp at Vorkuta,[18] most of them under sentences of from 10

---

[16] Avtorkhanov, *op. cit., Posev,* November 1950, pp. 14-16.

[17] *Ibid.,* p. 14.

[18] Among them were O. Butsenko, the former secretary of the Ukrainian Central Executive Committee, chairman of the Far Eastern Executive Committee, and chief of a section in the

to 25 years. Isolated from the rest of the world and without newspapers, we attempted to unravel the mysterious changes in the Soviet government on the basis of radio reports and the rumors which circulated in the camp. It was difficult for us to understand how such military leaders of the USSR as Tukhachevsky, Yakir and others, or a faithful *apparatchik* of Stalin's like Postyshev, could so suddenly have fallen into disfavor. From the accounts of several men who knew the inner world of the Party in the thirties, the following picture of the events of 1936–38 finally emerged and were preserved in my memory.

After the trial of Zinoviev and Kamenev, and after the announcement by Vyshinsky, on August 21, 1936, of the implication of Tomsky, Bukharin, Rykov, Uglanov, Radek, Pyatakov, Serebryakov and Sokolnikov in an anti-state plot, there followed widespread arrests of the associates and subordinates of these men. The new investigations, started by the Special Security Commission of the CC All-Union CP(b); the replacement of the NKVD chief, Yagoda, by Yezhov;[19] the dismissal of Rykov;[20] and a series of instructions from the Special Security Commission to the Army to root out "enemies of the state," all were portents of a new and broad purge. It became clear to the lowest Party chiefs of the District Committees that the purge was directed against the former theoreticians and oppositionists in the Party. Taking advantage of the confusion caused by the execution of the Zinoviev-Kamenev group, and hiding behind the slogans of the new liberal Soviet constitution, Stalin was preparing another slaughter of unprecedented magnitude. Many high officials of the Party and members of the CC All-Union CP(b) (Rudzutak, Chubar, Postyshev, Kosior, Eikhe, Petrovsky) saw in it a personal threat, since in the past they had on several occasions supported Bukharin and Rykov.

Previous attempts to indict Rykov and Bukharin had been rejected by the majority of the members of the CC All-Union CP(b) as inadequately supported by evidence. However, in spite of this, in January 1937, just before the trial of Radek and Pyatakov, who were accused of participating in a "Trotskyite center," Bukharin was dismissed from the editorship of *Izvestia*, his last prominent post. At the plenum of the CC All-Union CP(b) in February, the members of the Central Committee were asked to approve a recommendation that Rykov and Bukharin should be expelled from the Party. These moves by Stalin created an atmosphere of tension and insecurity among the top officials of the Party. Many members of the Central Committee, commanders of the Army, chiefs of indus-

People's Commissariat for Heavy Industry, (sentenced to 25 years for participation in the National Fascist Organization of the Ukraine); Ivan Mikhailovich Makeev, an aeronautical engineer, first deputy to the chief of the Airplane Construction Board of the USSR (sentenced to 25 years for Bukharinism); Safarov, one of the leaders of the Leningrad opposition; Grigorii Abramovich Vinokurny, director of the Moscow Trading Company; two top NKVD officials whose names I have forgotten; the chief of the NKVD in Grozny, and the Commissar of Internal Affairs in the Mari Autonomous Republic, and several professors from Moscow State University, among them Stadnik and Nekrasov.

[19] *Pravda*, September 27, 1936.
[20] *Ibid*.

trial enterprises, leaders of republican governments had, therefore, spontaneously agreed to defend Rykov and Bukharin at the February Plenum. Most of them were faithful followers of Stalin and could not be accused of any oppositionism. They objected to the methods which Stalin used in liquidating Bukharin and other deviationists. They wanted some protection against the indiscriminate charges and accusations which were being flung at leading Communists and against the brutal methods used in disposing of these men.

This agreement between various prominent Party men must not be regarded as a plot against Stalin. The members of the group were merely anxious to provide safeguards in Stalin's dictatorial system, to improve relations within the Party, and finally to remind Stalin that not he alone but the Central Committee ruled the Soviet state.

The agreement to oppose Stalin at the plenum was secret. The plan was in the course of the discussion of a keynote address outlining the main objections to bring into the open the disagreement with Stalin. Postyshev was chosen to deliver this address, for the obvious reason that Stalin was thought to have complete confidence in him. After his speech, demanding justice for Bukharin and Rykov, other members of the Central Committee were to join Postyshev, thus creating a majority demanding a re-examination of the case of the two accused leaders. This was the plan to stop Stalin. Perhaps it would have succeeded, had it remained a secret. However, Stalin learned about it in advance, and this gave him the opportunity to prepare his defense.

To a man like Stalin this opposition meant a serious threat, a conspiracy, high treason. Should it succeed, his dictatorial power would be severely curtailed, his prestige would be badly damaged. He, therefore, prepared himself thoroughly to counteract Postyshev's speech. Having mobilized all his native resources of craft and diplomacy, he composed a speech which he delivered before Postyshev's. In his speech, Stalin, very subtly, without being obvious, contradicted all the charges which Postyshev was later to make.[21] Stalin's argumentation was irrefutable, his appeal for unity and to the high responsibility of Communist leadership was overwhelming. The assembled members of the CC All-Union CP(b) were deeply impressed by the logic of their leader, by the acute mind which seemed to read their thoughts. Did they falter in their plan to oppose Stalin?

There might have been some who were already wavering when Postyshev went up to the rostrum to deliver his speech. In a dry, hoarse and unpleasant voice he began reading his prepared text. Tension was at the breaking point. At the critical moment, when Postyshev, after a careful preamble, was about to come to grips with Stalin's accusations against Rykov and Bukharin, Stalin, who was listening without apparent emotion, uttered a loud interjection, thus revealing to Postyshev that Stalin was aware of the opposition's plan, and knew what Postyshev was about to say. Postyshev faltered, and for a few moments the audience could feel

---

[21] Stalin's speech, as printed in *Pravda* (March 29, 1937), and his concluding report (*Pravda*, April 1937) bore no relation to the speech he actually delivered at the plenum.

the struggle within the speaker's mind. Then he suddenly departed from the prepared text of his speech and in the meek, humble voice of one who has been found out by the teacher, attempted to explain the doubts which he and his associates had of Stalin's tactics. He declared that after listening to Stalin's masterly analysis of the situation he was withdrawing the charges which he was about to make and he hoped that his associates would also see their errors.

This was a great anti-climax. The opposition was shattered. Like sheep, one by one, the men who only an hour before had been determined to check Stalin, now filed to the rostrum, humble and penitent. They had been beaten by Stalin, and they felt that all they could do was to save their own skins. But not all of them lost heart; some said that they saw no reason for admitting their errors or vacillations. Among these were Rudzutak, Chubar, Eikhe, and some military commanders. They argued that their doubts as to Stalin's policy were not signs of treason or weakness, but were the result of their deep concern for the welfare of the Soviet state. The most brilliant speech in defense of the opposition was reportedly delivered by Chubar.

Stalin watched this tragicomedy with an assumed indifference, smoking his pipe and taking notes. After the discussion, which lasted three days, he was called upon to deliver the final report. The audience was extremely apprehensive. They expected sharp words and criticism from their leader after such a display of "self-criticism."

Once more Stalin took everyone by surprise. His tone was mild; he scarcely mentioned the debates, but concentrated on describing the foreign threat to the USSR, the Trotskyite plots, the fascist schemes, and the conspiracies of such former fellow-travellers as Ruth Fisher, Maslov, Max Eastman and others. He also pointed out the shortcomings in Party work and organization, and made particular mention of the unsatisfactory conditions within the Kiev Party organization from which, quite unjustifiably, a good rank-and-file Communist, Nikolenko, was about to be expelled. Not until the very end did he refer to the critical discussion, thanking all the participants for their concern for the state. He concluded his report by saying that in spite of the difference of opinion the plenum had come to unanimous decisions and the Party had emerged stronger than before.

The plenum, it seemed, was to have a happy ending. The expulsion of Bukharin and Rykov from the Party, the "inner Party democracy," secret balloting, and the re-organization of Party work in accordance with the new Constitution had all been agreed upon. The delegates went home. We do not know whether they were convinced that the expulsion of Rykov and Bukharin was an act of great wisdom, or whether they believed Stalin's words acknowledging the contribution they had made by criticizing the Party. We do know, however, that soon after the plenum all the members of the Central Committee who had opposed Stalin were liquidated.[22]

---

[22] This has been confirmed by Khrushchev in his secret speech to the Twentieth Party Congress (*New York Times*, June 5, 1956, p. 14).

The Vorkuta version of the February Plenum cannot claim to be entirely authentic, but it offers a plausible explanation of the downfall of Postyshev.

In conclusion, it may be said that Postyshev's career was ended because he failed to live up to his task in the Ukraine and because he became involved with the anti-Stalin opposition in the spring of 1937.

Although Stalin came to despise his former protégé, he also showed him an unusual degree of mercy. Eleven days after the plenum Postyshev was relieved of his duties as secretary of the CC CP(b)U and expelled from the CC of the All-Union CP(b). A year later, accused of abetting Trotskyism and nationalism, he was expelled from the Party. And, according to one version, he, unlike all the other members of the Central Committee who had opposed Stalin at the plenum, was not arrested and executed, but was allowed to die a natural death in the Kremlin hospital.

Chapter IV

Storm Over Kiev

On the Eve of Vital Decisions

On January 25, 1937, when the first Moscow trial was about to begin, and the accusations against Pyatakov and Radek were connected with the Ukrainian problem, a special session of the Congress of Soviets of the Ukraine was convened in Kiev to approve the new constitution for the Ukrainian SSR.

The new constitution deprived the Ukraine of the last privileges of an independent internal administration which it had enjoyed under the old constitution. Outwardly, all the trappings of the independent Ukrainian SSR were left intact; thus, according to Article 14 of the new Constitution of the USSR, the Ukraine preserved the rights of a sovereign state.[1] But how could these rights be reconciled with other articles of the constitution? In accordance with Article 25 of the Constitution of the USSR, the government of the Ukrainian SSR consisted of the following People's Commissariats (Ministries):[2] food, light industry, forestry, agriculture, grain and cattle-breeding state farms, finance, commerce, internal affairs, justice, health, education, local industry, municipal economy, social insurance. However, matters of defense, foreign affairs, foreign trade, communications, transportation, heavy industry, defense industry, the engineering industry and the navy were all delegated to the All-Union Council of People's Commissars.

Even the fourteen ministries left to the Republic were not, according to Article 47 of the new constitution, entirely independent. They were either "union-republican" or "republican," which implied that, in some cases, they were merely branches of the All-Union Commissariats. Article 48 mentions the ministries which were only nominally republican and which were, in fact, subordinated to the All-Union government. They were: food, light industry, forestry, agriculture, grain and cattle-breeding farms, finance, commerce, internal affairs, justice and health. Hence, as Article 49 confirms, only the ministries of education, local industry, municipal economy, and social insurance were left under the jurisdiction of the republics.

Judging by the reports of the Soviet press, the Ukrainian people received this constitution as a great gift to their country from Stalin the wise. They did so in

---

[1] *Konstitutsiya (osnovnoy zakon) SSSR* (The Constitution [Basic Law] of the USSR), Moscow, GIZ, 1938, pp. 19-20.

[2] Three kinds of special agencies, the Committee for Provisions of the USSR, the Artistic Affairs Administration, and the branches of the All-Union Commissariats in Moscow, which enjoyed the rights of Commissariats in all the Republics, are not included in our discussion.

spite of the fact that the new constitution robbed the government of their country of practically all power. The new Soviet Ukrainian government was authorized only to supervise schools, local industry, the sanitation and cleanliness of Ukrainian towns, and to care for the sick! Indeed, the new constitution was the crowning glory of Stalin's new empire. Article 17 of the Constitution, guaranteeing the right of secession to all the republics, sounded like a mockery of the cherished dream of the conquered peoples in view of the impotence of the republic governments.

There are good reasons to believe that Panas Lyubchenko, the chairman of the Ukrainian Council of People's Commissars and the nominal head of the Soviet Ukrainian government, fully understood the significance of the new constitution for the Ukraine. He happened to be chairman of the Constitutional Commission and had written the chief report on the projected constitution to the Fourteenth Congress of Soviets in Kiev.

Although unable to change the draft of the Stalin Constitution in any way, Lyubchenko gave his own interpretation of it in a speech at the Congress. In his speech he stressed with extraordinary force and persuasiveness the fact that he believed the new constitution signified the preservation of the status of the Soviet Ukraine as a sovereign state. He reminded his audience of the tragic past of the Ukraine under tsarist oppression and stressed that this could never happen again. "The Ukrainian Soviet Socialist Republic," he said, "has voluntarily united on the basis of equal rights with other Soviet Socialist Republics into a united state—the Union of Soviet Socialist Republics ... In accordance with Article 14 of the Constitution, the Ukraine independently exercises the functions of her own government, preserving all her sovereign rights."[3] Further, Lyubchenko stressed the "feeling of national pride which sprang up in us at the birth of the Soviet Ukraine as a sovereign, proletarian state."

Was it possible that Lyubchenko was so deeply convinced of the strength of the Soviet Ukrainian state that he hoped for a certain modification of the constitution? Was his hope the illusion of the last Borotbist? The answer was provided by Lyubchenko himself eight months later on August 30 when, faced with arrest by the NKVD, he committed suicide.

Soon after Postyshev was removed from the Ukraine, Stalin delivered a second blow to the Ukrainian SSR. I. E. Yakir, the commander of the Ukrainian Military District, was transferred to the command of the Leningrad Military District.[4] At about the same time, quietly and unobtrusively, another important

---

[3] "Proekt konstytutsii UkSSR" (A Draft of the Constitution of the UkSSR), *Visti*, January 26, 1937.

[4] *Pravda*, May 11, 1937. This announcement was part of an extensive reshuffle in the military command which was preliminary to the arrest and execution of Marshal M. N. Tukhachevsky. Among other changes were the transfer of Marshal Yegorov from the post of chief of staff to that of first deputy of the People's Commissar of Defense; the appointment of B. M. Shaposhnikov in Yegorov's place, and the transfer of Marshal Tukhachevsky to the command of the Volga Military District.

figure in Postyshev's entourage disappeared from the Ukraine. Balitsky, the chief of the Ukrainian NKVD, was reported to have been transferred to the Far East. He was never heard of again.

On May 27, 1937, the Thirteenth Congress of the CP(b)U convened in Kiev. The public remained rather indifferent to the recall of Postyshev, Balitsky, and Yakir; people were growing accustomed to sudden changes in their government that they were supposed to elect and in the Party which still called itself the Communist Party of the Ukraine.

The usual political report to the Congress was read by Kosior. The usual resolution, approving the report and adopting several measures recommended by the Central Committee, was approved, and a new Central Committee was elected. On the surface it was a most uneventful Congress. Yet it had a certain historical significance. First, it was the last Congress of the CP(b)U to be attended by the national cadres of the Party, the last prominent participants in the Ukrainian revolution. Second, the Congress demonstrated some Soviet Ukrainian patriotism, with the emphasis on "Ukrainian." This was obvious, even from Kosior's report.[5] The first part of Kosior's speech was devoted to a historical survey of the oppression which the Ukraine had suffered under the tsarist regime. Great emphasis was laid on the development of Ukrainian culture and economic strength after the revolution. This growth, he said, could be explained only by the absence of the old colonial and Russification policies of Moscow on the one hand, and by the establishment of the Soviet Ukrainian state on the other. Third, the Congress would pass into history as one from which Postyshev was absent. Fourth, a veiled but tangible attempt was made at the Congress to vindicate the Borotbist point of view,[6] and criticism was expressed of the nationality policy in the Ukraine. These sentiments were prominent enough to be included in the resolutions of the Congress:

> The Congress finds that . . . in the work of several organizations of the CP(b)U less attention has been paid recently to the question of the nationality policy and the problem itself has been underestimated. This showed itself . . . in the insufficient Ukrainization of the Party, the Soviet, and particularly of trade-union and Komsomol organizations; in the inadequate promotion of Ukrainian Bolshevik cadres to leading Party, Soviet, economic and trade-union posts.[7]

Fifth, the unity and conservatism of the Party cadres in the Ukraine were striking. The new Central Committee and the Politburo of the CP(b)U consisted largely of old members, except for those who had been transferred from the Ukraine (Chubar, Postyshev, Balitsky) or had been arrested (Kotsyubynsky,

---

[5] "KP(b)U v borbe za sotsialisticheskuyu Ukrainu" (The CP(b)U in the Struggle for a Socialist Ukraine), *Pravda*, May 29, 1937.

[6] *Visti*, June 3, 1937.

[7] The resolution of the Thirteenth Congress of the CP(b)U, *Pravda*, June 6, 1937.

Yakir, Demchenko, Holubenko, Dudnyk, Kileroh, Mykhaylyk, Musulbas, Taran, and several others).[8]

The sixth and most important historic characteristic of the Congress was the fact that the new Central Committee, during the first plenum, held on June 3, elected the following representatives to the Politburo by secret ballot: Lyubchenko, the former Borotbist who had always been barred from the highest organ of the CP(b)U; M. Popov, a former Menshevik, a supporter of the Ukrainian national cadres within the CP(b)U, and a strong critic of Russian centralism who had never before been admitted to the Politburo; and S. O. Kudryavtsev and I. S. Shelekhes, who were both old members of the Central Committee, but who had never before been elected to the Politburo because of their anti-Stalinist sympathies.

The atmosphere in Kiev, after the election of the new Central Committee and the Politburo, was calm and confident. However, this was the calm before the storm which finally became a real tornado, sweeping away all the members of the Central Committee and the Politburo and leaving thousands of other victims in its wake.

The Rout of the CC CP(b)U and of the Soviet Ukrainian Government

Early in 1937, Stalin realized that neither Postyshev, in whom he had placed so much hope, nor the CC CP(b)U which Postyshev had purged, could fulfill his plan for the Ukraine. To do this, new men had to be found, men who would have no attachment to the Ukraine, and who could replace the Party chiefs in that stubborn country. This meant, of course, another and even bloodier purge of the CC CP(b)U, and one which would be final. Stalin did not shrink from this act. Stalin therefore sent no special representative to the Thirteenth Congress of the CP(b)U, as had been customary. There was no need to regroup the existing Central Committee nor to reshuffle the Soviet Ukrainian government. He had decided to liquidate them all.

After the removal of Postyshev, Yakir, and Balitsky from the Ukraine, and the arrest of the command of the Ukrainian Military District, Stalin made further moves to prepare the coup de grace for the Ukrainian government. The Special Security Commission of the CC All-Union CP(b), created on May 14, 1935, and consisting of Stalin, Yezhov, Vyshinsky and Malenkov, set to work to investigate the Ukrainians. First, scores of agents were sent into the country to collect information about "enemies of the people," or rather to fabricate and elaborate evidence which had already been prepared by the NKVD. When the CC CP(b)U learned of this, it was naturally perturbed about the decline of its prestige in Moscow. It requested, therefore, that the special investigators sent by the Kremlin to the Ukraine report to the Ukrainian authorities and keep them informed of

---

[8] For the list of members of the Central Committee of the CP(b)U (Twelfth Congress) see *Visti*, January 25, 1934; the composition of the CC CP(b)U (Thirteenth Congress): *Visti*, June 4, 1937.

their moves. The Kremlin replied evasively, finally stating, in August 1937, that a special commission consisting of Molotov, Yezhov, and Khrushchev was coming to the Ukraine. A special plenum of the CC CP(b)U was called in connection with their arrival.

It was clear from several attacks on the CC CP(b)U in *Pravda*[9] and from the general atmosphere which prevailed after the February plenum of the CC All-Union CP(b) that nothing good was to be expected from the visit of the special commission. The situation in Kiev on the eve of the arrival of the Kremlin guests was ominous. Avtorkhanov describes it as follows:

> At the same time [as the arrival of Molotov, Yezhov and Khrushchev] several trainloads of "special NKVD troops" arrived in Kiev from Moscow. Side by side with the Kiev NKVD, a new "mobile" Moscow NKVD was established; its purpose was known only to the emissaries of Stalin. Units of the Kiev Military District were replaced by Siberian military detachments.
>
> Kiev resembled a fortress, beleaguered by enemy troops. The district in which the plenum of the Central Committee was held was cordoned off from the rest of the city and patrolled by special Moscow NKVD troops. The local guards at the very entrance to the building of the Central Committee were replaced by sentries selected from the "special troops."[10]

It was obvious that Yezhov (the chief of the NKVD), Nikita Khrushchev (the future overlord of the Ukraine, but at that time almost unknown), and Molotov (who was to play the part of "diplomat") did not trust the Ukrainian Central Comittee and did not feel safe under the protection of the local NKVD. Perhaps they had good reason for their fears.

When the plenum of the CC CP(b)U convened, Kosior was the first to speak; he introduced the main speaker, Molotov. Molotov delivered a long report, full of accusations against the CC CP(b)U. He reinforced his charges with secret evidence collected by the agents of the Special Security Commission. In short, he declared that the CC CP(b)U had failed in the execution of its duty. He demanded, therefore, a vote of non-confidence in Kosior, the secretary of the CC; and in Khataevich and Popov,[11] two members of the CC; in Petrovsky, the Chairman of the Central Executive Committee of the Ukrainian SSR; and in the Chairman of the Council of People's Commissars, Lyubchenko. Molotov demanded, in addition, that all of them be expelled from the Central Committee, and that Khrushchev be "elected" secretary of the CC CP(b)U.

This pronouncement came as a profound shock to all the members of the Ukrainian Central Committee; the tone was even more cynical and ruthless than that of the declaration made by Postyshev in 1933. After Molotov's speech there was no doubt in the minds of those he had accused that their days were numbered.

---

[9] *Pravda*, Juli 9, 1937.
[10] Avtorkhanov, *op. cit., Posev*, 50, 1950, pp. 14-15.
[11] Avtorkhanov erroneously lists the name of Postyshev, who by then had been removed from the Ukraine.

Did they submit to Molotov's demand? Did Lyubchenko, Petrovsky, Popov, Kosior and others who knew that their fate depended on the fate of these men decide to capitulate, knowing very well that at any moment Molotov could call in his "special troops"? Their reply must have come as a surprise to Molotov. All of them refused to cast a vote of non-confidence in Kosior. They stood firm, in spite of the threats of Yezhov and the pleading of Khrushchev. This meant, of course, that the Central Committee of the CP(b)U was expressing a vote of non-confidence in the Kremlin.

Stalin's emissaries understood that they could not achieve their objective democratically and certainly not by secret ballot. They could have called in the troops and arrested the entire Central Committee, but before doing anything drastic they had to consult with Stalin. According to Avtorkhanov, Molotov held a long telephone conversation with Stalin, after the first day of debate at the plenum. Stalin's advice was to continue negotiations with the CP(b)U, in the headquarters of the "mobile" NKVD from Moscow.

The next day the plenum convened in new surroundings, much less auspicious for the Ukrainians. According to Avtorkhanov, who reconstructed the story of this plenum from reliable reports, Molotov repeated his ultimatum: the members of the Central Committee whom he had named must be expelled and Khrushchev must be accepted as the new secretary. This demand was again rejected. Only then did Molotov present an alternative: all the members of the Ukrainian Central Committee should go to Moscow to discuss the matter with the CC All-Union CP(b). This request was accepted by the majority, although with some dissension. Lyubchenko openly declared that he would not go to Moscow, since he felt very strongly that the problem must be decided in the Ukraine. This speech was his last. In it he defended for the last time the principle of Soviet Ukrainian sovereignty, insisting that the decision of the plenum should be binding on the emissaries from the Kremlin. However, the majority voted in favor of the journey to Moscow. The plenum was declared ended, and the next day the entire Central Committee of the CP(b)U was scheduled to leave for Moscow.

The mission of the "special commission" of Molotov, Yezhov and Khrushchev had suffered a defeat, if only a temporary one.

The Suicide of Panas Lyubchenko

After the plenum Lyubchenko went to his office on Funduklievska street. He was determined not to go to Moscow. This meant the end not only of his career, but also of his life. The Prime Minister of the Ukrainian Soviet Republic must have felt at that moment that neither the army, the navy, nor the police of his state could offer him any protection. He must have felt, too, that the people who were supposed to have elected him cared little about his fate. The choice before him had narrowed sharply: he decided to take his own life. He went to see his wife, who was also a former Borotbist. She agreed to die with him. After sending away their children, a daughter who was a student at the University and a thirteen-year-old son, Lyubchenko first shot his wife and then himself.[12]

The news of his death came as a bad omen to the other members of the Central Committee, who were boarding a special train for Moscow. On September 2, 1937, *Pravda* printed a brief note:

> Entangled in anti-Soviet schemes, and afraid of his responsibility to the Ukrainian people for his betrayal of the interests of the Ukraine, the former Chairman of the Council of People's Commissars of the Ukraine, Lyubchenko, ended his life by suicide on August 30.

The Results of the Moscow Conference

Nobody knows what went on at the meeting between the Ukrainian Central Committee and Stalin. Today the only living witnesses of this discussion are Molotov and Kaganovich. What is more important, however, is the result of these negotiations. The following figures speak for themselves:

1) Of 11 members and 5 candidate members of the Politburo of the CP(b)U, not one was left at liberty.

2) Of 8 members and 2 candidate members of the Orgburo of the Central Committee of the CP(b)U not a single one survived.

3) All 9 members of the Control Commission of the CP(b)U perished.

4) All three secretaries of the CC CP(b)U (Kosior, Khataevich, Popov) lost their lives.

5) Only two men (P. F. Kryvonos and M. D. Dyukanov) were left of 62 members and 40 candidate members of the Central Committee of the CP(b)U.

6) Not one of the 17 members of the Soviet Ukrainian government was left free.

7) Nearly all the secretaries of the district committees of the Party, the district executive committees, the city soviets, many managers of state enterprises,

---

[12] There are several other versions of Lyubchenko's suicide, each differing in detail, but agreeing in the essentials. Avtorkhanov remarks only that "the Chairman of the Council of People's Commissars of the Ukraine, Lyubchenko, refused to go to Moscow and, in protest, ended his life by committing suicide." See Avtorkhanov, *op. cit., Posev,* 50, 1950, p. 15.

P. Pavlov, a former official of the Council of People's Commissars of the Ukraine, gives the following account of Lyubchenko's death in his reminiscences. At the plenum, Lyubchenko realized from Yezhov's behavior and from the tone of Molotov's speeches that "his hour had struck." He excused himself, left the meeting, and went home. There he shot his wife and then himself. See P. Pavlov, "Razgrom Sovnarkoma Ukrainy" (The Rout of the Council of People's Commissars of the Ukraine), *Narodnaya Pravda,* No. 4, 1949, pp. 16-18.

A. Vysochenko, in his book "SSSR bez masky" (The USSR Unmasked), pp. 94-96, writes that during the lunch intermission Lyubchenko went home and after shooting his wife and daughter first, committed suicide.

A. Gaev, in his study of Postyshev, relates how Lyubchenko was told of his impending doom while he was about to deliver an address in a Kiev theater. He called off his appearance and went home, where he shot his wife and then himself.

directors of scholary institutions and chiefs of the Ukrainian Union of Soviet Writers[13] were purged.

As if struck by sudden plague, the top administrators and leaders of the Soviet Ukrainian Republic were wiped out. In this unprecedented hecatomb on the altar of Stalin's empire, it is difficult to establish the order of events.

The suicide of Lyubchenko and the breakdown of negotiations between the Ukrainian Central Committee and the representatives of the CC All-Union CP(b), was immediately followed by the arrest of Shelekhes, Kudryavtsev, Popov, Chernyavsky and several other members of the CC CP(b)U. In quick succession, Porayko, the deputy chairman of the Council of People's Commissars; Khvylya, the chief of the cultural section of the CC; Shlikhter,[14] the commissar of agriculture; Rekis, the commissar of finance; Kantorovich, the commissar of health; Zatonsky, the commissar of education; and Voytsekhovsky, the secretary of the Central Executive Committee, were arrested.

The young Communist, Bondarenko, who was appointed to take Lyubchenko's place as chairman of the Council of People's Commissars, was himself accused of being an "enemy of the people." Mass arrests of other members of the Soviet Ukrainian government and of the Central Committee continued without the election of a new "premier."[15]

After the arrest of his two aides, Popov and Khataevich, Kosior, secretary of the CC CP(b)U, was transferred to Moscow where he disappeared in 1938. The same thing took place in the CEC. Hryhoriy Petrovsky, one of the oldest Bolsheviks in the Ukraine, a member of the Duma before the Revolution, who for twenty years had been chairman of the Ukrainian Central Executive Committee, was also removed from the Ukraine.[16]

The violent tremor which shook the Soviet Ukrainian administration in 1937 occurred when the new Soviet constitution was supposed to guarantee the Soviet Union a democratic government, justice under the law, and sovereign rights to the Soviet Republics. The chaos that followed the mass arrests of the Ukrainian Communists was so great that all forms of Soviet law were abandoned. For instance, the Central Committee of the CP(b)U was not dissolved, it simply ceased to exist. For some time orders and announcements still bore the signature of Kosior, although he was no longer in the Ukraine. After the arrest of Lyubchenko's successor, Bondarenko, the post of chairman of the Council of People's Commissars remained vacant. The function of chairman of the Central Executive

[13] The chairman of the Ukrainian Writers' Union, I. Kulyk, was arrested, together with Mykytenko, Krylenko, Kovalenko, Koryak, Kolesnyk, Yosypchuk and other writers.

[14] Shlikhter was probably given a reprieve after his sentence in 1937. He was allowed to do some research in the Academy of Sciences of the Ukrainian SSR. On December 2, 1940, *Komunist* reported his death as an academician, and nothing more.

[15] P. Pavlov, *op. cit.*

[16] Kosior was rehabilitated, posthumously, in 1956 (see Khrushchev's speech, *New York Times*, June 5, 1956). Petrovsky, who died on January 9, 1958, was rehabilitated two months after Stalin's death and awarded the Order of the Red Banner.

Committee was carried out for a time by S. I. Andreev. He was an old, sick man, who was now chosen to sign the various decrees, some of which he read for the first time after their publication in the press.[17] From time to time unknown Party officials came to the Ukraine, all of them with Russian names (Starygin, Lunkov, Smirnov, Lyubavin, Shpilevoi, Teleshev), and replaced the Ukrainian Party chiefs who had been arrested.

The arrests of Ukrainian Communists in 1937 were carried out in connection with the uncovering of the fictitious National Fascist Organization of the Ukraine. What were the charges made against the participants in this organization? Some of them, extracted in Hrynko's confession, have already been dismissed as untrue. The Soviet press contains a number of more specific accusations than those of sabotage, diversion and terrorist activities made at the trial of the Right Trotskyite Bloc. After all, the disappearance of hundreds of men who held high public office had to be justified. One charge was that of criminal activity by the Broadcasting Committee of the Ukraine. Allegedly the Kiev, Kharkov, Moldavia and other broadcasting stations had transmitted funeral marches after the announcement of the verdict of the Supreme Court on the Zinoviev and Kamenev group on August 24, 1936, and on the Pyatakov and Radek group on January 31, 1937. In another instance, a broadcast from Kiev in German omitted references which Vyshinsky had made to the connections between the Trotskyites and the Gestapo. On April 4, 1937, the artist Kovalenko slandered the Red Army during a musical program. On June 12, when news of the verdict in the trial of Tukhachevsky, Yakir, and others was being transmitted from Moscow, the Kiev station went off the air. "Can it be doubted," asked *Pravda*, "that an enemy organization is active in the Kiev broadcasting station? This is not understood, by either the directors of the broadcasting committee, or by . . . the CC CP(b)U."[18] According to another *Pravda* report, the Commissariat of Education and many Ukrainian schools were "sullied with bourgeois nationalists."[19] Ukrainian museums were full of spies and nationalists, who were busily destroying all signs of Ukrainian dependence on Russia and stressing the independent character of Ukrainian culture. They were also wantonly destroying ancient monuments.[20] Further, *Pravda* charged that Ukrainian nationalists were trying to separate the Ukraine from Russia. The "enemy of the people, Khvylya," who had been used four years earlier to prevent Skrypnyk's linguistic policy, was now charged with nationalist deviation in matters of cultural and linguistic policy.[21] The Ukrainians had neglected to celebrate Peter the First's Victory over Charles XII at Poltava.[22] Ukrainian nationalists were wrecking the national

[17] Vysochenko, *op. cit.,* p. 84.

[18] "Kto rukovodit radioveshchaniyem na Ukraine" (Who Directs Broadcasting in the Ukraine), *Pravda,* July 9, 1937.

[19] *Pravda,* September 18, 1937.

[20] "Kto khozyaynichayet v muzeyakh Ukrainy" (Who Is the Boss of the Museums in the Ukraine), *Pravda,* September 25, 1937.

[21] *Pravda,* October 4, 1937, and December 29, 1937.

[22] "Politicheskaya tupost" (Political Stupidity), *Pravda,* October 4, 1937.

economy and commercial enterprises.[23] They were infiltrating the repertory of the Ukrainian opera-houses and of the theaters and had opposed visits of artists from other republics.[24]

It appears that the activity of the "Ukrainian fascists" was, after all, not as dangerous as one might have expected. The charges in *Pravda* hardly correspond to the upheaval which Stalin caused in the Ukraine. They are trivial incidents which in no way explain the events of 1937. The latter were the final methods used to subjugate the Ukraine and were decreed on January 24, 1933. It was not enough to destroy the national Communist cadres in the Ukraine, to annihilate the ex-Borotbists, to deport and execute hundreds and thousands of Ukrainian scholars, writers, and intellectuals and to starve millions of Ukrainian peasants. All the Ukrainian Bolsheviks, or those who had been in any way connected with the Ukrainian revolution, had to perish too. The purgers had to be purged, the most ardent followers of Stalin's new course who had remained in the Ukraine long enough to be infected with the fanatic spirit of Ukrainian resistance had to be liquidated. Stalin's new policy for the Ukraine could only be established by an entirely new set of men, by a complete re-staffing of all responsible posts.

---

[23] "Prestupnaya bespechnost Poltavskogo gorkoma" (Criminal Carelessness of the Poltava City Committee), *Pravda,* October 10, 1937.
[24] *Pravda,* January 3, 1938.

Chapter V

The Fulfillment of Stalin's Plan

The "New Men" from Moscow

Stalin's master-plan was engineered by the "leader of peoples" himself. The new executor of this plan in the Ukraine was not the diplomat Molotov, nor the policeman Yezhov, but the third member of the 1937 "special commission," Nikita Sergeevich Khrushchev. In spite of the setback he had received during his earlier Ukrainian visit, in spite of the fact that the Ukrainian Central Committee had rejected his candidacy for the post of secretary of the CP(b)U, Khrushchev was put in charge of the Ukraine. Soon after the affront he had suffered at the hands of the Ukrainian Communists, Khrushchev supervised the purge of the very men who had dared to oppose Stalin's protégé. He accomplished his task brilliantly.

Khrushchev's arrival in the Ukraine in his new capacity as secretary of the CP(b)U was not the result of his election to this post by the Central Committee. It was merely noted by *Pravda* as an accomplished fact. On January 28, 1938, the Party organ printed the following announcement on the first page:

> *Plenum of the CC CP(b)U.* In connection with the transfer to other work of Comrade S. V. Kosior, the plenum relieved him of the duties of first secretary and member of the Politburo of the CP(b)U. The plenum elected Comrade N. S. Khrushchev as acting first secretary of the CC CP(b)U.
>
> Comrade M. A. Burmistenko was elected acting second secretary of the CC CP(b)U.

Above the announcement was a large portrait of the new governor of the Ukraine, Khrushchev. Like his predecessor, Postyshev, he was wearing a Ukrainian embroidered shirt. On his face was a contented and confident smile.

It is difficult to imagine how the plenum of the Central Committee could have been held when there was no Central Committee. It is possible that some sort of rump plenum was convened with the help of two members of the old Central Committee (the Stakhanovites Kryvonos and Dyukanov) and the new nominee to the CC, General Timoshenko, who had replaced Yakir. One thing is certain; a lawful plenum of the last elected Central Committee could not be held, since all its members had been liquidated.

A similar puppet show may have been performed with the Council of People's Commissars. On February 22, 1938, *Visti* reported that Demyan Semenovych Korotchenko had been appointed by the Central Executive Committee of the

Ukrainian SSR to the post of Chairman of the Council of People's Commissars. How could this have been done legally, when, after the liquidation of the previous Council of People's Commisars no elections had been held to the new Council? The new chairman of the Council of People's Commissars, Korotchenko, was a little-known figure in the Party and almost unknown in the Ukraine. The Soviet Ukrainian press reported the changes which took place as if nothing had happened. Its readers, however, must have realized that their government from then on was to be a group of Stalin's men who were strangers to the Ukraine. Khrushchev, Korotchenko, Burmistenko and the new Ukrainian NKVD chief, A. I. Uspensky, were to govern a country completely unfamiliar with their names.

Their first task was to deal with the so-called "organization of the rear," which meant the mopping-up of all those connected with the old regime, while the new men surrounded themselves with trusted followers. Then Khrushchev and Korotchenko made preparations for new elections to the Supreme Soviet of the Ukrainian SSR and to the forthcoming Fourteenth Congress of the CP(b)U.[1] They realized that only a newly elected Supreme Soviet and Party Congress could give them, usurpers as they were, at least some semblance of legality.

June 14–18, 1938, the Fourteenth Congress of the CP(b)U was held in Kiev. It elected, or rather confirmed in office, the new Central Committee, headed by Khrushchev and Burmistenko. This was the legalization of the "Khrushchev era" in the Ukraine.[2] It also confirmed Korotchenko as Chairman of the Council of People's Commissars.[3]

Five weeks later on July 25, 1938, the first session of the newly elected Supreme Soviet of the Ukrainian SSR opened in the Franko Theater, in Kiev. An unknown, unimportant Party official from the Melitopol district in the province of Dnepropetrovsk, Leonid Romanovych Korniyets, was elected chairman of the Supreme Soviet. He was, undoubtedly, a protégé of Korotchenko, who had been for some time the secretary of the Dnepropetrovsk Provincial Committee of the CP(b)U.

---

[1] D. S. Korotchenko, "Sovetskaya Ukraina pered vyborami Verkhovnogo Soveta Respubliki" (The Soviet Ukraine before the Elections to the Supreme Soviet of the Republic), *Pravda*, April 24, 1938. "Plenum TsK KP(b)U o podgotovke k vyboram v Verkhovny Sovet USSR" (Plenum of the CC CP(b)U Concerning the Preparation for the Elections to the Supreme Soviet of the Ukrainian SSR), *Pravda*, April 28, 1938.

[2] "XIV sezd bolshevikov Ukrainy" (The Fourteenth Congress of the Bolsheviks of the Ukraine), *Pravda*, June 13, 1938. Khrushchev's speech, *Pravda*, June 16, 1938; Proceedings of the Fourteenth Congress of the CP(b)U, *Pravda*, June 17, 18, 19, 1938.

[3] According to *Pravda* of July 26 and 28, 1938, the following was the distribution of portfolios in the new Soviet Ukrainian government (the Council of People's Commissars): chairman, D. S. Korotchenko; deputy chairman, D. N. Zhyla; chairman of State Planning Commission, A. M. Usikov; internal affairs (NKVD), A. I. Uspensky; food, S. M. Balyka; light industry, N. I. Kirichenko; forestry, P. Ya. Ushakov; agriculture, I. F. Murza; grain and cattle-breeding state farms, V. S. Shylo; finance, N. A. Kurach; commerce, P. M. Borisov; justice, N. F. Babchenko; health, I. I. Ovsienko; education, H. S. Khomenko; local industry, L. I. Ulyanenko; municipal economy, V. S. Chernovol; social insurance, E. I. Legur; chief of the Office of Cultural Affairs, N. M. Kompaniets; highway administration, S. P. Mychev. Not one of these had previously occupied any government post.

By comparing the composition of the Central Committee of the CP(b)U, elected at the Thirteenth Congress in 1937,[4] with the new Central Committee, elected at the Fourteenth Congress,[5] we shall see that, apart from Kryvonos and Dyukanov, whom we have mentioned earlier, as well as General Timoshenko, none of the old members of the Central Committee was re-elected in 1938; not a single member of the new Committee was ever a well-known public figure or an active participant in the revolution and the civil war in the Ukraine. General Timoshenko's Party standing was nil. He was a professional soldier who had no relation to the events of 1917 in the Ukraine. The new Central Committee consisted of 59 members and 27 candidate members. Khrushchev was the first and Burmistenko the second secretary. The new Politburo consisted of Khrushchev, Burmistenko, Korotchenko, Timoshenko, Uspensky, Shcherbakov, and two candidate members, Osipov and Zodiochenko.

It is noteworthy that the new Politburo had 6 members and 2 candidate members, while the former Politburo had consisted of 11 members and 5 candidate members. The even number of members in the new Politburo was a departure from the democratic system of the uneven number of the Politburo. Obviously, voting was not regarded by the new Politburo as very important; orders from the Kremlin were accepted unanimously.

Political Profiles of the Leaders

The old Central Committee and the Council of People's Commissars had had many outstanding personalities. Petrovsky, Zatonsky, Lyubchenko, Shlikhter, Sukhomlin, Kosior all had a long record of revolutionary work. Many of them were talented organizers and speakers (Lyubchenko, Khvylya, Zatonsky); several were well-known writers (Kulyk); some were scholars (Popov, Shlikhter). They owed their position in the Party hierarchy in the Ukraine at least partly to their intellectual qualities. How did the new leaders of the Ukraine compare with them?

All that can be attempted here is a very brief characterization of the new rulers.

Nikita Khrushchev was born in 1894 in the Russian province of Kursk into a family of proletarianized peasants. Having received little formal education and having shown no original talent, Khrushchev failed to play an active part in the revolution. He was called up into the Red Army in which he served as a private.[6] After the Civil War he did not distinguish himself in any way. At a period when the new regime offered many opportunities to young Communists, Khrushchev went to work as a miner in the Donbas. It was some little time before he was sent by the local Communist cell to the Workers' Faculty (*Rabfak*), which was one of several adult education institutes created for those who had had no opportunity to receive a secondary education. After four years of study Khrushchev was given

---

[4] *Visti*, June 4, 1937.
[5] *Visti*, June 20, 1938.
[6] *Visti*, January 28, 1938.

his first Party job: he became secretary of the Petrov-Mariinsky district. Later he held a similar post in one of the districts in the town of Stalino, and still later he was put in charge of a small trade union in Kiev. From Kiev, where he also held the post of chief organizer of the Kiev area committee of the CP(b)U, he was sent in 1929 to the Stalin Industrial Academy in Moscow.

This was the turning point in Khrushchev's unspectacular Communist career. He entered the Academy just when Stalin was consolidating his power in the Kremlin and was looking for faithful *apparatchiks*. He recruited them from the ranks of colorless, mediocre Party members like Khrushchev. Through a lucky chance Khrushchev came to the attention of Nadezhda Allilueva, Stalin's second wife, who was then the secretary of the Communist organization of the Academy. She soon offered him her job, thus launching Khrushchev on a major Party career. After a time the work in the Academy became too narrow for him. With Stalin's recommendation, in 1931 he became secretary of the Bauman district and later of the Krasnaya Presnya district in the city of Moscow. In 1932 Khrushchev was second secretary of the Moscow City Committee of the Party, and in 1934 he became the first secretary of that committee and second secretary of the Moscow Province Committee. Finally, in 1935, Khrushchev climbed to the very top, as first secretary of the Moscow City and Province Committees of the Party.

During that time Khrushchev had not distinguished himself as an orator, writer, or thinker. It may perhaps have been because he was not any of these and was an ideal underling that he rose to such heights under Stalin's patronage. His obedience and devotion to his master earned him an important assignment: membership in the special commission which, in 1937, went to investigate the Ukrainian Central Committee. He played his part well enough to become elevated to the leadership of the CP(b)U.

Mikhail Burmistenko was born in 1902, in the province of Saratov, in Russia. His family origin was not mentioned by the official biographers. Burmistenko enrolled in the Party in 1919. His job was in the Cheka of the Tambov and Penza provinces, where, as his biographer stresses, he did the ordinary duties of a Chekist. One of the occasions on which he distinguished himself was the "suppression of the kulak uprisings." Apart from his work in the Cheka, he acted (perhaps on orders of the Cheka) as secretary of the local Komsomol. From 1923 to 1926 he joined the Red Army and was the political secretary of the provincial military commissariat. In 1927, still in the Cheka, Burmistenko was made responsible for the supervision of newspapers. A few months later he became the editor of the provincial newspaper in the Volga German Autonomous Republic. From 1928 to 1929 he studied journalism at the Moscow Communist Institute of Journalism. Later he continued his career as an editor. In 1932 he became the secretary of the Provincial Committee of the All-Union CP(b) for the Kalmyk Autonomous SSR. This post he held until December 1935. In January 1936 Burmistenko was chosen to be an instructor for the training program of the cadres in the CC All-Union CP(b), where he soon became deputy chief of the program. This program was closely connected with Stalin's personal secretariat and served as an intelligence center within the Party. At the height of the campaign of terror directed against the Old Bolsheviks, Burmistenko was made the chief of this private NKVD. There is little doubt that Burmistenko must have performed this task well, and that he could boast of the achievements of his men in the Ukraine. This fact might have been decisive in earning him high honor in the Ukrainian Party hierarchy. Apart from the time-tested qualities of a Chekist, Burmistenko had the advantage of a Ukrainian name.

His career came to an abrupt end in the middle of the Second World War. In 1942, when the Ukraine was already occupied by the Germans, Burmistenko was broadcasting to the Ukrainian people. His name suddenly disappeared from the Soviet press early in 1943. Vysochenko quotes a story, broadcast by the BBC in 1950, according to which Burmistenko was revealed to be a German agent and fled to the Nazis,[7] where he became one of the leaders of the Vlasov movement. An even more fantastic story of Burmistenko's end is given by Ivan Krylov, a former high-ranking Red Army officer. Krylov speaks of Burmistenko as a German spy and a Ukrainian nationalist.[8]

Both these versions are unrealistic; they do not explain, in our opinion, the mystery of Burmistenko's disappearance.

Demyan Korotchenko, third in importance in the new Soviet Ukrainian hierarchy, was born in 1894 in the village of Pohrebky, in the province of Chernigov, in the Ukraine. He came from a peasant family. Before the Revolution he worked in a bakery in the small town of Shostka. In 1914 he was mobilized and served in the army as a private soldier. During the Revolution he was elected to the Committee of Soldiers' Deputies in Tallinn. He then returned to his native village in the Ukraine, where he was active in the local committee and took part in the uprising against Hetman Skoropadsky. When the Red Army occupied the Ukraine at the end of 1918, Korotchenko joined the Communist Party.

From 1919 to 1924 Korotchenko occupied minor posts in the Shostka Party Committee. In 1924 he was the secretary of the Chernigov Regional Committee, and from then on he climbed steadily in the Party hierarchy. During his work in Moscow he came into contact with Khrushchev, with whom he worked as one of the secretaries of the Moscow District Committee. In June 1937, Korotchenko replaced the secretary of the Western Province Committee of the All-Union CP(b), who had been purged. He became the first secretary of the Western Province and Smolensk City Committees of the All-Union CP(b), using the Russian name of Korotchenkov.[9] In the fall of 1937, Korotchenko was transferred to the Ukraine, to take the place of the liquidated secretary of the Dnepropetrovsk Committee, Khataevich. From there he quickly rose to a highly responsible post in the

[7] Vysochenko, op. cit., p. 80.

[8] Ivan Krylov, The Soviet Staff Officer, New York, Philosophical Library, 1951, pp. 142-44.

[9] Cf. Merle Fainsod, Smolensk Under Soviet Rule, Cambridge, 1958, p. 60.

Party organization of the Ukraine. The career which this half-educated Red Army man forged was only possible under Stalin's and Khrushchev's guidance.[10]

Little is known about A. I. Uspensky and A. S. Shcherbakov. They had never worked in the Ukraine before and were strangers to that country. Uspensky was an old Chekist. At the end of January 1938, he was decorated for bravery as "a famous son of the fatherland, a fearless intelligence officer, vigilantly protecting peaceful labor."[11] This "fearless intelligence officer" was responsible for the last wave of terror which swept the Ukraine in 1938. In a few years, the "famous son of the fatherland" disappeared without a trace. According to Vysochenko, Uspensky was a German agent and fled to Rumania.[12]

Before coming to the Ukraine, Shcherbakov (born in 1901, in Moscow province) was secretary of the Irkutsk Province Committee of the All-Union CP(b).[13] When Sarkis (Sarkisov), an Old Bolshevik, a member of the CC CP(b)U and secretary of the Donbas Party Committee, was liquidated, Shcherbakov was sent to take his place. In a few months this little-known Party official became a member of the Ukrainian Politburo. His further career was truly meteoric. He was transferred to Moscow, where he became a favorite of Stalin. During the war he wore the epaulettes of a Red Army General—only to fall victim to the sinister plot of the Jewish doctors. Soon after Stalin's death, the story of the "doctor-poisoners" was officially denied; this, however, did not bring A. S. Shcherbakov back to life.

The gallery of new Ukrainian chiefs is not very imposing. The most outstanding of them were small and insignificant *apparatchiks*. Most of them were, no doubt, sufficiently competent for Stalin's purposes. They were incapable of taking sides in any ideological struggle, of succumbing to this or that tendency, because they were men of the new Stalin era, careerists and functionaries. As long as they reaped material benefits and enjoyed the confidence of their leader, they were ready to do anything and to go anywhere. They remained totally alien to the Ukraine and her culture. They were Stalin's empire-builders and colonizers, bringing Russification and reaction to all parts of the Soviet Union.

As has already been emphasized, their function in the Ukraine was to execute, down to the most minute detail, the old instructions issued to Postyshev in January 1933. The last vestiges of the independent spirit of the Ukraine, of its cultural, political, social and national traditions, had to be extinguished. Krushchev and his lieutenants finally completed Stalin's plan. By the time the Eighteenth Congress of the All-Union CP(b) had convened in March 1939, the Ukraine was no longer a country in its own right, but a Soviet colony, a mere province of the Soviet Empire.

---

[10] All biographical data on Khrushchev, Burmistenko and Korotchenko are taken from *Visti*, January 28, and February 22, 1938.

[11] *Pravda*, January 28, 1938.

[12] Vysochenko, *op. cit.*, pp. 77-78.

[13] "O bolshevistskoi bditelnosti i chutkosti" (About Bolshevik Vigilance and Sensitiveness), *Pravda*, January 29, 1938.

The Ukrainian language was no longer used by the new Soviet Ukrainian government. Few of the new rulers of the Ukraine could speak it. The official proceedings of the government in Kiev began to be conducted and printed in Russian. On January 1, 1938, the new daily organ of the CP(b)U, *Sovestkaya Ukraina* (The Soviet Ukraine), started publication. It was printed in Russian.[14]

After twenty years of Soviet Ukrainian statehood, the Ukrainian people found themselves back where they had been before the Revolution, when their masters had spoken to them only in Russian. This was a painful blow to the national pride of the Ukrainians, who realized very clearly that a gesture as cynical as this by their masters would have been impossible in the days of Skrypnyk or of Lyubchenko. The Ukrainian newspapers still being published merely reprinted the pronouncements of *Sovetskaya Ukraina*. Like Soviet Ukrainian literature, the press was forced to follow in the footsteps of the "Russian elder brother."

In April 1938, a special decree was published by the Soviet Ukrainian government, introducing Russian as a compulsory subject in non-Russian schools. Sometimes this meant that the Russian language received more attention than the Ukrainian. There was, of course, no time for foreign languages. Khrushchev reminded the Fourteenth Congress of the CP(b)U that

> the enemies of the people, the bourgeois nationalists, knew the impact and influence of the Russian language and culture on the Ukraine. They knew that this meant, too, that the teachings of Lenin and Stalin had influenced the minds of the Ukrainian people, the minds of the Ukrainian workers and peasants. That is why they removed the Russian language from the school curriculum. In many Ukrainian schools, German, French, Polish and other languages were taught, but no Russian... Comrades, now all the peoples will learn Russian.[15]

It is doubtful that Khrushchev really believed all the peoples would learn Russian, but he certainly knew this: the Ukrainians would learn Russian, because the latest turn of the Party line prescribed it for them.[16]

It was due to Khrushchev that Russian became firmly established in the Ukrainian schools. Although it was impossible to destroy or to forbid the Ukrainian language, its use was limited and its vocabulary, syntax, and grammatical structure were not to be determined by the Ukrainian Academy of Sciences, but by the police. Under their watchful eye Ukrainian was purged of many native characteristics, words, and expressions and became littered with Russianisms.

Russification of the Ukraine proceeded not only in the fields of language; Ukrainian history, culture, and even the history of the Ukrainian Communist

[14] *Pravda*, December 30, 1937, announced: "From January 1, 1938, a large daily newspaper in Russian, *Sovetskaya Ukraina*, will be published in Kiev as an organ of the CC CP(b)U and UCEC."

[15] Khrushchev's speech, *Pravda*, June 16, 1938.

[16] "Russky yazyk—dostoyanie sovetskikh narodov" (The Russian Language—Property of the Soviet Peoples), *Pravda*, July 7, 1938.

Party were excluded from the curriculum in schools and institutes of higher education. Instead, Ukrainian children were forced to learn Russian history and to regard Russian national heroes as their own. The Ukrainian press and books began to repeat one slogan ad nauseam: The Ukraine is an inseparable part of the USSR.[17] There were endless tributes to Stalin, to the great Russian culture, to the "eternal friendship of the Russian and Ukrainian peoples." Ukrainian literature, deprived of all contacts with the West, purged of its brightest talents, and chained to the Soviet Writers' Union, was reduced to exhibiting pre-revolutionary ethnographic themes of "local color" and to slavish imitation of Russian Soviet literature.

The era of Khrushchev closes the decade (1929–1939) in which Stalin's plans for the Ukraine were finally brought to a successful conclusion. On one side of the balance sheet we find collectivization, famine, terror, the extermination of millions of peasants and workers, intellectuals, scholars and Ukrainian Communists; one the other side, the fulfillment of Stalin's dream by Nikita Khrushchev.

---

[17] "Plenum TsK KP(b)U o podgotovke k vyboram v Verkhovny Sovet USSR" (The Plenum of the CC CP(b)U Concerning the Preparation for the Elections to the Supreme Soviet of the Ukrainian SSR), *Pravda*, April 28, 1938. D. Korotchenko's address, *Pravda*, April 24, 1938.

Chapter VI

Conclusion

The events in the political, economic and cultural life of the Ukraine since 1930 which we have surveyed were the product of Stalin's era. They were the consequence of his plans, unfolded at the Sixteenth Party Conference of the All-Union CP(b) and the Plenum of the CC All-Union CP(b) in April 1929. The decision to accept the so-called optimum variant of the First Five-Year Plan in industrialization, to begin the collectivization of agriculture, and to give warning to all oppositionist groups in the Party, which was taken at this conference in Moscow, determined the course of Soviet Ukrainian history for the next decade. The structure as well as the character of the Soviet state was also altered by postulating the creation of a powerful economic basis, complete centralization, and political obedience with Moscow as the base.

This meant, on the other hand, the concentration of all power in the hands of Stalin, necessitating a drastic abrogation of local government and of the national and political rights of the Soviet republics, finally leading to the abolition of almost every form of political, social and cultural independence at the behest of the Muscovite leadership of the Soviet Third Rome.

The fulfillment of the requirements of Stalin's plan took nine years (1929 to 1938). During that time industrialization and collectivization were accomplished, the dictatorship of Stalin was firmly established, and the political, cultural, and economic autonomy of the Soviet republics was abolished. All of these measures were achieved at the expense of millions of human lives, accompanied by purges in the ideological leadership of the Party and the destruction of native Communist cadres in the non-Russian Soviet republics. On the ruins of the hopes and ideals of the Revolution of 1917 there arose the new Stalinist state.

Because of her geographic and strategic location, her economic resources, her cultural life and vast man-power, the Ukraine was destined to play a major role in the creation of Stalin's empire. The new economic reforms, industrialization and collectivization (imposed against the will of the people and carried out in spite of widespread famine), the drastic repressive measures, and the economic exploitation of the country brought the Ukraine in 1933 to the brink of ruin.

These developments caused a crisis in the relationship between the Soviet Ukrainian government and Moscow, which was particularly conspicuous during the third All-Ukrainian Party Conference in July 1932. The conflict between Kharkov and Moscow was a matter of grave concern to the Kremlin, since the leading Ukrainian Communist Party officials found themselves in the camp of the Ukrainian opposition.

141

At that time the Communist Party of the Ukraine was far from monolithic; rather, it was a conglomerate of several elements. On the one hand there were former Borotbists, Ukapists, Western Ukrainian Communists, SR's, SD's, Bundists, the Federal-Communists (Lapchynsky's group,[1] as well as Skrypnyk's group), and some younger Ukrainian Communists, all forming, in spite of internal divisions, one ideological group of Ukrainian Communists. On the other hand, there was a numerically strong Russian camp, consisting of the Russians and Russified Ukrainians, hostile to the very idea of a Soviet Ukrainian state and nurtured by the remnants of the great-power tradition as well as by opportunist and philistine elements. By the late twenties the CP(b)U was polarized between these two camps, each having its own leaders. Behind the second of these groups stood the Russian Communist Party and Moscow, the center of the Bolshevik dictatorship; behind the first, the energies of the regenerated Ukrainian nation with its craving for freedom and independence.

The decision of the CC All-Union CP(b) of January 24, 1933, and the arrival of Postyshev in the Ukraine, with dictatorial powers and a sizeable staff, marked the beginning of violent interference by Moscow in the Ukrainian internal situation. This act was intended to forestall further "deviationism" in the CP(b)U and, with the help of widespread terror, to coerce the Ukrainians into accepting the new Stalinist regime. Postyshev's rule in the Ukraine lasted four years and it was brought to a conclusion by Nikita Khrushchev after Postyshev's fall. It was a period of wholesale massacre and destruction, with few parallels in the history of mankind. Here is a partial list of the victims of the Postyshev-Khrushchev era:

1) The Ukrainian Orthodox Autocephalic Church with all its clergy, and many members.

2) The Ukrainian Academy of Sciences.

3) The historical school of Professor Hrushevsky.

4) The historical school of Professor Yavorsky.

---

[1] The Group of Federalists of the CP(b)U with Yuri (George) Lapchinsky as its head, originated at an illegal (forbidden by the CC RCP) Party meeting in Gomel in November 1919. This opposition movement in the CP(b)U began as a protest against the centralization policy of the RCP in the Ukraine, against dissolution of the Ukrainian Soviet government and of the CC CP(b)U according to the resolution of the CC Russian CP(b), and against Stalin's open policy of complete liquidation of both the CP(b)U and of the Ukrainian SSR.

The basic demands of the Group of Federalists were as follows: 1) Re-establishment of the Ukrainian SSR as an independent socialist government; 2) Restoration of the dissolved CC CP(b)U; 3) Establishment of a separate Ukrainian Red Army); 4) Existence of the CP(b)U as an independent Party, separated from the Russian CP(b), and its merger with the Borotbists.

The CC Russian CP(b) after acquainting itself with the demands of the Federalist Group, formally accepted the first three points for realization, while the fourth point was dismissed and the Group of Federalists was gradually liquidated. Lapchinsky left the CP(b)U and became a member of the just then organized (May 1920) Ukrainian CP.

After the merger of the UCP and CP(b)U (December 1924), Lapchinsky was for a rather long time Ambassador to Poland and Czechoslovakia. During the period of terror (1933-1938) he disappeared without a trace.

142

5) The Institute of Philosophy, headed by Professor Yurynets.

6) The Bahaliy Historical Research Institute.

7) The Shevchenko Research Institute, headed by Serhiy Pylypenko.

8) The Institute of Linguistics of the Academy of Sciences.

9) The Agricultural Academy and the Economic Research Institute.

10) The Ukrainian Institute of Eastern Studies, headed by Professor Velychko.

11) The Research Institute of Soviet Construction, headed by Professor Trublaevych.

12) The Research Institute for the Deaf and Dumb, headed by Professor Sokolyansky.

13) The Ukrainian literary organizations (over two hundred writers arrested and deported or executed).

14) The school of painting of Professor M. Boychuk.

15) The *Berezil* theater.

16) The Editorial Board of the Soviet Ukrainian Encyclopedia.

17) The Ukrainian Chamber of Weights and Measures directed by Mazurenko.

18) The All-Ukrainian Marx and Lenin Institute (VUAMLIN).

19) The School of research on the history of the CP(b)U.

20) The *Rukh, Chas, Knyhospilka* publishing companies, the Ukrainian State Publishing House, and *Molodyi Bilshovyk*.

21) The Ukrainian Film Company (VUFKU).

22) A significant portion of the faculty members of all Ukrainian higher educational establishments were arrested.

23) The Ukrainian Conference for the Establishment of a New Ukrainian Orthography.

Most of the members of these institutions were arrested and deported. By the end of 1938, the following categories of people were excluded from political, scholarly and public life in the Ukraine:

1) All former members and associates of the government of the Ukrainian People's Republic.

2) All former Ukrainian SD's, SR's, SF's, "Postupovtsi" (Progressives) and Hetmanites.

3) All former Borotbists, Ukapists, members of the Communist Party of the Western Ukraine, and all Galicians.

4) All those associated with the deviations of Shumsky, Khvylovy and Volobuev, and Skrypnyk's entire group.

5) All former emigres who had returned to the Soviet Ukraine.

6) A large part of the old non-Party intelligentsia working in the cultural, literary and scholarly fields.

143

7) A large number of the younger generation of the intelligentsia.

8) All Ukrainian sympathizers with Trotsky and the Right Opposition.

9) The entire Ukrainian Soviet government and the leadership of the CP(b)U (in 1937).[2]

The terror of 1933–38 resulted in the extinction of native Ukrainian Communism as a political idea; it also destroyed all the leading representatives of this idea. Moreover, it claimed thousands of other victims who were neither Communists nor, as was charged, "bourgeois nationalists," but men and women devoted to Ukrainian culture, scholarship and literature. Ukrainian peasants and workers who dared to voice opposition to the exploitation and subjugation of their country also perished. The methods used in this mass destruction of the Ukrainian people and the intelligentsia were disguised behind fictitious charges of "counter-revolution" and "bourgeois nationalism," as well as of belonging to the mythical "underground organization" to which we have devoted special attention in our study.

Tragic as it was, the end of Ukrainian Communism contains a practical lesson in history which Ukrainians are not likely to forget. There were two reasons for the destruction of the Ukrainian Communists. On the one hand they committed an unpardonable political error in accepting on faith the Bolshevik guarantee of "the right to self-determination" without attempting to safeguard this right in any effective way. By allowing themselves to be entirely dependent on the Russian Bolsheviks and by failing to create an effective government of their own, they signed away the independence of the Ukraine. On the other hand, because of their close collaboration with the Russian Bolsheviks, they isolated themselves from the masses of the Ukrainian people and lost their confidence. Thus, at the moment of crisis, when they were subjected to the direct onslaught of the mighty machine of Muscovite centralism, they found themselves deserted by the people.

When considering the mass liquidation of Ukrainian political leaders, scholars, writers, intellectuals, and ordinary men and women during 1933–38, one question remains unanswered. It is this: Why was Stalinist terror in the Ukraine so harsh and widespread? Or, in other words, why was the Ukraine so dangerous to Stalin? We have attempted to supply a detailed answer in the course of this study. It remains to sum up some of the general conclusions.

---

[2] Following the Twentieth Congress of the Communist Party, many prominent political and literary figures who had been purged in the thirties were rehabilitated. Among the political and military leaders in the Ukraine we find, in addition to Petrovsky, Kosior, Postyshev, and Yakir. Skrypnyk's rehabilitation has been, so far, only partial. His name has been mentioned as a historian of the Communist movement and as a victim of Stalin's "cult of personality." In the literary field some associates of Khvylovy (Blakytny, Kulish, Dniprovsky, Kurbas) have been reinstated, although, so far, their works have not been republished. The plays of Ivan Mykytenko have, however, been republished. So far, the "rehabilitation," meaningful as it is, has not brought about any substantial restoration of the purged political or intellectual elite of the thirties, and it is too early to assess its full extent or significance.

It is clear that in planning to place the Soviet state under his dictatorship, Stalin sought the support of Russian nationalism. This made him at once the enemy of the "internationalist" wing of the Communist Party (Trotsky, Bukharin, Rykov, Smirnov, Mrachkovsky, Radek, Rakovsky, and others), and of the various republics. In particular, the national Communist leaders of the non-Russian republics viewed with great apprehension any attempt to reinstate Russian supremacy. For them these attempts smacked of the familiar imperialist policies of tsarist Russia.

The Ukraine, the second largest republic after Russia, became the foremost center of resistance to Stalin's revived imperialism. Partisan warfare against the Bolshevik regime during the Civil War became widespread in the Ukraine. There were many non-Communist scholars in the Ukraine (Hrushevsky, Yefremov, Krymsky, Chechel, Khrystyuk, Slabchenko, Hermayze, Zerov, and many others). There was public pressure for a sovereign state in the Ukraine. The Soviet Ukrainian leaders, Skrypnyk, Shlikhter, Ravich-Cherkassky, Shumsky, Volobuev, Richytsky, Hrynko, Khvylovy and others provided, in their writings, a solid foundation for the unity of Ukrainian culture and the economy. The Ukraine produced outspoken critics of Russian culture and arts (Khvylovy's idea of "Romantic vitaism," and an "Asiatic Renaissance"). Finally, the Ukraine's national problems were often discussed at international forums (the Ukrainian issue was debated by the Comintern five times in the years 1920–28).

The sources of Ukrainian strength were to be found in the long history of the Ukrainian struggle for independence, and in the Ukrainian Revolution of 1917, which led to the creation of the Ukrainian People's Republic.[3] Much of this heritage was preserved in the Soviet Ukraine. The Red Army, which, in 1920, destroyed the democratic Ukrainian republic, could not destroy the idea of statehood nor the spirit of the people. Ever since 1920, the Ukraine was a battleground between the centralist forces of the Russian CP(b), later the All-Union CP(b), and the national forces within the CP(b)U and the Soviet Ukrainian government. During the course of this struggle a center of Ukrainian opposition to the Kremlin policy was formed in the CP(b)U (Skrypnyk, Chubar, Zatonsky, and others). The existence of this opposition became extremely dangerous for Stalin's centralist policy after 1930.

Stalin realized this danger as early as 1926, when he wrote his letter to Kaganovich condemning Shumsky and Khvylovy. However, Shumsky's deviation was only the first major protest against Moscow centralism. Other such uncompromising tendencies in the Ukraine manifested themselves with even greater force during the late twenties, strongly supported by the CP(b)U, in the person of Skrypnyk. The widespread peasant rebellions against collectivization in 1930 could, if unchecked, have had the most serious consequences. These were the reasons why Stalin regarded Ukrainian intransigence as a mortal danger, and why he used such extreme measures to suppress it.

---

[3] Cf. John S. Reshetar, Jr., *The Ukrainian Revolution*, Princeton, Princeton University Press, 1952.

This poses another question which is also germane to the present inquiry. If the Ukrainian opposition was so strong, why was an attempt not made to return Stalin's attack blow for blow? Why was this opposition merely passive, why did its leaders not organize an uprising against Moscow? It is not easy to supply a satisfactory answer to this question.

In the opinion of the present writer, the reasons for the impotence of the Ukrainian opposition lay in the internal differences within the CP(b)U and in its isolation from the people at the critical period of collectivization. The differences within the Ukrainian camp were cleverly exploited by opponents of Ukrainian nationalism, who prevented the various Ukrainian groups within the CP(b)U from forming a core of active opposition. On the other hand, the Ukrainian people had little faith in the CP(b)U because of its collaboration with the Russian Bolsheviks. The hatred and anger of the people, aroused during collectivization, was primarily directed against the local authorities of the CP(b)U who were fulfilling orders from above. The CP(b)U failed at that critical moment to dissociate itself from Kremlin policy and to come to the defense of the Ukrainian people. Therefore, it lost the remaining support of the people and the ability to form any policy of its own. Indecisive attempts to do this (the Third Party Conference in 1929) were quickly and successfully quashed by the Kremlin. Several Ukrainian Communists, seeing the tragic and inescapable consequences of Soviet policy, and feeling their own inability to remedy the situation, committed suicide (Khvylovy, Skrypnyk, Lyubchenko). Others, whose personal integrity was not as great, remained at their jobs, doomed to be liquidated in due course.

Was Stalin's policy in the Ukraine crowned with final success? The answer to this question is contained in the events after 1938. In spite of the violent extermination of the Ukrainian opposition, the Kremlin found it impossible to kill the idea of Ukrainian independence, which has continued to plague it up to the present day. Even the most radical methods of Stalin's NKVD proved helpless.

After the Second World War, Stalin's tactics in solving this problem to his own satisfaction changed somewhat. In addition to the stick, the carrot came into play. Concessions were made to the Ukrainian SSR in many outward forms (the recreation of the Ukrainian Ministries of Defense and Foreign Affairs, admission to the United Nations, the institution of a Ukrainian flag and national anthem) which, no matter how fictitious, have a deeper meaning. The Russification and economic exploitation of the country proceeded at a greater pace than before, but these traditional Stalinist measures threatened to boomerang against the Kremlin as soon as Stalin was dead and the struggle for the succession began. Beria's fall meant a return to the old centralist policies, but it still remains to be seen whether Khrushchev can afford to sit quietly on the volcano of the Soviet nationality problem while promising a better standard of living to all the peoples.

The Ukrainian problem is still unsolved. The Ukrainian people, their culture, their political and social aspirations, are destined to play an important role in the future history of Europe. It is not amiss to recall here Eugene Lyons' report of the penetrating observation of a German officer in conversation with an American journalist. "Do you know where we lost the war in Russia?" the German asked.

"In Stalingrad," the journalist answered promptly.

"No, we lost it long before that—in Kiev, when we hoisted the swastika instead of the Ukrainian flag!"[4]

---

[4] Eugene Lyons, *Our Secret Allies: The Peoples of Russia*, New York, Duell, Sloan and Pearce, 1954, p. 232.

APPENDIX NOTE

The Assassination of Kirov

Several theories have been advanced by writers who have tried to elucidate this assassination. We shall disregard here the theory put forward by the Russian emigre group—the National Labor Alliance (NTS), which claimed the responsibility for Kirov's murder. We regard this claim as too naive to deserve serious consideration. Explanations current in the USSR have been summarized in an article by B. Usinovsky:[1]

Version 1: Nikolaev was a member of the Zinoviev opposition inside the All-Union CP(b). For this he was expelled from the Party. However, he twice appealed unsuccessfully against this decision. Disappointed and frustrated, Nikolaev decided to avenge himself on the man who was blocking his readmission. This he did on December 1, by assassinating Kirov.

Version 2: The assassination of Kirov was engineered by Stalin himself. "Kirov," writes Usinovsky, "was the most influential and active member of the Central Committee ... He was undoubtedly dangerous to Stalin, as a possible rival."[2]

Both these versions have been given some credence in a recently published book of dubious authenticity by Alexander Orlov, allegedly one of the top NKVD men, who deserted the regime in 1938 in Spain.[3] The first version has all the earmarks of having been created by the NKVD—in order to justify the terrorist campaign against Stalin's enemies. The second explanation is even less convincing, since it is impossible to regard Kirov as a serious, or even potential, rival of Stalin. Kirov was Stalin's choice to lead the Leningrad Party Committee after the purge of Zinoviev. Unlike Zinoviev, Kirov was a man with no outstanding intellectual gifts; he was a typical *apparatchik*, a creature of Stalin. There was no reason why Stalin should feel alarmed by the activity of this man who was his obedient protégé. No record of any disagreements between them has been preserved. Those who accepted this view were, to some extent, confirmed in it by Khrushchev's disclosures in his secret speech before the Twentieth Congress.[4] Nicolaevsky, in a series of articles in *Sotsialistichesky vestnik*,[5] argues that Kirov perished as Stalin's

---

[1] B. Usinovsky, "Nemnogo skromnosti, gospoda" (A Little Modesty, Gentlemen), *Sotsialistichesky vestnik*, No. 11, November 1938.

[2] *Ibid.*

[3] Alexander Orlov, *The Secret History of Stalin's Crimes*, New York, Random House, 1953. Orlov's book, like that of W. G. Krivitsky (*In Stalin's Secret Service*, New York, Harper, 1939), contains little information on Kirov which is not guesswork.

[4] "The Kirov Purges," *New York Times*, June 5, 1956, p. 14, col. 3-4.

[5] *Sotsialistichesky vestnik*, No. 5, 1956, pp. 91-94; No. 10, 1956, pp. 185-188; No. 12, 1956, pp. 239-243.

rival. Yet at no point in this argument is new evidence produced to support this view. Nicolaevsky's arguments about "the long duel between Stalin and Kirov"[6] are based mostly on the "letter from an old Bolshevik" which was published in December 1936.[7] This anonymous source can hardly be regarded as a reliable document. Khrushchev's revelations about Stalin only confirm one point in the Kirov case: that, in some degree, Stalin was implicated in the latter's murder. However, Khrushchev does not offer any explanation as to why Stalin should have been anxious to dispose of Kirov. He states that "still today, many circumstances of Kirov's murder remain mysterious and unexplained and require most thorough investigation."[8] Nicolaevsky's contention must, therefore, be regarded as hypothetical.

There was yet a third version of Kirov's death current in the Soviet Union, one which so far has received little attention in the Western literature on the subject. According to this version, Kirov was shot by a jealous husband. Nikolaev's wife, famous for her beauty, worked as Kirov's secretary while her husband was a member of the Leningrad Party Committee. Having convinced himself that his wife was being unfaithful to him with Kirov, Nikolaev first tried to put a stop to this liaison by talking to his wife and to Kirov. His attempt to win back his wife from his superior proved unsuccessful. Only then did Nikolaev resort to the desperate act of killing Kirov.

This version was first presented by the present author, a former inmate of the Vorkuta concentration camp.[9] There the author met a cousin of Nikolaev, whose name was also Nikolaev, and from him heard the details of the assassin's personal tragedy. In 1950 this story was confirmed in Avtorkhanov's work[10] and in 1952 by Eduard Dounet, formerly an active member of the opposition group of Democratic Centralism (group of Sapronov and Smirnov),[11] who escaped from the USSR during the last war and died in France in 1953. Dounet wrote to the present author in 1949 that he had heard the same story of Kirov's assassination from his wife, who worked as a consultant at the Central Executive Committee of the USSR, and that he had no doubt that Nikolaev killed Kirov out of jealousy.

It seems most likely, therefore, that the last version of Kirov's assassination is true. The reasons which prompted Nikolaev to fire at Kirov were personal, not political.

---

[6] *Ibid.*, No. 12, 1956, p. 243.

[7] "Kak podgotovlyalsya moskovsky protsess; iz pisma starogo bolshevika" (How the Moscow Trial Was Prepared; From a Letter of an Old Bolshevik), *ibid.*, December 1936, pp. 20-23 and January, 1937, pp. 17-27.

[8] "The Kirov Purges," *New York Times*, June 5, 1956, p. 14, col. 3.

[9] B. P. "Za shcho bulo vbyto Kirova" (Why Kirov Was Murdered), *Vpered* (Forwards), No. 1, April 1949, pp. 11-12.

[10] Avtorkhanov, *op. cit.* Professor F. L. Schuman also asserts that there were rumors about a love affair between Kirov and Nikolaev's wife (*Soviet Politics*, New York, Knopf, 1946, p. 259). Similar reports were current among the Russian emigres, particularly in Prague.

[11] R. A., "Pamyati E. M. Dounet," *Sotsialistichesky vestnik*, No. 2-3, February-March, 1953.

How, then, can we explain Khrushchev's unmistakable hint as to Stalin's complicity in Kirov's death? Perhaps Trotsky's remark, made in 1929, may provide the key to this mystery. In connection with the execution of Blumkin, an agent of the GPU who allegedly met Trotsky in Constantinople in order to transmit his letter to his followers in the USSR, Trotsky wrote:

> Stalin was left with one choice: to attempt to draw a bloody line between the official party and the opposition. It was imperative for him at any cost to link the opposition with attempts and preparations for an armed uprising...
>
> This is why after the expulsion of the leaders of the opposition it is certainly to be expected that Stalin's clique will try to involve one or the other opposition group in an adventure, and, in case of failure, will fabricate an "attempt" or "a military conspiracy" by this opposition.[12]

Trotsky's remark proved to be prophetic. After 1930, and especially after the "Ryutin case" in 1932,[13] Stalin looked for every opportunity to discredit and destroy opposition. In order to justify purges and indiscriminate terror it was necessary for him to uncover "plots" and "conspiracies." The murder of a prominent member of the Politburo would serve this purpose better than anything else. It might have been this search for situations which could be exploited in just such a way which led Stalin to make use of the romantic triangle: Nikolaev—his wife—Kirov. Only in this sense is Stalin implicated in Kirov's murder. The political accusation against Nikolaev was made only in order to justify the purges of all potential opposition groups in the USSR.

---

[12] *Byulleten oppozitsii*, No. 1-2, July 1929, p. 2.
[13] B. Nikolaevsky, "Stalin i ubiystvo Kirova" (Stalin and the Murder of Kirov), *Sotsialisti-chesky vestnik*, No. 5, 1956, pp. 91-94.

BIBLIOGRAPHY

Artemsky, A. Ya., *Shcho take Vseukrainska Akademiya Nauk* (What Is the All-Ukrainian Academy of Sciences), Kiev, 1931.
[Avtorkhanov, A.], *The Reign of Stalin*, London, 1953.
[——], *Staline au Pouvoir*, Paris, 1951.

Bahriany, Ivan, *Sad hetsymansky* (The Garden of Gethsemane), Neu-Ulm, 1950.
Batschinsky, Julian, *Memorandum to the Government of the United States*, 1919 (Columbia University Library).
Bilshovyk (The Bolshevik), Kiev.
Bilshovyk Ukrainy (Ukrainian Bolshevik), Kiev.
Bolshaya sovetskaya entsiklopediya (Large Soviet Encyclopedia), Moscow, 1st ed., 65 vols., 1926-47; 2nd ed., 51 vols., 1949-58.
Bolshevik (Bolshevik), Moscow.
Boritesya-poborete! (Fight and You Will Conquer!), Vienna.
Borotba (The Struggle), Kiev.
Budivnytstvo radyanskoi Ukrainy—Zbirnyk (The Organization of the Soviet Ukraine. A Compendium.), 2 parts, Kharkov, 1929.
Byulleten oppozitsii (Bulletin of the Opposition), Paris, Berlin.

Case of Leon Trotsky, The; Report of Hearings on the Charges Made Against Him in the Moscow Trials by the Preliminary Commission of Inquiry, New York, Harper Bros., 1937.
Chamberlin, W. H., *The Ukraine—A Submerged Nation*, New York, 1944.
Chaplenko, Vasyl, *Bilshovytska movna polityka* (Bolshevik Linguistic Policy), Munich, 1956.
Chervony shlyakh (The Red Pathway), Kharkov.
Czapski, Josef, *Na Nieludzkiej ziemi* (In an Inhuman Land), Instytut literacki, Paris, 1949.

Druha konferentsiya komunistychnoi partii (bilshovykiv) Ukrainy, 9-14 Kvitnya 1929 roku (The Second Conference of the Communist Party (Bolshevik) of the Ukraine 9-14 April 1929). *Stenohrafichny zvit*, Kharkov, DVU, 1929.

Entsiklopedichesky slovar russkogo bibliograficheskogo instituta Granat (Encyclopedic Dictionary of the Granat Bibliographic Institute), Moscow, n. d.
Entsyklopediya ukrainoznavstva (The Ukrainian Encyclopedia), Munich-New York, 1949.

Fainsod, Merle, *Smolensk Under Soviet Rule*, Cambridge, 1958.
Filomelya, O., *Ukrainsky litopys abo Kalendar istorychnykh podii* (A Ukrainian Chronicle or a Calendar of Historic Events), Winnipeg, 1950.

[Gaev, A.], *Soviet Political Personalities: Seven Profiles*, New York, Research Program on the USSR, 1952.
God that Failed, The, New York, Harper Bros., 1949.

Han, O., *Trahediya Mykoly Khvylovoho* (The Tragedy of Mykola Khylovy), Augsburg, Promotey, n. d.
Hirchak, Ye. F., *Shumskizm i rozlam v KPZU* (Shumskism and the Split in the CPWU), Kharkov, Ukrainian State Publishing House, 1928.
Hirniak, Yosyp, "Birth and Death of the Modern Ukrainian Theater," in *Soviet Theaters; 1917-1941*, ed. M. Bradshaw, New York, Research Program on the USSR, 1954.

Horlis-Horsky, Yuriy, *Ave Dictator*, Lvov, 1941.

Hromadyanka (The Woman Citizen), Munich.

Hrushevsky, M., *A History of the Ukraine*, New Haven, Yale University Press, 1941.

Istorik-Marksist (The Marxist Historian), Moscow.

Istoriya Vsesoyuznoi Kommunisticheskoi Partii (bolshevikov). Kratky Kurs (History of the Communist Party of the Soviet Union (Bolshevik). Short Course), Moscow, *Gospolitizdat*, 1950.

Izvestia (News), Moscow.

Jacobs, Lewis, *The Rise of the American Film: A Critical History*, New York, 1939.

Kalendar kommunista, Moscow, 1931.

Khmuryi, V., Yu. Dyvnych, Ye. Blakytnyi, *V maskakh epokhy* (The Masks of an Era), Germany, 1938.

Khrushchev, N., *Otchetny doklad Tsentralnogo Komiteta Kommunisticheskoi partii Sovetskogo Soyuza XX sezdu partii; 14 fevralya 1956 goda* (Report of the Central Committee of the Communist Party of the Soviet Union to the Twentieth Party Congress, February 14, 1956), Moscow, 1956.

Khvylya, A., *Vykorinyty, znyshchyty natsionalistychni korinnya na movnomu fronti* (To Uproot and Destroy the Nationalist Roots on the Linguistic Front), Kharkov, 1933.

Klen, Yuriy, *Spohady pro neoklasykiv* (Reminiscences of the Neoclassicists), Munich, 1947.

Koestler, Arthur, *Darkness at Noon*, London, Cape, 1941.

Kommunistische Partei der West-Ukraine (KPZU) — Die Ukrainische Nationale Frage (Materialen zur Frage der sogenannten ukrainischen Abweichungen »Schumskismus« in der Kommunistischen Partei der Ukraine und der Kommunistischen Partei der West-Ukraine), Lemberg, im Selbstverlag des ZK der KPZU, 1928.

Komunist (The Communist), Kharkov, Kiev.

Konstitutsiya (osnovnoy zakon) SSSR (The Constitution (Basic Law) of the USSR), Moscow, *GIZ*, 1938.

Kovalevsky, Mykola, *Ukraina pid chervonym yarmom: Dokumenty, fakty* (The Ukraine under the Red Yoke: Documents and Facts), Warsaw, Lvov, 1936.

——, *Polityka narodowosciowa na Ukraine* (Nationality Policy in the Ukraine), Instytut Badań Spraw Narodowościowych (Institute for the Study of Nationality Problems), Warsaw, 1938.

Krakivski visti (Cracow News), Cracow.

Krivitsky, W. G., *In Stalin's Secret Service*, New York, Harper Bros., 1939.

Kubanska, H., *Ternystym shlyakhom, spohady* (Along a Thorny Path-Recollections), Winnipeg, 1948.

Kulish, Mykola, *Tvory* (Works), New York, 1955.

Leites, Nathan and Elsa Bernaut, *The Ritual of Liquidation: The Case of the Moscow Trials*, Glencoe, The Free Press, 1954.

Lenin, V. I., *Sochineniya* (Works), 3rd ed., Moscow, 1926-37.

——, *Stati i rechi ob Ukraine* (Articles and Speeches Concerning the Ukraine), Kiev, *Partizdat TsK KP(b)U*, 1936.

Leytes, A. and Yashek, M., *Desyat rokiv ukrainskoi literatury* (Ten Years of Ukrainian Literature) Kharkov, 1928.

Literaturno-naukovy zbirnyk (Literary and Scientific Symposium), New York, I, 1952.

Literaturny yarmarok (The Literary Fair), Kharkov.

Litopys revolyutsii (Chronicle of the Revolution), Kharkov.

Luckyj, George S. N., *Literary Politics in the Soviet Ukraine: 1917-1934*, New York, Columbia University Press, 1956.

Lyons, Eugene, *Our Secret Allies: The Peoples of Russia*. New York, Duell, Sloan and Pearce, 1954.

Majstrenko, I., *Borot'bism: A Chapter in the History of Ukrainian Communism*, New York, Research Program on the USSR, 1954.

Malaya sovetskaya entsiklopediya (Small Soviet Encyclopedia), 2nd ed., 10 vols., Moscow, 1933-41.

Manuilsky, D. and S. Dukelsky (ed.), *Delo chlenov Tsentralnogo Komiteta Ukrainskoi Partii Sotsyalistov-Revolutsionerov Golubovicha, Petrenko, Lyzanivskogo, Chasnyka, Yaroslava i dr.* (The Case of Holubovych, Petrenko, Lyzanivsky, Chosnyk, Yaroslav and Other Members of the Central Committee of the Ukrainian Party of Socialist-Revolutionaries), Stenographic Report, Kharkov, 1921.

Moloda Ukraina (Young Ukraine), Toronto.

Movoznavstvo (Linguistics), Kiev.

MUR, Almanakh, I, Augsburg, 1946.

Narodna volya (The People's Will), Zhitomir, Kamenets-Podolsk.

Narys istorii Ukrainy (An Outline of the History of the Ukraine), Kiev, 1923.

Narysy z istorii revolyutsiinoi borotby na Ukraini (Sketches in the History of the Revolutionary Struggle in the Ukraine), 2 vols., Kharkov, 1927, 1928.

Nasha borotba (Our Struggle), West Germany.

Nashi dni (Our Days), Lvov.

Nauchnye rabotniki SSSR bez Moskvy i Leningrada (Scientific Workers of the USSR without Moscow and Leningrad), Moscow, Academy of Sciences of the USSR, 1928.

New York Times, The, New York.

Nova Ukraina (The New Ukraine), Prague.

Novi dni (New Days), Toronto.

Novi shlyakhy (New Paths), Lvov.

Novoe russkoe slovo (The New Russian Word), New York.

Novy shlyakh (The New Path), Winnepeg.

Ocherki istorii KP(b)U (A Sketch of the History of the CP(b)U), Kharkov, 1929.

Orlov, Alexander, *The Secret History of Stalin's Crimes*, New York, Random House, 1953.

Orwell, George, *Animal Farm*, London, 1946.

Osnovnye direktivy partii i pravitelstva po khoz. stroitelstvu (Basic Directives of the Party and Government on Economic Construction), Moscow, 1934.

Ouralov, Alexander, [Abdurakhman Avtorkhanov], *Stalin au Pouvoir*, Paris, 1951.

Pidhayny, S., *Islands of Death*, Toronto, Burns and MacEachern, 1953.

——, *Ukrainska intelligentsiya na Solovakh — Spohady 1939-1941* (Ukrainian Intellectuals on the Solovetsky Islands — Recollections 1939-1941), Neu-Ulm, Prometey, 1947.

Pokrovski, M. N., *Brief History of Russia*, translated by D. S. Mirsky, London, 1933.

Polonska-Vasylenko, N., *Ukrainska Akademiya Nauk: Narys istorii — Chastyna I, 1918-1930* (History of the Ukrainian Academy of Sciences: Part I, 1918-1930), Munich, Institute for the Study of the USSR, 1955.

Popov, M. M., *Ocherk istorii kommunisticheskoi partii (bolshevikov) Ukrainy* (An Outline of the History of the Communist Party [Bolshevik] of the Ukraine), Kharkov, 1929.

Posev (Sowing), Limburg-Frankfurt.

Prapor marksyzmu (Banner of Marxism), Kharkov.

Pravda, Moscow.

Proletarska pravda (Proletarian Truth), Kiev.

Radyanska Ukraina (The Soviet Ukraine), Kharkov-Kiev.

Ravich-Cherkasky, M., *Istoriya Kommunisticheskoi Partii (bolshevikov) Ukrainy* (A History of the Communist Party (Bolshevik) of the Ukraine), Kharkov, 1923.

——, edited and with introduction by, *Pervoye maya: Yuzhno-russkie rabochie soyuzy* (The First of May: The South-Russian Workers' Unions), Kharkov, 1925.

——, *Revolyutsiya i KP(b)U v materialakh i dokumentakh. Khrestomatiya* (The Revolution and the CP(b)U — Collected Materials and Documents), Vol. I, Kharkov, 1926.

Reshetar, John S., Jr., *The Ukrainian Revolution*, Princeton, Princeton University Press, 1952.

Richytsky, A., [Pisotsky, A.], *Do problemy likvidatsii perezhytkiv koloniyalnosty ta natsionalizmu — Vidpovid Mykh. Volobuyevu* (Concerning the Problem of the Liquidation of the Vestiges of Coloniality and Nationalism — Reply to Mykhaylo Volobuyev), Kharkov, 1928.

Schachtman, Max, *Behind the Moscow Trial, the Greatest Frame-up in History*, New York, Pioneer Publishers, n. d.

Schuman, Frederick L., *Soviet Politics*, New York, Knopf, 1946.

Sedov, Leon, *Livre rouge sur le proces de Moscou*, Paris, published in German under the title *Rotbuch über den Moskauer Prozess*.

Serge, Victor, *The Case of Comrade Tulayev*, New York, 1950.

Sistematicheskoe sobranie zakonov RSFSR (Systematic Collection of the Laws of the RSFSR), Moscow, 1929.

Skrypnyk, M., *Dzherela ta prychyny rozlamu v KPZU* (Origins and Causes of the Split in the CPWU), Kharkov, 1928.

——, *Pereznaky tvorchoho terenu — rekonstruktyvni linii v literaturi, muzytsi, obrazotvorchomu mystetstvi* (Changing Marks in the Creative Field — Trends of Reconstruction in Literature, Music and Painting), Kharkov, 1930.

——, *Statti i promovy* (Articles and Speeches), 2 vols., Kharkov, 1929-1931.

Smal-Stocki, R., *The Nationality Problem of the Soviet Union*, Milwaukee, 1952.

——, *Ukrainska mova v sovyetskii Ukraini* (The Ukrainian Language in the Soviet Ukraine), Warsaw, 1936.

Sobranie-zakonov i rasporyazhenii Raboche-Krestyanskogo Pravitelstva SSSR izdavaemoe Upravleniem Delami SNK SSSR, 7 yanvarya 1935 goda (The Collection of Laws and Regulations of the Workers' and Peasants' Government of the USSR published by the Administration of the Affairs of the Council of People's Commissars, January 7, 1935), No. 1, *otdel pervy*.

Solovey, D., *Holhota Ukrainy* (The Calvary of the Ukraine), Winnipeg, 1952.

——, *Stezhkamy na Holhotu* (Along the Paths to Calvary), New York, Detroit, Scranton, 1952.

Sotsialistichesky vestnik, New York and Paris.

Sotsiyalistychna Ukraina. Statystychny zbirnyk upravlinnya narodnohospodarskoho obliku USSR (The Socialist Ukraine: A Statistical Compendium of the Office of National Economic Statistics of the UkSSR), Kiev, January 1937.

Sotsyalistychna Ukraina (Socialist Ukraine), Kiev.

Soviet Political Personalities; Seven Profiles, New York, Research Program on the USSR, 1952.

Spilka vyzvolennya Ukrainy; stenohrafichny zvit (The Union for the Liberation of the Ukraine: Stenographic Report), Kharkov, 1930.

Stalin, J. V., *Sochineniya* (Works), 13 vols., Moscow, 1946-54.

Suchasna Ukraina (Contemporary Ukraine), Munich.

Svoboda (Liberty), New York.

Trotsky, L., *Moya zhizn* (My Life), 2 vols., Riga, Bereg, 1930.

Trudy pervoi vsesoyuznoi konferentsii istorikov-marksistov (Proceedings of the First All-Union Conference of Marxist Historians), 28, XII. 1928-4. I. 1929. Vol. I. Moscow, *Komakademiya*, 1930.

Ukraina (The Ukraine), Kiev.

Ukraina v epokhu kapitalizmu (The Ukraine in the Era of Capitalism), Kharkov, Poltava, 1924-25.

Ukrainian Review, Munich.

Ukrainian Trend, The, New York.

Ukrainska literaturna hazeta (Ukrainian Literary Gazette), Munich.

Ukrainsky derzhavnyk, kalendar-almanakh (Ukrainian Statesman: Calendar and Almanac), Berlin, 1942.

Ukrainsky holos (Ukrainian Voice), Winnipeg.
Ukrainsky Prometey (The Ukrainian Prometheus), Detroit.
Ukrainsky zbirnyk, Munich.
Uralov, Alexander, [Abdurakhman Avtorkhanov], *The Reign of Stalin*, London, 1953.

Vaplite. Literaturno-khudozhniy zhurnal (Vaplite. Literary and Art Journal), Kharkov.
Vechernyaya Moskva (The Evening Moscow), Moscow.
Vestnik instituta po izucheniyu istorii i kultury SSSR, Munich.
Vilna Kuban (The Free Kuban), Toronto.
Visti Vseukrainskoho Tsentaralnoho Vykonavchoho Komitetu (News of the All-Ukrainian Central Executive Committee), Kharkov.
VKP(b) v rezolyutsiyakh i resheniyakh sezdov, konferentsii i plenumov (The CPSU in Resolutions and Decisions of Congresses, Conferences and Plenums), Part II, 1925-35, 5th ed., Moscow, *Partizdat TsK VKP(b)*, 1936.
Vpered (Forward), Winnipeg.
Vysochenko, A., *SSSR bez masky* (The USSR Without a Mask), Buenos Aires, 1951.

Zamitky i materiyaly do istorii ukrainskoi revolyutsii (Notes and Materials Concerning the History of the Ukrainian Revolution), Vienna, 1921-22.
Zatonsky, V., *Natsionalna problema na Ukraini* (The National Problem in the Ukraine), Kharkov, 1926.
Zerov, M., *Do dzherel. Literaturno-krytychni statti* (To the Sources. Literary-Critical Articles), Kiev, 1926.
——, *Nove ukrainske pysmenstvo* (Modern Ukrainian Literature), 1924.
Zhyttya i revolyutsiya (Life and Revolution), Kiev.

XI sezd Rossiiskoi KP(b) (Eleventh Congress of the Russian CP[b]), Kiev, 1922.
XII sezd Rossiiskoi KP(b) (Twelfth Congress of the Russian CP[b]), Moscow, 1923.
XVI sezd VKP(b) (Sixteenth Congress of the All-Union CP[b]), 2nd ed., Moscow, 1931.
XVII sezd VKP(b) (Seventeenth Congress of the All-Union CP[b]), Moscow, 1934.

INDEX OF NAMES

159

161